MARTIN LUTHER

ROMAN CATHOLIC

PROPHET

by

Gregory Sobolewski

MARQUETTE
UNIVERSITY

PRESS

Marquette Studies in Theology
No. 25

Andrew Tallon, Series Editor

Library of Congress Cataloguing in Publication Data

Sobolewski, Gregory, 1955-
Martin Luther, Roman Catholic prophet / by Gregory Sobolewski.
p. cm. — (Marquette studies in theology; no. 25) Includes bibliographical
references and index.
ISBN 0-87462-649-8 (pbk. : alk. paper)
1. Luther, Martin, 1483-1546. 2. Catholic Church—Doctrines—
History—20th century. 3. Catholic Church—Teaching office—History—
20th century. I. Title. II. Marquette studies in theology ; #25.
BR334.3 .S63 2001
284.1'092—dc21
2001005254

Cover design by Andrew J. Tallon

Special thanks to Amy Schlumpf Manion
for editing and proofreading this text.

MARQUETTE UNIVERSITY PRESS
MILWAUKEE

The Association of Jesuit University Presses

To Susan

Contents

1

INTRODUCTION

Arise, O Lord, and judge thy cause. . . . A roaring sow of the woods has undertaken to destroy this vineyard, a wild beast wants to devour it. . . . Since these errors, as well as many others, are found in the writings or pamphlets of a certain Martin Luther, we condemn, reject and denounce these pamphlets and all writings and sermons of this Martin, be they in Latin or other languages, in which one or more of these errors are found. For all times do we want them condemned, rejected and denounced.

—Pope Leo X, 1520[1]

For the Catholic Church the name of Martin Luther is linked, across the centuries, to the memory of a sad period and particularly to the experience of the origin of deep ecclesiastical divisions. For this reason the 500th anniversary of Martin Luther's birth should be for us a reason to meditate, in truth and Christian charity, on that event fraught with historical significance which was the period of the Reformation. Because time, by separating us from the historical events, often permits them to be understood and represented better.

—Pope John Paul II, 1983[2]

Roman Catholic attitudes toward Martin Luther (1483–1546) have changed. Whether popular, scholarly, or magisterial, twentieth-century Catholic viewpoints about Luther have generally abandoned a tradition of contempt for the German reformer. The alternate perspectives, however, are not nearly as sharply defined or as single-minded. The contemporary Catholic opinion towards Luther *is* genuinely positive. Today few would choose the latter of Avery Dulles's options, given at a sermon during the Chair of Unity Octave (a period of prayer for Christian unity held annually from January 18 to 25) in 1965: "What are we to think of Martin Luther? Was he a reformer sent by God to recall the Church to its true vocation or a false prophet impelled by Satan to lead the faithful astray?" Rather, the current state of the question for Catholics remains as it was given in

Dulles's next inquiry: "What is the meaning for us today of Luther and the movement which he began?" (1965, 32).

In order to advance the Roman Catholic search for Luther's meaning, this study investigates the contemporary Catholic magisterial view of Luther, focusing on the period from the Second Vatican Council (1962–65) through the quincentennial of Luther's birth (1983). "Roman Catholic magisterial view" refers to the teachings of the Holy See—that is, the teachings of the Pope and of the congregations and offices that are under his immediate jurisdiction. The teachings of local bishops are noteworthy for their immediate pastoral intent, their novelty of expression and circumstance, and their consistency with or modification of Roman magisterial positions. However, the infrequent statements about Luther by diocesan ordinaries are given to express ecumenical interest or to assist in development of ecumenical features by diocesan newspapers rather than for the clarification of long-standing issues in the Catholic perception of Luther's person or work.[3]

I proceed from the conviction that any integral Roman Catholic ecumenical perspective appreciates the charism of teaching authority in the church according to the nature of the church's self-understanding given in the Second Vatican Council. While the historical events including Luther and various ecclesial authorities are important in themselves, their evaluation by the magisterium is vital for authentic Catholic envisioning of Christian unity (Tanner 1990; *Lumen gentium* §§ 18–20; *Unitatis redintegratio* §§ 2–3). Roman Catholicism is clearly more than a collection of scholarly or popular convictions; its identity as an ecclesial communion is grounded in the abiding presence of Providence guiding its leadership. Notably, the magisterium welcomes scholarly studies as a fundamental and preliminary first step in its own ecumenical conversion and development.[4]

I contend that Roman Catholic magisterial opinion in regard to Martin Luther has undergone a fundamental shift from the mid-sixteenth to the mid-twentieth centuries, now portraying Luther as a prophetic reformer rather than a misguided renegade.

Illustration of this claim begins in chapter two with an overview of how the vast majority of Roman Catholic scholars have abandoned the polemical assessments of their predecessors in order to establish a generally positive appraisal of Luther. While in-depth surveys of this theological reassessment are available elsewhere, familiarity with their general lines of thought will provide an essential awareness of the issues and approaches which inform all Catholic thought on Luther, including magisterial authorities.[5] The significance of an investigation into Catholic magisterial teaching on Luther is confirmed by the rare attention paid to magisterial reassessment in Catholic theological literature on the reformer.

In chapter three an evaluation of papal and conciliar appraisals of Luther in the sixteenth century will explore the first official Catholic responses to the reformer from Wittenberg. This assessment will identify constitutive elements of a magisterial appraisal that continues without modification through the mid-twentieth century, animating negative attitudes about Luther in ecclesiastical, theological, and popular circles. Fundamental concerns expressed in this early appraisal must be considered as major interests for contemporary magisterial revisions, especially in view of Roman Catholicism's remarkable reference to ecclesial tradition as a source of wisdom.

In the context of Catholic theological reappraisal and the initial magisterial posture regarding Luther, chapter four deliniates official Catholic positions in the twentieth century. Focusing on statements about Luther within a much larger body of ecumenical pronouncements, this evaluation necessarily integrates the developments during and after the Second Vatican Council where, as the Synod of Bishops said on the occasion of the council's twentieth anniversary in 1985, "Basing itself on the ecclesiology of communion, the Catholic Church . . . fully assumed her ecumenical responsibility" (449).

Finally, chapter five clarifies causes of this magisterial shift toward a positive appraisal of Luther, exploring magisterial positions in terms of a social analysis of prophecy. Like intermediaries in many societies, Luther's stature in Roman Catholic society is authorized by its officials in terms of his spiritual authority for the community, not merely in appraisal of his personality and orthodoxy, factors that do not in fact disappear across the centuries.

This concluding perspective is especially relevant when reviewing charges of Catholic ecumenical stagnation. Albert Outler (1908–89), a Methodist theologian and observer for the World Methodist Council at the Second Vatican Council, stated that:

> On the ecumenical front, however, it has to be said (and with great sadness) that *Unitatis Redintegratio* has turned out to be one of the least productive of all the landmark documents of Vatican II. It committed the Roman Catholic Church to a new ecumenical vision and horizon, but to few creative programs that have hastened the day of organic reunion. (1986, 256)

This sentiment is exemplified also by Heinrich Fries, a Catholic priest and Professor Emeritus of Fundamental and Ecumenical Theology at the University of Munich, who has argued that a "this far and no farther" attitude impedes the common Catholic reception and implementation of ecumenical advances (1986, 107–111). One of the most stinging criticisms comes from Hans Küng who, while recapitulating twenty years of ecumenical theology presented in *Concilium*, stated that: "The capital of trust that accrued to it [the church] in the time of John XXIII and the council has mostly been squandered" (1983, 51). Thus, my analysis of the current magisterial attitude toward Luther asks: What are meaningful ways, if any, to appreciate Roman Catholic magisterial reappraisal of Martin Luther?

Finally, with the conviction that theology must listen to the voices of the all the faithful and not only those who are most thoughtful, I note this book's limits. Given the focus on Roman magisterial regard for Luther and related Catholic theology, an analysis of the popular Catholic attitudes toward him would complete his Catholic portrait. A popular preconciliar view of Luther was given in *St. Jude Magazine* in 1961: "The man whom he [the Lutheran] reveres as, in the words of Carlyle, 'The Prophet and Hero,' remains in the eyes of Catholics a failure and a villain" (Jabush 1961, 33).[6] What, if anything, has changed about the Catholic grassroots attitude about Luther, given its solidly negative past? How have the ecumenical initiatives of theologians and bishops, in addition to other less formal factors such as greater collaboration of Christians in everyday life, promoted an enhanced positive view about Protestants by Catholics?

Answers are not provided here. One would likely begin with opinion polls—a project demanding a socio-theological approach rather than the historical-theological approach utilized here. National surveys of Catholics in the United States have focused on their attitudes about intercongregational relations (e.g., the viability of intermarriages, cooperative worship services and intercommunion, and general views of "likableness") rather than seeking to discover Catholic attitudes about Protestant personalities and doctrines (Wuthnow 1988, 91–95; Castelli and Gremillion 1987, 176–180). Generally, surveys reveal that American Catholics support strongly the ecumenical endeavors brought by the Second Vatican Council. The 1977 Gallup–Catholic Press Association study found that eighty-four percent of Catholics agreed with the statement: "The Catholic Church should become more ecumenical, that is, should try to develop closer relations between Catholics and non-Catholics." Again in 1986, ecumenical performance was a high mark of American

Catholic opinion about the Church (Gallup and Castelli 1987, 49). Prospects for such research are tantalizing not only because such data are rare but also because much of Catholic knowledge and sentiment about Protestant denominations derives from an awareness of the personalities and actions of their founders offered in the Catholic media.[7]

Given the understanding of the Catholic magisterial attitude toward Martin Luther that is accomplished here, one could begin to assess one aspect of the popular Catholic image of Luther—that shown in the Catholic media. As Catholic media present magisterial and scholarly teaching to many Christians, the following brief review of its practices from Vatican II through Luther's five-hundredth birthday is illuminating.

A positive assessment of ecumenism in general, and Luther specifically, is normative for the American Catholic press between 1965 and 1983. This is demonstrated cursorily by scanning article titles of popular newspapers, magazines, and journals in the *Catholic Periodical and Literature Index*. One detects a positive and expectant Catholic approach towards both non-Catholic Christians and the various ecumenical initiatives intending to advance Christian unity.

This constructive outlook was exemplified in two events concerning Luther's work and his person in 1983: the statement on justification by the U.S. Lutheran-Catholic Dialogue, involving representatives of the Lutheran World Ministries and the National Conference of Catholic Bishops, and the celebration of the five-hundredth anniversary of Luther's birth (11 November 1483). International and national dialogues are a major fixture in the Catholic ecumenical vanguard and this is underlined consistently in periodic assessments by Catholic media. Thomas Stransky, CSP, a founding member of the Vatican's Secretariat for Promoting Christian Unity, reported in an article in *America* entitled "Surprises and Fears of Ecumenism: Twenty Years After Vatican II" that the dialogues, while expected at the conclusion of the Council, have moved forward with surprising scope and speed, reducing confessional barriers by a "flood of results, with various degrees of consensus, convergence and agreements or disagreements" (47). Cardinal Jan Willebrands, a founder of the Secretariat and its president from April 1969 to December 1989, echoed Stransky's sentiments in *Origins*, the less circulated but influential documentary service of the National Conference of Catholic Bishops, with publication of his comments to ecumenical leaders on 12 September 1987, the day after Pope John Paul II's visit with them in Columbia, South Carolina (1988, 565–573).

Reports on the November 1983 release of the U.S. Lutheran-Catholic Dialogue's "Justification by Faith" prompted *Our Sunday Visitor*, a long-standing Catholic newspaper, to produce this headline: "Catholic-Lutheran Consensus Climaxes 20 Years' Work." With a front-page article the *National Catholic Register* presented a succinct and irenic report of both the historical circumstances of the sixteenth-century controversy about justification and the ecumenical signifi-cance of the 1983 agreement (Sly 1983, 1+). *America* responded with a major article by Kilian McDonnell, OSB, a member of the dialogue, who in a measured response stated that "After five years the scholars on the commission . . . still believe that the issue should not divide the Church, but we have more respect for our ancestors who during 400 years saw in it reason to live in a divided church" (1983, 345). Further, with indirect reference to popular Catholic sensibilities shaped by previous polemical attitudes about Luther, he stated, "The heart of the Lutheran Reformation was not freedom of conscience, individual autonomy, or even the principle 'sola scriptura' (scripture alone), but justification by faith, by which, Luther said, 'the Church stands or falls'" (346).

The *New York Times* reported Pope John Paul II's letter to Cardinal Willebrands on the five-hundredth anniversary of Luther's birth in a Sunday edition with a page-one headline: "Pope Praises Luther in an Appeal For Unity on Protest Anniversary." The article mentioned in a euphoric fashion the pope's appreciation of Luther as a theologian and reformer as well as his candor about a lack of comprehension of Luther by Catholics in the sixteenth century, Catholic and Protestant studies on Luther, and the Catholic commitment to Christian unity (Kamm 1983, 1+). *America* noted the Pope's letter to Willebrands in an editorial entitled "Luther's Justification" and said

> The fathers of Vatican I [1869–70], in fact, would probably dismiss as ludicrous any suggestion that one century and one council later Roman Catholics would join Lutherans in noting the fifth centen-nial of the Reformer. Yet this is precisely what has happened. (1983, 322)

Several Catholic publications linked the quincentennial birthday with reviews of contemporary ecumenical efforts. The *National Catholic Register* presented extensive reviews of Luther's life, subse-quent elements in the division of Catholics and Protestants, and ecumenical advances in national and international dialogues (Sly and Hays 1983, 1+). *St. Anthony Messenger* presented an historical summary of events that galvanized Luther and led to the Council of Trent along with a commentary on interconfessional dialogues and commitments to Christian unity; it exhorted its readers to anticipate convergence on key issues (Horgan 1983, 12–15; McBride 1983, 17–18). *Our Sunday Visitor* reported "Luther: Catholic 'Heretic' now 'Reformer'" with an overview of Catholic scholarship on Luther and the conclusions of various international and national dialogues, including the U.S. dialogue on justification. Only thirty years earlier the same newspaper printed an assessment of Reformation Sunday that stated "It is quite certain that the Founding Father of Lutheranism was an impure man who, because he was unwilling to check his own lechery, thought to devise a religious system that would accommodate it" (Ginder 1955, 4–5).[8] The *National Catholic Reporter* presented a feature-length article on some of Luther's perspectives and their compatibility with Catholicism after the Second Vatican Council, incorporating comments of Avery Dulles, SJ, a Catholic representative to the U.S. Lutheran-Catholic Dialogue (Finley 1983, 9+). The *National Catholic Reporter* characterized the entire "Luther year" with the headline: "At Luther Fest; a Good Word Was Said by All" (Hebblethwaite 1983, 4).

However, Catholic publications were not unanimous in promoting a positive ecumenical attitude and Luther-image in 1983, a momentous year in Roman Catholic relations with the Lutheran church. The *Wanderer* commemorated Luther's birthday with an indictment of Archbishop John F. Whealon's efforts as Director of the Bishops' Committee for Ecumenical and Interreligious Affairs to promote American episcopal involvement in the quincentennial celebrations.[9] Author Carol Jackson Robinson imagined a dialogue between Luther and a messenger to him in purgatory, if not hell. The harbinger informs him of Whealon's effort and Luther responds: "I would like to feel free again to use my masterful invective. But I shall restrain myself, remembering my own sins" (1983, 7). In the next issue, an article by Farley Clinton castigated Hans Küng for his criticisms of Catholicism and Christianity by depicting Küng as a new and more invidious manifestation of the reformer's anima (1983, 1+). A few months later, Robinson again chided Whealon and Rev. Richard P. McBrien, head of the Department of Theology at the University of Notre Dame which sponsored a celebration of Luther's birth in November 1983, by arguing that "if Martin Luther were alive today he would be especially pleased with the cunning our progressive theologians and bishops use in destroying the Holy Catholic Church by first reducing it to Protestantism" (Robinson 1984a, 4).

The *Wanderer* subsequently ran articles critical of modern theologians by correlating assertions of Luther's apostasy. In her article entitled "Who Is the Common Doctor of the Church: Thomas Aquinas or Martin Luther?," Robinson resented the spiritual authority attributed to Luther by Jared Wicks, SJ, of the Pontifical Gregorian University and Cardinal Joseph Bernardin of Chicago (1928–96), claiming an abandonment of the Catholic tradition and the Tridentine catechisms of Robert Bellarmine and Peter Canisius for false ecumenical goals (1984b, 5). In October 1985 Robinson vilified Karl Rahner, SJ, (1904–84) by comparing him to Martin Luther, asserting a common theological abandonment of Aquinas and common personality traits of arrogance and imperiousness (1985, 6). Curiously, the *Wanderer* did not report Pope John Paul II's quincentennial letter to Cardinal Willebrands and also avoided any similar editorializing when it reported the pope's visit to Rome's largest Lutheran church in December 1983 (Pope Preaches 1983, 1+).

With a similar focus on Luther's personality, John J. Kelly, OSA, argued that the reformer's messiah complex prompted the revolution of the sixteenth century in the April 1984 edition of *Homiletic and Pastoral Review*. Kelly wrote that "Brother Martin, bedeviled by his own scruples and doubts, simply used that occasion [abuses in the selling of indulgences] as a springboard to denaturalize and eviscerate the doctrinal structure of the Catholic faith, and bring thereby the thinking of the Catholic Church into line with his own" (1984, 61).[10] While not modeled strictly on polemics that had reduced Luther to a slave of fame, lust, alcohol, or psychosis, this evaluation maintained that a malevolent motive was operative in Luther's theology.[11]

Both the *Wanderer* and the *Homiletic and Pastoral Review* publicly pledge firm allegiance to Roman magisterial teaching as part of their editorial principles. Yet their opinions exaggerate the criticism of Luther expressed in *L'Osservatore Romano*, the semi-official publication of the Holy See. For example, Battista Mondin's article in the Roman newspaper admitted the existence of abuses in the sixteenth century and Luther's courage in face of them while still rejecting Luther's initiative on ecclesiological grounds:

> Now every Christian knows, he believes it on Christ's promise, that the Church cannot succumb to corruption in anything that belongs to her essence, therefore, he knows that he can never demand a reform of the Church in this regard, as Luther did. This was Luther's greatest and most tragic mistake.[12] (1972, 11)

Two conclusions emerge from this brief consideration of Catholic media's coverage of the Luther quincentennial and the U.S. Lutheran-Catholic statement on justification in 1983. First, the media generally have been enthusiastic about ecumenical progress between Catholics and Lutherans and have provided stories giving an historical and doctrinal context for the change in Catholic magisterial and theological consideration of Luther and Lutherans. Second, significant resistance to enhancement of the Catholic image of Luther has been posed by a segment of the media that represents itself to be most faithful to the magisterium of the Church. Magisterial reconsideration of Luther is underreported and centuries-old polemics are reinforced. A clear and accurate statement of what the magisterium itself teaches and explores can illuminate this practice.

In summary, this delineation of change in Roman Catholic magisterial opinions of Luther responds to a lack of scholarly study thereof, increasing scholarly concern about stagnation in Roman Catholic ecumenical efforts, and uninformed reporting and editorializing about Luther and his teachings in popular Catholic media.

2

LUTHER AND ROMAN CATHOLIC THEOLOGIANS IN THE TWENTIETH CENTURY

Luther, there is no ounce of godliness in you.
> —Heinrich Suso Denifle, OP[1]

At the core of Luther's religious experience we find God.
> —Joseph Lortz[2]

Incognito, Luther is present in an extremely efficacious way in the present-day Catholic experience of faith.
> —Otto Hermann Pesch[3]

Catholic theological assessments of Martin Luther have changed in the twentieth century, especially since World War II. The solidly negative appraisal of Luther initiated by Sylvester Prierias, OP, in 1517, enshrined by Johann Cochläus in 1549, and reaffirmed with near unanimity by Catholic scholars in succeeding centuries has disintegrated in the face of the ecumenical movement in general and, more specifically, in recognition of Roman Catholic Luther-studies in Germany. Contemporary Catholic theologians do not invoke a litany of psychoses, felonies, or sins of the flesh as was routine in past generations. Further, the majority of theologians evince a genuine respect for Luther's religious motivations, theological insights, and ability to communicate.

More important, Catholic theologians have not abandoned, in ecumenical zeal, the long-standing theological or doctrinal issues that were obscured or ignored in past polemics. The primary benefits of freeing Catholic theology from this legacy of character assassination has been to promote honest appreciation of existing Christian unity and candid consideration of the confessional divergences that remain to be resolved.

The following review of major elements in twentieth-century Catholic historiography about Luther chronicles the basic features of a reconfigured historical and theological understanding of Luther. Contemporary magisterial invitations for scholarly ecumenical research are rewarded with an academic consensus that places Luther inside Roman Catholic society, locating him in various ways away from the periphery and nearer to central convictions held by faithful Catholics after the Second Vatican Council.[4] This Catholic theological reappraisal of Luther can be understood in three phases: (1) denigration of Luther, (2) respect for Luther, and (3) dialogue with Luther.[5]

DENIGRATION OF LUTHER

In *The Righteousness of God: Luther Studies*, Gordon Rupp stated that "To every age there belong mental patterns, involving assumptions about causes and persons, for the most part accepted without reference to the canons of historical criticism, and even the expert in one particular field of historical investigation is bound to take over certain general assumptions when he considers matters beyond his own exact knowledge" (1953, 3–4). The negative assumptions by Catholics about Martin Luther emerge, to a great degree, from a consistent pattern of theological belittling that began with Luther's Catholic opponents from the universities in Germany and the papal court in Rome. While a few theologians exercised charity and restraint in their opposition to Luther, for example, Robert Bellarmine (1542–1621) and Francis de Sales (1567–1622), the vast majority supported their substantive criticisms of Luther by documenting and embellishing the less favorable aspects of his personality.[6] Their concern with his personality regularly overshadowed attention to the substance of his theology.

Foundations

The disparaging focus on Luther's character was set primarily by Johann Cochläus (1479–1552) and, to a lesser degree, by Johann Pistorius the Younger (1546–1608).

Cochläus, a parish priest at Frankfurt and later a canon at Breslau, had supported Luther's efforts at reform until the treatises of 1520 and the reformer's subsequent burning of *Exsurge Domine*, the papal bull proposing Luther's excommunication. After that event Cochläus became increasingly concerned about Luther's potential for harm to the church because of the latter's reconfiguration of essential doctrine and his ability to influence public opinion. Cochläus's *De gratia sacramentorum liber unus Ioani Cochlaei adversus assertionem M.*

Lutheri (1522) was one of the first of many Catholic rebuttals of Luther. However, his *Septiceps lutherus, ubique sibi, suis scriptis, contrarius in visitationem saxonicam* of 1529 and *Commentaria de actis et scriptis Martini Lutheri Saxonis* of 1549 have earned Cochläus pride of place among the sixteenth-century Roman Catholic controversialists. While the tone of condemnation in these works was not uncommon, the influence that they exercised afterward on centuries of Catholics is unique (Atkinson 1983, 8; Wicks 1983a, 15).

Written to awaken those who thought Luther was being forthright and upright in his criticisms, these works quoted over 140 of the reformer's own writings to document Cochläus's estimation of Luther's crimes: destroying church unity, betraying monastic vows, and perpetuating a madman's revolution at the expense of the common believer (Jedin 1966, 54; Rupp 1953, 19–20). Perhaps the most enduring image is the woodcut print of the seven-headed Luther which accompanied the 1529 work. The demon-like figure represented seven phases of Luther's alleged criminal activity, for example, theologian, preacher, and church administrator.[7] Cochläus emphasized the divisive outcome of Luther's actions rather than the reformer's motives or theological arguments. Motivation, however, was not missing in Cochläus's analysis:

> Luther is a child of the devil, possessed by the devil, full of falsehood and vainglory. His revolt was caused by monkish envy of the Dominican, Tetzel; he lusts after wine and women, is without conscience, and approves any means to gain his end. He thinks only of himself. He perpetuates the act of nailing up the theses for forty-two gulden—the sum he required to buy a new cowl. He is a liar and a hypocrite, cowardly and quarrelsome. There is no drop of German blood in him. (Lortz 1968, 296)

Elsewhere Cochläus claimed that Luther had secret communion with a demon as an Augustinian novice and had earlier engaged in sexual relations with his benefactress at Eisenach (Rupp 1953, 19; Swidler 1965, 202). Assignation of gross moral culpability would become a standard feature when Catholics undermined Luther. During the sixteenth century such denigration would discredit Luther; in later centuries it would be used to counter any Lutheran claim of spiritual legitimacy. Surely, the logic concluded, nothing good can come from someone so vile.[8]

Johann Pistorius the Younger, a convert from Lutheranism to Calvinism, and then to Catholicism in 1588, published his *Anatomia*

Lutheri from 1595 to 1598.[9] Given the successes of the Reformation and the establishment of Protestant congregations, Pistorius's work exemplifies a genre of Catholic evaluation of Luther that was strictly concerned with demonstrating the reformer's complete moral corruption. Pistorius considered seven devils whom he thought to have possessed Luther, including the spirits of whoredom, blasphemy, and laziness. Originally a doctor of medicine, Pistorius claimed to have read Luther's literary corpus three times. His citing the reformer in an incendiary style provoked serious and vehement reaction from Protestants. Even in 1966 Richard Stauffer could write that "This work ... is, after Cochläus' book, the most vehement, gross, and unjust indictment ever pronounced against the Wittenberg reformer" (Stauffer 1966, 12).

Gordon Rupp summarizes the effect of these and similar works: "This bitter seventeenth-century polemic can almost be described in Hegelian dialectical terms as: Catholic work evoked Protestant counterblast, which in turn gave rise to another Catholic exposition." While the production of vitriolic literature lapsed because it gave offense to the common believer, the caricature of Luther was firmly in place (1953, 21).

The Catholic image of the corrupt, divisive, and consequently unprovidential Luther was, with rare exception, *the* Catholic image of Luther until the twentieth century. Opinions outside this norm, however, can be found in the work of Maimbourg, Bossuet, Möhler, and Döllinger.

An Interlude

By the end of the seventeenth century more sophisticated presentations of the issues of the Reformation and Luther himself claimed a larger share of controversial literature. The writings of Louis Maimbourg, SJ, (1610–86), a church historian at Paris, presented evidence of a shifting Catholic focus. While Luther's personal liabilities still outweighed his good traits (oratorical and early academic work), Maimbourg spoke about sorrowful ecclesiastical conditions that coincided with Luther's efforts. Abuses in the preaching of indulgences and a preoccupation with political machinations by the church were acknowledged as contributing factors to spawning Luther's revolution (Dickens, Tonkin, and Powell 1985, 109–110).

More influential than Maimbourg was Jacques Benigne Bossuet (1627–1704). Like Maimbourg, Bossuet, the bishop of Meaux from 1681 and formerly bishop of Condom in Gascony from 1670, was not an unbiased historiographer.[10] His *History of the Variations of the Protestant Churches* (1688) was written to refute Protestant errors and proceeded from the claim that the multiplicity of sects in Protestantism was "a mark of falseness and inconsistency" that brought individualism and near chaos to society. On the other hand, he argued, Catholicism presented truth that was uniform and integral. Bossuet understood the Reformation as yet another manifestation of heresy within history and not merely as the single consequence of Luther's own initiative. While he considered Luther to be eloquent, passionate, and tough, the reformer was but another victim of the human predilection for novelty (Dickens, Tonkin, and Powell 1985, 110).[11] Consequently, Bossuet's work discussed the respective truth and falsity of the Catholic and Protestant doctrines of the church, Eucharist, and ecclesial authority and exhorted Protestants to return to the Catholic church.[12]

   Johann Adam Möhler (1796–1838), professor of church history at Tübingen from 1826 and at Munich from 1835, had a lifelong preoccupation with Christian reunion as did Bossuet. However, many scholars differentiate the two insofar as Möhler "was almost the first Catholic to treat Protestantism with anything approaching a scientific spirit" (Faulkner 1905, 360). Influenced by the zeal for the study of history brought on by German Romanticism, Möhler recognized the need for the sixteenth-century Reformation but concluded that it had been overly revolutionary and destructive (Dickens, Tonkin, and Powell 1985, 180). His *Symbolics, or Exposition of Doctrinal Differences between Catholics and Protestants as Evidenced by Their Symbolical Writings* of 1832 was a comparison of Lutheran confessional writings and Roman Catholic doctrines. Rather than seeking out polemical grist in the former, he engaged the central principle of Protestantism, justification by faith alone, one of the first Catholics to demonstrate an assumption that a viable system of belief can be found in the Reformation.

   Möhler saw the Lutheran doctrine of justification by faith alone as the Archimedean point of the system and, in accord with his Hegelian sympathies, posited an inherent dualism as the principal deficiency. He stated that the Lutheran anthropology of a radically corrupt person incorrectly modifies the early patristic anthropology which defined man as partially corrupt. The Lutheran understanding of persons losing both the image and likeness of God expands incorrectly the patristic notion of the corruption of will (loss of likeness), adding the corruption of reason (loss of image).[13] Thus, Luther is praised for his vigorous piety and inspiring thought, yet is criticized roundly for his intellectual myopia and role in the destruction of church unity (Dickens, Tonkin, and Powell 1985, 180–18).

Johann Joseph Ignaz von Döllinger (1799–1890), professor of church history at Munich from 1826 to 1872, wrote his *The Reformation, Its Interior Development and the Results It has Produced in the Heart of Lutheran Society* (3 vols., 1845–48) with the explicit purpose of refuting Lutheran Leopold von Ranke's *History of the Reformation in Germany* (6 vols., 1839–47).[14] Döllinger, who lost his professorship after being excommunicated for opposing Vatican I's definition of papal primacy and infallibility, held Luther responsible for the moral and cultural decline of Germany, especially its long-suffering in the Thirty Years' War (1618–48).[15] More significant from a historiographical point of view is Döllinger's focus on psychobiography, a distinctive feature of Catholic Luther-studies emphasized by Heinrich Denifle and Hartmann Grisar in the twentieth century (Jedin 1966, 56).[16]

Döllinger determined Luther's inner motives and dispositions by reference to the reformer's own writings, especially those of later years which included his own critical assessment of the Reformation. This shift from a concern with external factors to a preoccupation with the psychological cause of Luther's teachings allowed Döllinger to conclude:

> [Luther] himself admitted that he was constantly plagued by distrust, doubt, despair, hatred and blasphemy. Overwhelmed by such a gloomy, depressing state of mind, wildly confused by contradictory and destructive ideas about divine grace and human will, as well as about sin and faith, he gradually developed views which eventually would dominate his whole life and thought. (Dickens, Tonkin, and Powell 1985, 176)

While he presented a generally negative appraisal of Luther, Döllinger's work demonstrates that attention to historical sources was reemerging among Catholic historians and that the caricatures of earlier polemicists was yielding to an analysis of primary texts.

In 1872, Döllinger's *Lectures on the Reunion of the Churches* provided a revised assessment of Luther, viewing curial neglect of disastrous conditions in the church as the key factor in causing the division of the church. He stated that

> The force and strength of the Reformation was only in part due to the personality of the man who was its author and spokesman in Germany. It was Luther's overpowering greatness and wonderful

many-sidedness of mind that made him the man of his age and his people. Nor was there ever a German who has such an intuitive knowledge of his countrymen, and was again so completely possessed, not to say absorbed, by the national sentiment, as the Augustinian monk of Wittenberg. The mind and spirit of the Germans was in his hand what the lyre is in the hand of a skilled musician. . . . And yet still more powerful than this Titan of the world of mind was the yearning of the German people for a deliverance from the bonds of a corrupted Church system. (60–62)

Overall, this turn for a more respectful Catholic view of Luther was stillborn. The initiative for more respectful Luther studies among Catholics by Maimbourg and Bossuet did not influence the academy or church of France. Möhler's work was stymied by the increase of confessional polemics in late nineteenth-century Germany and intramural Catholic concern over Pius IX's *Syllabus of Errors* (8 December 1864). Coming on the heels of his own criticism of doctrines of papal infallibility and primacy at the First Vatican Council (1869–70), Döllinger's reappraisal was generally unheralded and subsequently overshadowed by his earlier estimation (Jedin 1967a, 84–86).

The Neo-Classical Image of Luther

While the next generation of Catholic scholarship about Luther continued the predominant mode of vilification, the superficial and reactionary approach that typified the sixteenth and seventeenth centuries was left behind. Catholic scholars now affirmed the principles of historical objectivity and attention to the sources. However, the assumptions about Luther given in the sixteenth century, and reaffirmed by the continuing opposition of Lutherans to Catholic doctrine thereafter, still provided the dominant perspective for the new assessments even though the method demanded a more impartial investigation.

Johannes Janssen (1829–91), professor of history for Catholic students at the Gymnasium of Frankfurt, produced his eight-volume *History of the German People at the Close of the Middle Ages* from 1876 to 1894. Taking his lead from the early Döllinger, Janssen asserted that Luther was the destroyer of German culture and piety. Janssen saw the church of the fifteenth and sixteenth centuries as a flourishing segment of German society. He considered various sermons, devotional writings, religious art, and the increase in translations of the Bible as clear evidence of ecclesial vitality. Janssen contended that Luther's error, arising from an ignorance produced by his immature character and moral weakness (as evident in his monastic incompetency, for example) was in failing to acknowledge the resources for reform already in place in the church (Dickens, Tonkin, and Powell 1985, 183–184).

Janssen admitted that conditions caused by political interference in church affairs with ecclesial complicity, by clerical abuses, and by nationalistic differences presented challenges to the church. Nevertheless, he maintained that the existing spiritual reserves could have resolved these problems, save the egotistical interference of Luther who nipped nascent reforms in the bud. Luther's great personal gifts of religious insight and oratory, squandered in the service of a confused purpose, resulted in the destruction of the church's unity.[17]

Janssen's work was a standard for generations of Catholic scholars until it was displaced by Heinrich Suso Denifle's *Luther und Luthertum in der ersten Entwicklung quellenmässig dargestellt* (*Luther and Lutherdom from Original Sources*) (1904–09), the single most important Catholic work on Luther in the first third of the century and the most ferocious attack since Pistorius (Jedin 1967a, 86). Denifle (1844–1905), a German Dominican who taught in the monastery at Graz from 1870 to 1880 and then worked as a sub-archivist at the Vatican's Archives from 1883 until his death, was an accomplished medieval historian who concentrated on scholasticism and the development of medieval universities.[18] His three-volume study of Luther, begun in 1883 and fully published after his death, received immediate attention not only because of his scholarly reputation among Protestants and Catholics but also because of the work's harsh tenor and attention to primary sources. Written in response to the Protestant apotheosis of Luther during the quadricentennial of his birth in 1883 and to the consequent renaissance in Luther-studies, the stinging recriminations in the work "dropped a bomb into the veneration for Luther current at the end of the nineteenth century" (Iserloh 1966, 9).[19] The inclusion of material garnered from notes taken originally during Luther's lectures on Romans in 1515–16, which Denifle himself discovered in the Vatican Archives and were unavailable to scholars previously, heightened his authority.

Denifle rejected Janssen's rosy picture of the late medieval church, claiming that the church exhibited two currents: renewal *and* decadence. Accordingly, Denifle estimated Luther's career by analogy, utilizing the Pauline dichotomy of flesh and spirit: Luther began in the spirit of renewal but succumbed to the decadence of the flesh (Rupp 1953, 23). Denifle claimed that Luther's tragedy occurred because he was blinded by pride and incapacitated by theological ignorance and moral failure.

Denifle emphasized that Luther's claim for enlightenment, based on his understanding of a strictly gratuitous justification according to Romans 1:17, is unacceptable. In a separate work of 1905, Denifle had argued that more than sixty doctors of the church interpreted Romans 1:17 to demonstrate a gratuitous justice rather than retributive justice.[20] He concluded that either Luther was theologically uninformed or, more probably, he knew the tradition and lied by claiming originality for his own breakthrough [*Turmerlebnis*] (1917, 430–441). Thus, in the context of reviewing several liturgical prayers of Luther's time, Denifle stated:

> So here again does Luther express the verdict on his later calumnies, when he spoke as if the Church, prior to him and he with her, had known God only as a stern judge, whom man was obliged to propitiate by his own achievements. Apart from this, almost to the time of his apostasy, when he had long since found his gospel, Luther cited several of these liturgical prayers, *against* merit, against the notion that we or our achievements, of whatever kind they might be, were the cause of our salvation. (1917, 464)

Consequently, for example, Luther's account of the vacuity of the monastic vocation, underscoring its unfounded baseless demand for moral perfection, was based on Luther's allegedly deceptive claim that the monastic focus was concerned strictly with works to the exclusion of faith. Denifle posited that Luther embraced the doctrine of justification by faith alone to compensate for his moral depravity and monastic ineptitude.[21]

The preponderance of Denifle's work was spent qualifying the spiritual state of the reformer according to this presupposition of a diseased soul. Thus Luther was accused, among other things, of pride, hypocrisy, forgery, slander, drunkenness, licentiousness, and vulgarity. The assertion of Luther's moral corruption was documented by references to the reformer's own claims to sin and by correlation with his understanding of the doctrine of concupiscence. Denifle maintained that Luther understood concupiscence as sexual disorder.[22] He concluded that Luther's self-examination yielded a life of sexual preoccupation and his admonition to Melanchthon to "sin boldly" can be construed as an exhortation to a licentious lifestyle. In addition to the positions on Luther declared in the work, Protestant scholars were enflamed when Denifle belittled all of his detractors, including Catholic critics. In the preface to the second edition he stated:

> *On the reception accorded my replication* I can also be brief, thanks to the conduct of the opponents whom I fended off. . . . For I could not expect that they would lack the courage to take up the gauntlet which I had thrown down to them before the whole world in a special work—a work in which blunders of the worst description in so many passages of their defensive writings were evinced to them as under a spot-light, a work which did not merely warm over things already said, but contained numerous *new ideas*. The declaration of bankruptcy which, at the close of my brochure, I clinched upon Protestant Luther-research, especially that of Harnack and Seeburg, now counts the more against them. (1917, xxii)

A resurgence of Protestant scholarship in rejection of Denifle followed.[23] Ironically, Denifle had set out a new agenda for Luther-research with his focus on the development of the early Luther and Luther's relationship to scholasticism (Iserloh 1966, 9; Jedin 1966, 57). As Denifle's evaluation of Luther waned, his intent to place Luther in an historical context also stimulated Catholic research. His Catholic peers distanced themselves from his positions but not his recognition of the historical method (Dickens, Tonkin, and Powell 1985, 200–201).

Hartmann Grisar, SJ, (1845–1932), professor of church history at Innsbruck from 1871 to 1895 (when he was relieved of duties to pursue special historical and archaeological research in Rome), took issue with Denifle on two counts. He rejected both Denifle's assertions of moral turpitude and the narrow interpretation of Luther's understanding of concupiscence, stating that both do not stand up under rigorous examination (Grisar 1916–17, xxxviii–xxxix). Based in large measure on several articles about Luther published in the 1880s and 1890s, Grisar produced his three-volume *Luther* in 1911 and 1912, also dismissing many of the calumnious Catholic legends about Luther in his effort to conduct a psychobiographical investigation. Calumnies were not absent in Grisar although they are not as obvious or forceful as in Denifle. For example, he speculated that in 1523 Luther suffered from syphilis and he opined that Luther's religious breakthrough occurred in the lavatory (Grisar 1955, 290; Reu 1930, 49).

Grisar's 2,600-page work, condensed into one volume in 1926 and thereafter a standard Catholic resource on Luther, saw Luther's efforts as the result of mental instability rather than the moral incapacity alleged by Denifle.[24] Presuming Luther's upbringing by an alcoholic father and a melancholic mother, Grisar alleged that the monastery was the incubator for a number of psychological problems which prevented Luther from recognizing legitimate criticisms of his theology. Grisar asserts that Luther is more to be pitied than blamed because:

> With regard to his self-image, he is under the influence of ideas which disclose various pathological symptoms, all of which together raise serious questions as to the nature of his changing state of mind. Since he feels chosen by God to do great things, since he is not only "the prophet of the Germans" but also the restorer of the gospel for the whole Christian world, he thinks that he has been equipped by providence with faculties which hardly anyone else has received. He frequently says so, even though he insists that God is behind it all. He likes to compare himself not only to his papistical opponents but also to the most famous figures of the Church of the past. In the same fashion he likes to measure the opponents in his own camp against his own personal greatness. Thus it happens that he talks and sounds like a megalomaniac; and he likes himself so much in this role that he does not even notice how tasteless and offensive some of his exaggerations are. (1916–17, 3:650)

Coupled with an education in the decadent scholasticism of Ockham and a fascination with the mystical assertion of persons' passivity before God, this instability, Grisar claimed, suffused itself into Luther's rejection of works-righteousness. The Jesuit stated that "With ever increasing confidence he imputed to the Apostle [Paul] the ideas to which he was urged for the sake of the supposed quieting of his scruples. Simultaneously, an arsenal of new weapons against the self-righteous Pharisees within the Church seemed to open itself up to him" (1955, 71). Grisar's Luther is gifted with oratorical skills, motivated by sincere desires to reform the faith but ultimately doomed by the pride and egoism which serve as compensations for serious mental problems and which also prevent him from responding to the correction of the church and her theologians.

Gordon Rupp stated that "Between them, Grisar and Denifle present a documented indictment for which all students must be grateful. Anyone who cares to work through their thousands of pages will emerge knowing that he has heard all that can possibly be said against the character and work of Martin Luther" (1953, 26). In the final analysis, scholars have concluded that the differences between the two were marginal, often saying that Denifle attacked Luther with a club while Grisar did so with pinpricks (Loewenich 1959, 270). Their research considered Luther's writings and also admitted the need for reform during the sixteenth century. Both were respected scholars and pledged fidelity to the canons of historical research in their massive investigations. Nevertheless, Protestant and subsequent Catholic scholars rejected their work as modern versions of centuries-old invective. Yves M.-J. Congar concluded that "In all this exposition, in which the erudition was often admirable and much of which must, upon any hypothesis, be retained, the real motives and the true range of Luther's work are fundamentally overlooked, passed over in silence and smothered by the asides of a history which was unfortunately all too rich in scandals and contradictions" (1964, 366).

While German-speaking scholars debated or dismissed the double-barreled indictments of Denifle and Grisar, French-speaking and English-speaking scholars converted those allegations into a strong tradition by perpetuating them in numerous scholarly and popular works. The chief proponents of Denifle and Grisar in France were Léon Cristiani, Jacques Paquier, Marie-Joseph Lagrange, OP, and Jacques Maritain.[25]

Cristiani (b.1879), professor at the Grand Seminary of Moulin from 1903 to 1914 and at the Catholic Faculties of Lyon from 1919 to 1947, was the most influential, publishing dozens of monographs and studies during the fifty-year period after his introduction of Denifle to France in 1908 with his *Luther et le Lutheranisme: Études de psychologie et d'histoire religieuse.* Cristiani was impressed with Luther's childhood, often documenting the baneful effects of his heritage (impulsive, coarse, vulgar, impulsive, excessive) and his upbringing (excessively strict, gloomy). Thus, like Denifle, he posited that Luther's doctrine focuses on certainty of salvation to compensate for his own moral failures (1936, 31–40). As late as 1962 Cristiani would consider Denifle an historian of the "front rank" and, in Grisarian overtones, presented these conclusions about Luther:

> He then [1512] began to consider the Bible as his own personal domain, his private preserve. He plunged into it with delight. But his biblical study was not of the same kind as that of men like Erasmus and Lefèvre d'Étaples, his contemporaries. He read it with his own personal problems in mind. What he sought more than all else in it was comfort and spiritual security. (1962, 62)[26]

Paquier translated Denifle into French, frequently amending the Dominican's text with more excoriating commentary. In *Le*

protestantisme allemand: Luther, Kant, Nietzsche, written in the midst
of World War I, he asserted that the Reformation and subsequent
German intellectual developments had created much of the egoism
and brutality attributable to German nationalism.[27] In 1918 he
envisioned Luther as the Muhammed of the West and Lutheranism
as German Muhammedanism; together they present a gross deforma-
tion of true Christianity (Stauffer 1966, 28–30).

Lagrange (1855–1938), a principal catalyst behind modern Catholic biblical studies and founder of the L'École Pratique d'Étude
Bibliques at Jerusalem (1890) and the journal *Revue biblique* at Paris
(1892), examined the early Luther with "Le commentaire de Luther
sur l'Epitre aux Romaines de apres des publications recentes" in 1915
and 1916.[28] He began by rejecting Bossuet's claim that the posting of
the *Ninety-five Theses* was a first step focused on the abuses in the
selling of indulgences. Rather, he argued that Luther was in possession
of a theological system by October 1517 when "If all the details were
not formulated, the principles had been laid down clearly and with
assurance. The monk had his doctrine and his plan of reform. It was
now clear that the new religion is not the result of circumstances"
(Lagrange 1918, 2). Thus he studied Luther's commentary as an
exegetical work, mindful of the need to clarify the questions raised by
Denifle and Grisar about Luther's moral and mental capacities as well
as his understanding of Saint Paul. He concluded that Luther misin-
terpreted Paul:

> It is true that theologians, with a view to more precision, had
> distinguished these two aspects, following the example of Paul
> himself in the Epistle to the Corinthians where he distinguishes so
> clearly faith and charity (1 Cor. 13). But to understand faith as St.
> Paul did, it had to be taken with charity; and Luther would not do
> so. To understand it with theological precision was to make it a
> disposition which could not distinguish Christians who are justi-
> fied from those who are not. (Lagrange 1918, 9)

Further, while not wholly endorsing Denifle's picture of a thoroughly corrupt man, Lagrange attributed Luther's biblical deductions
and subsequent implementation to the reformer's tortuous struggles
with concupiscence, excessive pride, and constant immoderation.

Maritain (1882–1973), who taught at the Institut Catholique de
Paris from 1914 to 1933 and the Institute of Medieval Studies at
Toronto from 1933 to 1945, wrote his *Trois Reformateurs: Luther-
Descartes-Rousseau* (1925) with the conviction that it is "right that we
should go some distance into the past in our search for the roots and

first germinative principles of the ideas which rule the world to-day" (1929, 3).[29] Maritain presented his subjects, respectively, as a reformer of religion, a reformer of philosophy, and a reformer of morality. Relying on Denifle and Grisar, he stated that "from the very beginning his [Luther's] life was off the axle" and that Luther let himself go with the tide of sin (Maritain 1929, 3).

Consequently, Maritain contended that Luther marked the advent of modern individualism and the denial of legitimate Christian personalism, the apotheosis of affectivity at the expense of reason, and the installation of the principle of immanence, which exalts the "interior energy of man the master of his judgment against dead ideas and lying conventions imposed from without" (1929, 45).[30]

Notable English-speaking advocates of the Denifle-Grisar tradition are Hilaire Belloc, Joseph Clayton, Henry Outram Evenett, and Philip Hughes in Great Britain and Henry George Ganss and Patrick F. O'Hare in the United States.

(Joseph-Pierre) Hilaire Belloc (1870–1953), London-based author, journalist, and poet, popularized a negative caricature of Luther with his *Europe and the Faith* (1920). Overall, Belloc argued that the Reformation was a necessary consequence of three simultaneous forces, all promoting change in the status quo: the corruption of medieval society, including the church, which brought about a drive for reform; an increase in technical power which fostered human confidence and an appetite for change; and, the advent of "Absolute Government" which advanced nationalism and the decline of spiritual authority. In the face of the crisis that emerged, Martin Luther was, Belloc stated,

> one of those exuberant sensual, rather inconsequential, characters which so easily attract hearty friendships, and which can never pretend to organization or command, thought certainly to creative power. What he precisely meant or would do, no man could tell, least of all himself. He was "out" for protest and he floated on the crest of the general wave of change. . . . Luther (a voice, no leader) was but one of many: had he never lived, the great bursting wave would have crashed onward much the same. (1920, 206–224)

Joseph Clayton (1868–1943), English journalist and biographer, introduced his *Luther and His Work* (1937) as an impartial history together with the estimation that "inevitably is the work of Luther deplored and his name a word of reproach where it is held that the unity of Christian peoples—'one Lord, one faith, one Baptism'—is part of the divine plan for salvation of mankind, and that the guarantee of that unity resides in a common obedience to the spiritual authority of the Pope" (xxiv). Clayton, a Catholic convert from Anglicanism in 1910, relied more on Grisar than Denifle. "Turbulent and disquieted in mind, and therefore unhappy because of internal trouble, not because of external corruptions in the Church," he stated, "Luther continued in this state till he believed he had found in certain epistles of St. Paul the healing his soul sought" (32). Clayton posited that despite his courage, literary genius, and capacity for understanding human nature, Luther led his adherents to "a wasteland, littered with abandoned hopes and discarded creeds" (262).[31]

Henry Outram Evenett (1901–64), fellow of Trinity College, Cambridge, wrote a series of pamphlets for the Catholic Truth Society which included an account of the Reformation published in 1957. He cast Luther as the creator of a novel doctrine of justification, which spawned from the reformer's mental anguish and advanced by his genius as a pamphleteer. Evenett credited Luther's success to the standard set of external factors which fostered the Reformation generally (political, social, ecclesiastical), especially emphasizing the ready disposition of many believers to accept a doctrine which promoted moral laxity and confrontation with non-German ecclesial authorities (1957, 80).

Philip Hughes (1895–1967), archivist for the Archdiocese of Westminster from 1931 to 1943 and professor of church history at the University of Notre Dame from 1955 to 1963, published his *Revolt Against the Church: Aquinas to Luther* in 1947 and *A Popular History of the Reformation* in 1957. Both works were circulated widely in Britain and America.

In the earlier work Hughes stated that Luther was a false prophet who could not provide the correct remedy for the political, moral, and religious ills of the age. He concluded that while much can be said in Luther's favor,

> It is the deepest criticism of Luther's famous theory—and the explanation of the unending, ever-developing miseries that have come from it—that it goes against the nature of things, and against nothing more evidently than against the nature of the spiritual. The new religion introduced, or rather established as a permanent part of the permanent order of things, a whole series of vital antagonisms to perplex and hinder man already too tried by his own freely chosen wrong-doing, to fill his soul with still blacker thoughts about the hopeless contradiction and futility of all existence, to set him striving for centuries at the hopeless task of bringing happiness

and peace out of a philosophy essentially pessimistic and despair-
ing. (Hughes 1947, 528)

Anchoring his interpretation in Grisar's thesis that Luther's tor-
tured mental life was the matrix that linked the soothing doctrine of
justification by faith alone and all other doctrines, Hughes argued that
Luther has little relevance for Christianity at large. The reformer's
immediate success was due to his great literary and oratorical skills. In
the later work, more dedicated to describing the emergence of the
Reformation than an analysis, Hughes opined that while Luther's
motives were not impure they were self-serving (1957, 108).

Henry George Ganss (1855–1912), priest of the Diocese of Pitts-
burgh and an accomplished musician, may have exercised the most
influence on American Catholic attitudes towards Luther with his
biographical article in the *Catholic Encyclopedia* of 1913.[32] Relying
heavily on Denifle, Ganss also cited the early Döllinger and Janssen
as trustworthy interpreters. Integrating some of the damaging legends
about Luther that Protestants scholars themselves acknowledged, and
which Grisar later debunked, Ganss described Luther as a liar (about
his difficulties with monastic life), psychotic (from his severe upbringing and subsequent scrupulosity), and ecclesiastical malcontent (according to his theological, political, and pastoral activity produced by
unyielding confidence and pride). As one would expect, the mention
of Satanic manifestations and sexual appetites was not absent (Ganss
1913, 457).

Patrick F. O'Hare (1848–1926), priest of the Diocese of Brooklyn,
presented *The Facts About Luther* as a popularized account of Janssen,
Denifle, and Grisar. Written as a countermeasure to the continuing
wave of Protestant enthusiasm following the fourth centenary of
Luther's birth in 1883, O'Hare reiterated the charges of moral
corruption and mental incapacity. He concluded in a vein typical of
the Catholic denigration of Luther that

> When we now turn to Luther and ask him why he claimed to be a
> religious reformer and why he posed as one entrusted by Heaven
> with a great and holy mission, we are not only astonished, but
> dumbfounded to discover that his title was self-assumed and
> without warrant, and, that, moreover, his qualifications for the
> work of reform were of such a nature as to impress the wise with the
> conviction that he received no call from Heaven to inaugurate and
> carry out a moral rejuvenation in either Church or State. Unlike the
> saintly preachers of God's truth of all times, he was in no way ever
> under a sense of his own personal need of improvement and was in

consequence utterly incapable and unfitted to elevate unto righteousness any among the brethren. . . . that he was a deformer and
not a reformer is the honest verdict of all who are not blind partisans
and who know the man at close vision for what he was and for what
he stood sponsor. (1916, 329–330)

Respect for Luther

While the denigration of Luther by Catholic theologians was nearly
unanimous, it was not maniacal. They concluded that Luther's
behavior was aberrant, his theology was inadequate, and his results
were deficient but, save Denifle, they understood that Luther was also
genuinely gifted. Ultimately judged as the destroyer of the church's
unity, Luther's remarkable literary and oratorical talents, profound
zeal, and a dedicated pastoral sense were noted nonetheless. This
recognition of positive personal attributes and an increasing recognition of the church's need for reform in the early sixteenth century
became key themes in the radical revision of Catholic Luther-
scholarship that occurred between 1917 and 1940. This realization
provides avenues for perceiving Luther's prophetic role in Christianity and Catholicism that would make Catholic observance of Luther's
birth in 1983 so very different from that of 1883.

The emergence of Catholic assessments based on a genuine respect
for Luther's professional and religious performance occurred primarily in Germany. In addition to the obvious importance of Luther
from a cultural and national point of view, German Catholic scholarship also operated from a continuing inspiration by Rankean
historiography. The conclusions of Denifle and Grisar became unten-
able as Protestant and Catholic scholars considered and refuted their
claims with attention to the texts and contexts of the principal figures
of the reformation (Dickens, Tonkin, and Powell 1985, 179–180).
Too, the emergence and growth of the ecumenical movement also
required the reexamination of previous Catholic attitudes towards
Luther. The increased dialogue between German theologians in the
face of the Third Reich especially stimulated inter-confessional dialogue on all issues of faith, including the Luther-image.[33]

This movement in Catholic Luther-studies was initiated by Kiefl,
Fischer, Merkle, and Jedin. It gained permanent status with the work
of Lortz, and, to a lesser degree, Herte. Today it continues with the
historical scholarship of Iserloh and Manns.

Franz Xavier Kiefl (1869–1928), professor of dogmatic theology at
Würzburg and later dean of the cathedral at Regensburg, initiated
Catholic reappraisal of Luther with the claim that Luther's psyche was

actually the source of a providential movement to cleanse the church (Minus 1976, 52). With his article in the Catholic review *Hochland*, Kiefl thus challenged Denifle and anticipated Joseph Lortz by stating that Luther's motives were religious and theological. He asserted that Luther's awareness of God's might was the key factor in his thought, propelling his emphasis on faith and imputed righteousness as well as his denial of free will. Kiefl concluded that Luther's emphasis on faith did not imply moral slackening in Luther or, by extension, Lutheranism (Dallman 1943, 481–487).

Given his radical change from the previous Catholic assessment of Luther with this attribution of religious motives, Kiefl shared his predecessors' focus on Luther's inner life. In a more irenic fashion, he continued to raise a concern with Luther's morbidity. Likewise, Luther was still judged to be a heretic. However, as had been attempted earlier by Möhler and Bossuet, Kiefl's presupposition of a religious motivation brought a less inflammatory and more histori-cally reliable tone to the Catholic evaluation of Luther (Stauffer 1967, 37–38).

The presupposition of Luther's religious motivation was also evi-dent in the collection of essays by Protestants and Catholics edited by Alfred von Martin in 1929, *Luther in ökumenischer Sicht*.[34] Of the four essays by Catholics, those of Anton Fischer and Sebastian Merkle (1862–1945) are especially notable. Fischer argued that Luther's religious genius could only be appreciated by recognizing the reformer as a man of prayer. While realizing that Luther was also a fighting man, responsible for the division of the church, Fischer stated that "Though a Church be ever so rich in truly great Christian men of prayer it should nevertheless find room for the special gift of the praying Luther; it should not pass by unnoticed this great man of prayer with his priceless statements on prayer and his incisive instructions on how to pray." Fischer thus located Luther in the company of Augustine and Francis of Assisi (Atkinson 1983, 22).[35]

Merkle, professor of church history at Würzburg from 1898 to 1933, argued for historical justice in the Catholic treatment of Luther with his essay "Good Points in Luther and Bad Points in His Critics."[36] Criticizing Denifle especially, for which he was repri-manded by his bishop, Merkle considered Luther's religious motiva-tion in context of the low state of the church in the sixteenth century (Stauffer 1967, 73). Stating that Luther may have exaggerated the church's deficiencies, Merkle also judged that his critics have been overly optimistic in their reading of ecclesial conditions. Otherwise, he stated, "[Luther] would have to appear much more as the greatest

wonder-worker of history, if he had brought about the mass defection
from a flourishing church, a church at the zenith of fulfilling its task"
(Swidler 1965, 193). Consequently, Luther is said to have initiated a
spiritual movement, and not a revolution that inhibited a positive
Catholic response to the problems at hand (Dickens, Tonkin, and
Powell 1985, 205). Merkle, while affirming that Luther was objec-
tively wrong by virtue of his break with the church, sought to provide
a subjective understanding of his efforts by an accurate reading of both
Luther's context and aspirations (Iserloh 1966, 8).[37]

In 1931 Hubert Jedin (1900–80) reported that Denifle's argument
for Luther's moral incapacity had lapsed among German Catholic
scholars. Affirming the presupposition of Luther's religious motivation to be the norm, Jedin stated that Catholics should forget previous
understandings of Luther.[38] Echoing Merkle, he wrote later that "I do
not believe that we can make Luther Catholic or even canonize him.
But what we can and must do is this: we must not only let him be
historically justified, give him that justice which was understandably
denied him in an age of religious strife" (1966, 63). Nevertheless, the
general reappraisal of Luther achieved little attention outside Germany as these occasional essays did not command international
attention (Stauffer 1967, 40). With Joseph Lortz (1887–1975), a
student of Merkle who held appointments in church history at
Münster (1935–47) and Mainz (1947–50), such attention was gained.
Lortz's now-classic comprehensive statement of the revised view of
Luther came in 1939 and 1940 with his two-volume *The Reformation
in Germany*.[39] Lortz stated that: "Merkle basically considered Luther's
teaching to be, as a whole, quite clearly anti-Catholic. His work of
conciliation was mainly, if not wholly, directed at acknowledging
Luther's good intention, at interpreting, historically and psychologi-
cally, his person, his growth, and the possibility of his theses and at
understanding Luther subjectively" (Jedin, 1967a, 89).

Born in Luxembourg, Lortz became deeply engaged in Reformation
history in 1917 when he was appointed scientific secretary for the
Görres Society's *Corpus Catholicorum*, a project dedicated to the
publication of important documents of Catholic tradition at the
University of Bonn (Swidler 1965, 195). Lortz developed the fundamental positions of this work during seminars in the 1930s at
Braunsberg and Münster (Lukens 1988, 5). More historical interpretation than documentation, *The Reformation in Germany* has a
threefold structure: a description of the church on the eve of the
Reformation, a consideration of Luther's theological development to
1525, and an account of Lutheranism and Catholicism up to the

Peace of Westphalia (1555). Essentially, Lortz understood Luther to be a religious man (*homo religiosus*) who acted according to his understanding of the Bible and reacted to the corrupt environs and practices of the late medieval church. While the Reformation therefore had a certain inner necessity, it was nonetheless unjustifiable, he argued, insofar as Luther "overthrew a Catholicism that was not Catholic" (Lortz 1968, 1:200).

Lortz's description of the church on the eve of the Reformation recounted a dissolution of medieval Christendom with fracturing in ecclesiastical, doctrinal, and pastoral dimensions. On an ecclesiastical level, he argued that the hierarchy provided ineffective leadership due to institutional and individual factors. For example, the papacy had lost much of its spiritual and temporal power with the dislocation to Avignon (1309–77), the subsequent manifestation of antipopes (1378–1415), and an avaricious Roman bureaucracy. Combined with the peccadilloes of individual popes and their delegates, including local bishops, the hierarchy's attention to spiritual matters lapsed. Important factors in the diminishment of ecclesiastical authority are also found in the increased vitality of national churches and the consequent dissipation of the Holy See's temporal influence, often amidst ill-conceived political alliances (Lortz 1968, 3–164).

Lortz demonstrated doctrinal confusion with reference to Desiderius Erasmus (1466–1536) and William of Ockham (1285–1347). He alleged that Erasmus introduced doctrinal relativism into the church with the elevation of the individual conscience, anthropocentric theology, and subjectivism. He stated that "Erasmus represented the threat of dogmatic dissolution within the Church. Luther called men to a profession of faith. He shook people awake" (Lortz 1968, 155). More important for Lortz was Ockham's contradiction of the Catholic tradition by separating faith and reason. A consequent emphasis on the salvific activity of the human will was matched with a portrait of an utterly transcendent God. Lortz concluded: "In what way was it [Ockhamism] uncatholic? (*a*) The system bears no existential relationship to truth; (*b*) it makes grace virtually a superfluous accessory" (Lortz 1968, 196; cf. Bagchi 1991, 63). American Denis R. Janz corroborated Lortz's assertions in *Luther and Late Medieval Thomism*, concluding after reflection on theological anthropologies of five late medieval Thomists as well as Aquinas and Luther that "the fully Augustinian teaching of Thomas was not adequately represented by Luther's Thomist contemporaries" (Janz 1983, 157).[40]

Janz has argued further that Luther's indictment of Aquinas himself as a theologian of glory, who did not appreciate the paradoxical revelation of God on the cross of Christ, is wrong. Aquinas revels in the claim that God is mystery even as he applies syllogistic reasoning with great vigor. For Aquinas, states Janz, "syllogism here clarifies and to some extent makes intelligible, teases out the implicit, and really nothing more" (Janz 1998, 13). Thus Aquinas is faithful to biblical knowledge, expressed in paradoxical style, even as he communicates in a conclusive philosophy later misrepresented to Luther.

Pastoral decline in the church is evident to Lortz in the increased clericalization and simultaneous alienation of the laity from their leaders and the life of the church, especially the sacraments. A spiritual malaise intensified in the church because "there may have been far too many monks whose god was in their belly, and who were not nourished on the Word of God" (Ibid., 105). Reaction against ecclesial taxation, especially in the form of indulgences, is therefore seen as a reaction against pastors. Lortz summarized his view of the pre-Reformation church:

> No one would still want to deny that the possibilities of revolution in the Church had become unusually great. The failure of those really holding responsibility had been proved on all sides, in a manner that we rarely find in history. The opposition had infil- trated all classes of society and was loudly expressed in many forms. There was a universal expectancy of a coming revolution, even within the Church. The storm broke as soon as the man appeared who knew how to unleash the forces of the age. (Ibid., 164)

Lortz's Luther is a man of profound spiritual intensity whose greatest accomplishments were as a preacher of the Gospel and reform rather than as a theologian. Luther was remarkably energetic, bold, and persuasive. He was immersed in scripture and prayer, dedicated to the temporal as well as to the spiritual needs of the faithful, and fought for the preservation of doctrine. He is to be admired above all for his constant assertion of the sovereignty of God, faith in Jesus Christ as savior, and the real presence of Christ in the eucharist (Ibid., 428–488).

Lortz argued that Luther's myopia is due to his overly subjective reading of scripture as well as his training in and subsequent rejection of Ockhamist theology. He contended that Luther was not fully attentive to the Bible insofar as the reformer was preoccupied with his own personal needs—the means and status of his own salvation. Luther was unable to grasp the fuller sense of the faith as maintained by the church. Luther's rejection of a Catholicism known through

Ockham's perspective demonstrates that the Reformation resulted from a misunderstanding.

> Occamism [Ockhamism] with its overstress on the will is the classic formulation of that which Luther designated *work-righteousness*, and which he asserted was Catholic doctrine. We do well to note that Luther was not thinking merely of the well-known abuses and extravagances of Church life. Nor had he in mind the exaggerated affirmations of boorish polemics. This was Luther's conviction about Catholic teaching. (Ibid., 198)

If Luther would have been more fully aware of the Catholic tradition and less attached to his own scrupulosity and pride, Lortz posited, he may have grasped the full meaning of the tradition as well as scripture.

Lortz's respect for Luther was not diminished by his assertion of Luther's failure to respond properly to the impetus for reform that was evident in the church and in himself. In fact, his estimation of Luther became more positive in his later years:

> (1) We Catholics have gradually come to realize the Christian, indeed the Catholic richness of Luther's thought and we are deeply impressed by this; (2) we have come to realize also how greatly Roman Catholicism is responsible for Luther's expulsion from the Church with the result that the church became divided; (3) we are strongly moved by the desire to bring home to the Catholic church all the great and positive substance of Luther's thought. (Lortz 1970, 6–7; cf. Manns 1984, 10–16)

Lortz has been remarkably influential in Catholic Luther-studies due, in part, to the fact that he traveled in ecumenical as well as academic circles. He was particularly active in the Una Sancta movement and worked to promote the Catholic Conference for Ecumenical Affairs (*Conference catholique pour les questions oecuméniques*) with Monsignor Jan Willebrands (Swidler 1965, 200–201; Lortz 1948–49, 455–461). Also, his publications were widely distributed—in 1982 *The Reformation in Germany* continued in a sixth German edition. A summary of the original work and responses to critics was given in *Die reformation als religiöses Anliegen heute* (1948) and a popular version, *Wie kam es zur Reformation?*, appeared in 1950.[41] Recognition of his stature came in 1950 when he was appointed director of the newly founded *Institut für europäische Geschichte* at Mainz, a post he held until his death in 1975.

Dickens, Tonkin, and Powell state that while his impact on
Catholic Luther-studies has been exaggerated occasionally, "Lortz's
differences from these polemicists were more than variations of
emphasis. He understood it as the product not of base motives, moral
depravity, or psychic collapse, but of a one-sidedness born of an
earnest and godly spirit" (Dickens, Tonkin, and Powell 1985, 206).[42]
    While Lortz's reappraisal of Luther became the centerpiece of a
general Catholic theological reconstruction, the concurrent work of
Adolph Herte (1887–1970) was, from an historiographical perspective, no less important (Dickens, Tonkin, and Powell 1985, 206;
Jedin 1967a, 80). Herte's *Das katholische Lutherbild im Bann der
Lutherkommentare des Cochläus* (1943) considered over five hundred
Catholic interpreters of Luther from Cochläus to Grisar and argued
that Cochläus's calumnious invective exercised a controlling influence throughout, including modern popes and churchmen.[43] Of
Cochläus's commentaries he says: "Like a comet they have drawn the
whole of Catholic literature in their train, and have determined in the
last resort its whole character and appearance" (Loewenich 1959,
279). While the work was confined to an academic audience and was
more laborious to read than Lortz, Herte's study was a decisive call for
Catholic scholars to develop an historically accurate picture of Luther,
forsaking any reliance on legend and polemic. Stauffer claimed that
Herte was relieved of his position at the Archepiscopal Academy at
Paderborn for his views (1967, 73).
    The historical reassessment established by Lortz and confirmed by
Herte has continued and expanded with the efforts of Lortz's two
most notable students, Erwin Iserloh and Peter Manns.
    Iserloh (b.1915), professor of church history at Trier (1954–64)
and thereafter the director of the Catholic Ecumenical Institute at the
University of Münster, extended Lortz's perspective, with his history
of the Reformation in the ten-volume *Handbook of Church History*,
edited by Hubert Jedin.[44] In 1966 Iserloh became the first Catholic
scholar to address the International Congress on Luther Research
(Wicks 1970, 35–58). He considered the "inner historical necessity"
of the Reformation, including an analysis of the ecclesial context and
Luther's own development. He observed that

> To establish historical necessity does not mean to make a pro-
> nouncement on truth or error. A thing can be significant—that is,
> it can fit into a larger context—without being true. Furthermore,
> historical blame does not also mean moral blame. Something
> which was said and done with the best intention and was also good

in itself can turn out unfortunately and become "guilty" of an unhappy development. (1980, 3)

Thus Luther became the author of a new church although he did not intend to be such a catalyst. The combination of his one-sided Catholic philosophy and temperament with the abuses in piety and theology of the church helped establish a divided Christianity (Ibid., 10).

Iserloh, who has devoted much of his scholarly life to the study of Luther's Catholic controversialists, has also added to Luther-studies with the assertion that Luther did not post the *Ninety-five Theses* on 31 October 1517. In *The Theses Were Not Posted* (1966), Iserloh argued that Luther presented the theses to Archbishop Albrecht of Mainz and Bishop Schulz of Brandenburg in order to urge correction of abuses in the sale of indulgences.[45] The lame reaction of the bishops became an outstanding catalyst in Luther's inauguration of a movement:

> If Luther did turn first to the competent bishops with his protest, or better, with his earnest pleas for reform, and if he did give them time to react as their pastoral responsibilities called for, then it is the bishops who clearly were more responsible for the consequence. If Luther did allow the bishops time to answer his request then he was sincere in begging the archbishop to remove the scandal before the disgrace came upon him and the Church. Further, there was clearly a real opportunity that Luther's challenge could be directed to the reform of the church, instead of leading to a break with the church. But such reform would have demanded of the bishops far greater religious substance and a far more lively priestly spirit than they showed. (1968, 100)

As Lortz had argued previously, Iserloh concludes that Luther began the ultimately schismatic movement quite unintentionally. The Reformation began as a private affair and not a momentous public event as would have been caused by nailing them to the door of Castle Church on the eve of the feast of All Saints.[46]

Manns (b.1923), professor of church history at the University of Mainz and director of the Institute for European History since 1981, is the most prominent heir of Lortz's legacy (Gritsch 1988, 7). Manns became a consultant to the Institute shortly after his ordination in 1951 (Wicks 1970, 119). Lortz's earlier consideration of ecclesial debility and Luther's initiatives toward reform are likewise trademarks of Manns's thought. Manns affirmed that Luther's work was a tragic necessity and he proceeds from the paradoxical image of Luther that Lortz described, that is, a Luther who discovered genuinely Catholic doctrine in scripture and tradition yet who exaggerated or shortened it with his interpretation. However, he criticized Lortz for overemphasizing Luther's rejection of an Ockhamistic Catholicism and ambiguous use of the term 'subjectivism' (Manns 1984, 9).

Manns's description of Luther as a 'father in the faith', recharacterizing Lortz's 'holy and heretical' Luther, is a distinctive aspect of his contributions to contemporary Luther-studies. Luther's ecumenical value is imaged by Paul in 1 Corinthians 4:15: "For though you have countless guides in Christ, you do not have many fathers. For I became your father in Christ through the gospel" (RSV). Manns stated that

> What is exciting about Luther is that he bursts the framework of the old church without therefore leaving it, and that he does not establish a "new church" whose "reformist configuration" would be a function of its rejection of Catholicism. From this perspective, the uncommon and pronounced ecumenical potential of Luther's fundamental concerns becomes apparent. He resembles Abraham with whom, as with Paul, he identified throughout his life. . . . A person who goes along with Luther's questions and accompanies him on Abraham's path will quickly realize that in Luther also, he has found a "father in faith". (Manns 1983, 86)

Manns argued that Luther's theology of justification is more Catholic than previously acknowledged. Arguing that Luther's emphasis on faith alone necessarily includes a simultaneous recognition of love of God and love of neighbor *(agape)*, and thus a significant concern with good works, Manns stated that

> If God wants our love as a condition of salvation then he is thereby indicating to us a way of salvation that can be followed in communion of life and destiny with Christ and only through grace. Such a course still remains pure grace when we have fulfilled the law of charity through the power of new life. As a consequence, we do not succumb to the faulty argumentation Luther ascribed to the sophists, who saw the passage from precepts to eternal life as simply a matter of external performance. . . . Along with Luther, we understand the mystery of love through grace in terms of the mystery of righteousness to be advanced and revealed, whereby through faith we now possess love—the perfection of which we

struggle for in hope against ever-present sin. (Manns 1970, 155–156)

Manns claimed that this concern for pure love has profound ecumenical potential insofar as it cannot be restricted to either a "catholic" or "reformatory" category (1984, 17–18).

Manns also asserted that Luther never abandoned the clerical priesthood with his emphasis on a priesthood of all believers and that Luther did not absolutely define the papacy as inimical to the faith with the application of the term *antichrist* to his papal opponents (Ibid., 18–19).[47]

While German theologians have primarily fostered the Catholic historical reassessment of Luther, significant contributions have been made by French, English, and American theologians as well.

Louis Bouyer, COr, (b.1913), a Protestant convert to Catholicism in 1939 and professor of church history at the Institut Catholique de Paris, published *The Spirit and Forms of Protestantism* in 1954.[48] A personal witness to his own conversion, Bouyer explored intellectually what is positive and negative in Protestantism as well as elements of Catholicism that are necessary for the Christian faith. He became Catholic "not in order to reject any of the positive Christian elements of his [Protestant] religious life, but to enable them, at last, to develop without hindrance" (Bouyer 1956, xiii).

Bouyer considered Luther's affirmations of justification by faith in God's grace, personal religion, and the sovereign authority of scripture as keystones of the Protestant rediscovery. He admitted that the historical conditions of the sixteenth century fostered the advance of these propositions, although he still considered the break in Christian unity to be indefensible. Bouyer listed these negative factors in Luther's distortion of the Catholic faith: justification as external to persons rather than transformative, rejection of good works, radical debasement of the person, and the rejection of church authority (Minus 1976, 207).

Bouyer's Luther is thus a paradox, holding authentic elements of the faith even in its betrayal. Bouyer concluded that "it was Luther himself, and not only the stupidity of his followers, who provided all the elements of the system which was to imprison, rather than protect, the original doctrine" (1956, 166).

Daniel Olivier, AA, a student of Lortz and professor of Lutheran studies at Institut Superior d'Études Oecumeniques at Paris, has presented enthusiastically the results of the historical reassessment in a more popular, though not simplistic, fashion. *The Trial of Luther*

(1971) reviewed the estrangement of Luther and ecclesial authorities because of indulgences, integrating large segments of primary texts. Like Johannes Hessen of Cologne, Olivier considered the category of "prophet" an appropriate one to describe Luther's role in the sixteenth-century church.[49] Olivier's *Luther's Faith: The Cause of the Gospel in the Church* (1978) posited Luther as a source for contemporary Catholic evangelism and reviews major themes of the reformer.[50] Reaffirming his earlier judgment that Rome's refusal to listen during the indulgence controversy was a sign of the church's woeful state, Olivier highlighted Luther's understanding of self-abandonment in faith, salvation through Christ, and the creeds. It is Luther's retrieval of the Pauline-Augustinian emphasis on grace in face of a recalcitrant church that particularly impressed Olivier. The book also rejected the recurring psychopathological explanation of Luther by R. Dalbiez in his *L'Angoisse de Luther* (1974) (Tinsley 1983, 539; Wicks 1980b, 214–216).

The renewal of Luther-research in English-speaking countries dawned with the appearance of George H. Tavard's *The Catholic Approach to Protestantism* in 1955, the author's translation from the French original of 1954. Tavard introduce the book as a primer in European ecumenical studies and criticized Edward F. Hanohoe's *Catholic Ecumenism* (95).[51] Tavard recounted the basic events of the sixteenth century, subsequent developments of Protestantism and Catholicism ecclesiology, and posited fundamental principles for a Catholic ecumenical attitude. Echoing the historical reassessment of German Catholic theologians, he concluded that

> Had Luther alone been involved, he would have provided one more lopsided theology. The Church would have provided shelter to a new system, probably located next to the limit of orthodoxy. Communion with the universal church, however, would have gradually mended it. But Luther was not by himself. There were dissatisfied theologians. Among the aristocracy and middle classes many angrily watched German gold filling up the treasure chest of an Italian Pope. A whole people waited and waited for a true reform of ecclesiastical mores. (1955, 23)[52]

In 1983 Tavard argued more vigorously than he had in 1954 that Luther's doctrine of justification by faith alone is a legitimate interpretation of the Catholic tradition and hence the key to ecumenical reconciliation (Maddox 1984, 736–737).

Other notable contributions in the English-speaking world have been made by Thomas McDonough, OP, John Murray Todd, and

Jared Wicks, SJ. McDonough's *The Law and the Gospel in Luther: A Study of Martin Luther's Confessional Writings* (1963) argued that Luther's central doctrine is the soteriological relationship of Law, demonstrating one's inability to meet God's demands, and the Gospel, proclaiming God's merciful forgiveness.

He claimed that this most fundamental conviction of Luther stems from his experience of despair and faith during his monastic years which promoted understandings of humanity's enduring sinfulness, its passive role in justification by faith alone, and the external quality of righteousness (Parker 1964, 439–441). McDonough rejected the positions of Denifle, Grisar, and Maritain, maintaining a position consistent with Lortz that "Luther may not have experienced temptations of the flesh beyond the ordinary, if measured by a saner and more wholesome theology than Nominalism" (Stauffer 1967, 64).

Todd, a British layman, wrote for the nonspecialist with *Martin Luther: A Biographical Study* (1974) and *Luther: A Life* (1983). The earlier work was compiled from secondary studies, mainly Gordon Rupp's *The Righteousness of God*, and accounts for Luther's theological and spiritual development with an ecumenical design (Gritsch 1966, 257–258). The latter book was published during the quincentennial of Luther's birth, a biography that focused on the affective aspect of Luther by paying considerable attention to the reformer's correspondence and the *Table Talk* (Brown 1983a, 58–62).

Wicks (b.1929), a student of Iserloh and a professor at the Pontifical Gregorian University in Rome, has continued and advanced upon the Lortzian positions through various genres. His *Man Yearning for Grace: Luther's Early Spiritual Teaching* (1969) is a scholarly study that proceeded from Lortz's thesis of Luther as a religious man, arguing that Luther's eagerness to advance in holiness, which was demonstrated in his Augustinian life between 1509 and 1517, was a typically Catholic monastic discipline despite Luther's strong self-accusation. Wicks contended that the indulgence controversy of 1517 initiates Luther's non-Catholic deviation insofar as he becomes increasingly pre-occupied with the certainty of being forgiven of sins. The essential corruption of the tradition occurred because the latter concern, stated Wicks, "is not the conviction that opens itself to a new life by selfless giving (*fides caritate formata* in the pale language of one systematic theology), but a faith specified by the certitude that 'I am forgiven' (*fides certitudine remissionis meae formata*, in a possible comparative formula)" (1969b, 7).[53]

In 1970 Wicks edited and partially translated a collection of innovative reflections on Luther by Catholic scholars in *Catholic*

Scholars Dialogue with Luther.[54] As an introduction of Lortz, Iserloh, Manns, and others into the English-speaking world, Wicks stated, that "What our contributors seek is not a simplistic rehabilitation of Luther among Catholics, but rather a more sensitive treatment freed from pseudo-problems and alert to the deeper intention and peculiar style of his work" (1970, viii).

During the quincentennial of Luther's birth in 1983 Wicks presented a popular consideration of Luther's career, focusing on the theological themes of theology of the cross and conversion, with *Luther and His Spiritual Legacy.* Luther was appraised as a "prophetic figure" whose legacy is flawed due to his overemphasis of human passivity before God, denial of the Sacrifice of the Mass, and elevation of the self-interpretation of scripture.[55]

In 1978 Wicks presented an anthology of Cajetan's writings to the reformers. Cajetan, papal legate to the Diet of Augsburg, had been Luther's chief adversary there in 1518. Subsequently, *Cajetan Responds: A Reader in Reformation Controversy* (1983) emerged as a very significant scholarly consideration of the legate's life between 1517 to 1521, including a consideration of Cajetan's political and diplomatic concerns as well as his theological premises at Augsburg. Wicks asserted that while Cajetan judged Luther to be in error, the legate did not consider the reformer to be a heretic. Wicks asserted that, for Cajetan, "Differences about right doctrine should in his opinion be met by wisdom and openness to possibly legitimate differences in formulation of official truth" (Christopherson 1985, 387).[56]

In summary, the evolution of respect for Martin Luther by Roman Catholic scholars has emerged from serious attention to the principles of historical craftsmanship which demanded fidelity to textual sources and contextual factors. The tradition of Cochläus-Denifle-Grisar was expressly rejected with Lortz's thesis that Luther's motivation was religious. Nevertheless, judgments as to the exact dimensions and legitimacy of that religious motivation have varied. The psychopathological criterion has virtually disappeared in Catholic scholarship with the recognition that Luther's thought, while reflecting profound personal experience and exhibiting idiosyncratic expression, is the product of serious theological reflection. Nevertheless, debate as to the location of the reformer's fundamental axioms within Catholic tradition continues. Twentieth-century Catholic scholars have detached cleanly from the polemical opinions of their predecessors but have not simply whitewashed his image.

DIALOGUE WITH LUTHER

Catholic and Lutheran scholars have criticized the historical-Lortzian approach to Luther for never having considered seriously the essential *theological* issues raised by the Reformation. Generally, they fault the historical approach for continuing a negative assessment of Luther by creating excuses for Luther's theology and actions, thus denying the possibility of constructive Catholic engagement of reformational theology and doctrine. Otto Hermann Pesch (b.1931), formerly Docent for Dogmatic and Ecumenical Theology at the Albertus Magnus Academy at Bonn and then Catholic professor of systematic theology at the University of Hamburg, has concluded that "this [Lortzian] discussion, however, does not go beyond the basic assumption that one can only *discuss* with the 'Catholic' Luther, or with the Luther *to the extent* that he was (still) Catholic—which has become easier today because the Catholic church has been able to eliminate the defects which drove Luther to the Reformation" (1966, 307). Pesch noted the reaction of Danish Lutheran Leif Grane who asserts that Lortz went beyond Denifle in style but not substance.

Consequently, one can speak of a second strain of the Catholic theological reassessment of Luther, that is, a systematic-theological dialogue with him. Pesch characterizes this hermeneutic as an "ecumenical-theological breakthrough" which is demarcated by two movements: (1) a systematic study of Luther's theological questions in themselves, without great concern for his development or our defense of it, and (2) the "attempt to discover a hidden consensus between the Lutheran and Catholic positions by thinking through one's own position more thoroughly as well as that of Luther" (Ibid., 309).

Pesch, who is the most prominent representative of this approach, has stated that this direction in Catholic Luther-studies was initiated generally by Hessen and Stakemeier and deepened by Brandenburg, Küng, Pfürtner, McSorley, and Hasler (Ibid., 308).

Johannes P. Hessen (1889–1971), professor of religious philosophy at the University of Cologne, considered Luther to be a prophet who assailed the intellectualism, moralism, sacramentalism, and institutionalism of the sixteenth-century church. More than a religious man, Luther-as-prophet represents a biblical-historical type whose genius must be appreciated together with that of the Old Testament's prophets (Stauffer 1967, 44–46). Hessen's seventy-page booklet *Luther in katholischer Sicht: Grundlegung eines ökumenischen Gespräches* (1947) argued further that Luther's appeal to concrete biblical-historical insights in criticism of an abstract scholasticism promoted the use of *sola fide* as the reformer's primary critical principle. Thus Luther emphasized the correction of dogma before piety and developed a theology that was antischolastic but not antinomian. Luther sought to correct sacramental practice, Hessen claimed, and to foster the relationship of the individual with Christ; thus he practically ignored the visible dimension of the church (Congar 1964, 367–368). Like Lortz, Hessen determined that Luther went too far in his criticisms. While he may have been "the greatest of the spiritual sons of Augustine" he was also a heretic. However, Hessen criticized Lortz's assertion of Luther's subjectivism. While Luther's *experience* was formally subjective, Hessen argued, the *content* of the experience was absolutely objective, that is, a real meeting of God in Christ. He stated that "Nothing stands so in contradiction to the innermost spiritual structure of the reformer as the modern subjectivism which makes the human subject the measure of all things" (Swidler 1965, 203).

Pesch argued that Hessen's consideration of Luther according to the prophetic category was a first step in taking Luther's full range of thought seriously. Congar notes that Hessen's study was made easier by focusing on the young Luther, the Luther who established the religious quest (1964, 368). A significant advance of Catholic dialogue with Luther occurred with Adolf Stakemeier's *Das Konzil von Trient über die Heilsgewissheit*, also published in 1947. Stakemeier argued that very few bishops at the Council of Trent really understood Luther and subsequently presented a thorough examination of Luther's doctrine of the total passivity of man before God in justification. In so doing, Pesch stated, he made "it once and for all, if not actually, at least de jure impossible for future Catholic theologians to seek Luther's teaching in Denzinger" (Pesch 1966, 308).

If Hessen and Stakemeier authorized Catholic theological interaction with Luther, then Brandenburg, Küng, and Pfürtner actually engaged in the dialogue that Pesch characterized as an ecumenical-theological breakthrough.

According to Pesch, Albert Brandenburg (1908–78), professor of confessional studies at the Johann Adam Möhler Institute at Paderborn and an editor of *Catholica*, was the first to accomplish the systematic discussion of Luther's theology itself, leaving behind a strict concern for Luther's development as a means of his contemporary defense (1966, 310). In his *Gericht und Evangelium: zur Worttheologie in Luthers ersten Psalmvorlesung* (1960) Brandenburg argued that Luther's most novel idea is his understanding of the Word of God and not the principle of justification. In concert with Gerhard Ebeling's existential hermeneutic, Brandenburg stated that Luther's genius was to insist on the primacy of the proclamation of the Word of God over the facts of salvation themselves. Thus, he contended, the literal sense of scripture is subsumed by Luther into the moral decision demanded by one's engagement with scripture. For Brandenburg, a line can then be traced from Luther to Rudolf Bultmann's demythologizing of the New Testament (Pesch 1966, 310–311).

Hans Küng (b.1928), formerly professor in the Catholic theology faculty at the University of Tübingen and now professor of ecumenical theology and director of ecumenical research there, presented his *Justification: The Doctrine of Karl Barth and a Catholic Reflection* as a doctoral dissertation directed by Louis Bouyer at the Institut Catholique de Paris in February 1957.[57] In what Pesch considers to be the first step in attempts to discover a hidden consensus between Lutheran and Catholic thought, Küng stated that no fundamental differences exist between Barth's position and the Catholic teaching on justification. Küng argued that Catholicism teaches, in harmony with Barth, that justification is God's act of sovereignty in Jesus Christ and that Barth, in unison with Catholicism, posited that persons are justified in such a way that they can be characterized as new creatures because of faith, who through love want to be active in works (Küng 1964, 275–284). Küng's analysis of both parties has not been seriously contested, as Barth himself confirmed this understanding of his own position in a laudatory preface (1964, xix).[58]

While Luther's thought is not directly considered by Küng, the reconciliation of Barth's orthodox Evangelical thought and Catholicism on the doctrine of justification, the article of faith by which Luther claimed the church stands or falls, was the first installment in an emerging genre of ecumenically appreciative theological dialogues.

Stephen Pfürtner, OP, (b.1922) argued that the Tridentine Fathers misunderstood Luther's doctrine in regard to the certainty of salvation by construing the reformer to have a vain certainty of the *effect* of God's grace in the believer. Rather, Pfürtner claimed in his *Luther and Aquinas on Salvation* (1961) that Luther's sense of certainty corresponds to Thomas Aquinas's sense of Christian hope insofar as both speak of the unshakable trust that God forgives sins and brings about salvation. Pfürtner stated that

> For the believer as such there remains neither uncertainty in regard to what he believes nor in regard to his own believing. And the case is similar with one who hopes, in so far as he hopes. For the life unfolded in the theological virtues is the life of Christ in us. And in Christ nothing is uncertain. . . . Nevertheless, the uncertainty

bound up with this possibility of losing the virtue does not belong
to faith or hope as such. These are infallible. The danger threaten-
ing them is external, *per accidens*, coming namely from those
spheres in man which are not touched by the theological virtues
and are still subject to the law of sin. But if either Catholic or
Protestant maintains that there is a decisive difference between
Luther and Aquinas in this doctrine of man's peril or uncertainty
on his way of salvation, then he is mistaken. (Pfürtner 1964, 134–
135)

Divergences can be attributed to differing modes of expression in
the two theologians as well as confusion of their terms by subsequent
interpreters.

While these efforts have inaugurated Catholic theological assessment into new systematic and post-Lortzian frames of reference, the
works of McSorley, Hasler, and Pesch himself accelerated the effort,
stimulating intense intramural Catholic debate on Luther.

In 1965 Harry J. McSorley, CSP, defended his doctoral dissertation
for the Catholic faculty at the University of Munich as *Luthers Lehre
vom unfreien Willen nach seiner Hauptschrift De Servo Arbitrio im
Lichte der biblischen und kirchlichen Tradition*.[59] In his analysis of
Luther's *De Servo Arbitrio* (1525), the reformer's response to Erasmus
of Rotterdam's *De libero Arbitrio* (1524) which contended that all
persons have the freedom to choose or refuse God's grace, McSorley
argued that Luther's claim for the unfree will is simultaneously
Catholic and un-Catholic. Insofar as Luther rightly defended the
biblical position that apart from grace, persons have no freedom,
McSorley believed that Luther

> was one of the few theologians in Germany who unhesitatingly
> defended the biblical and Catholic teaching on man's bondage due
> to sin. He proclaimed that fallen man could do nothing whatever
> without grace to prepare himself for salvation. This he did at a time
> in which many Catholics—including Erasmus—had either lost
> this truth or were uncertain about it. (McSorley 1967, 293)

However, McSorley claimed that Luther departed from the Catholic tradition insofar as the reformer maintained a philosophical
position which argued that the foreknowledge and will of God-as-
creator places an absolute necessity on all events concerning persons-
as-creatures. In this reaction against nominalism, argued McSorley,
Luther places himself outside the Catholic theological and authentic

ecclesial tradition by denying one's personal decision. McSorley stated that

> If the spirit of God is absent, man cannot change his will from willing evil to willing good. This assertion of Luther is in full conformity with the biblical and Catholic tradition, which insists that the liberating grace is necessary for such a change of will. But when Luther says that the change of our wills from sin to justice depends solely on the overcoming and the defeat of Satan by someone stronger—Christ—and neglects entirely to mention that the personal, free decision of the sinner—made possible, to be sure, only by the healing and liberating grace of God—is essential to justification, then he is no longer on biblical or Catholic ground. (Ibid., 334)

Also in 1965, August Hasler, then a member of the Holy See's Secretariat for Promoting Christian Unity, presented a dissertation to the Pontifical Gregorian University, contending that Catholic manuals of theology published or revised since 1945 showed virtually no consideration of or dialogue with the authentic positions of Martin Luther. His *Luther in der katholischen Dogmatik: Die Darstellung seiner Rechtfertigungslehre in den gegenwärtigen Manualien der katholischen Dogmatik* concluded that these manuals, which often served as textbooks for seminarians, misrepresented Luther by drawing mostly from the polemical works of Cochläus, Möhler, Denifle, and Grisar as well as secondhand and partial glimpses of the reformer's theology given in Leo X's *Exsurge Domine* (1520) and various decrees and canons of the Council of Trent (1545–63).[60] Whether these manuals were overtly polemical or, in rare instances, showed limited familiarity with Luther, they all failed to grasp the essential dimensions of the reformer's thought and idiomatic language. Thus, for example, Luther's admonition to Melanchthon to "be a sinner and sin boldly, but believe and rejoice in Christ even more boldly" is reduced to its first injunction and categorized as antinomian and blatantly blasphemous (*Luther's Works* 48: 282). More important, Luther's positions on justification and sanctification, original sin, and the sacraments are fundamentally distorted. The Council of Trent's definitions of what is not to be believed often have been construed incorrectly as reverse statements of the reformer's teachings (Spitz 1971, 139–141; Wicks 1969c, 140–142).

In 1966 Pesch emerged as a Catholic Luther-scholar by reporting on twenty years of Catholic Luther-studies at the International Congress for Luther Research at Järvenpaa, Finland. He chronicled the emergence of the systematic school of Catholic Luther scholars, distinct from the historical school of Lortz–Iserloh–Manns, and concluded that "it cannot be doubted that Lortz's method of treating Luther has definitely been superseded. The Lortz school was not slow to protest, but it was not able to stop the new trend" (1966, 311). Thus Pesch drew notice to the new methods of Catholic scholarship on Luther and also the ire of the Lortzian school, especially Manns.

Pesch had established great credibility among scholars a year earlier with his systematic comparison of Thomas Aquinas (1225–74) and Luther, arguing that a consensus about the essentials of faith existed between the two, although this is often veiled by differing terminologies and conceptualizations.[61] His 1,500-page dissertation at Munich, *Die Theologie der Rechtfertigung bei Martin Luther und Thomas von Aquin: Versuch eines systematisch-theologischen Dialogs*, directed by Heinrich Fries, argued that two very different styles of intellectual performance yielded the diverse formulas that expressed the common faith. Aquinas's "sapiential" approach focused on the ontological appreciation of God as creator and human responsibility in creation. Luther's "existential" approach revealed a person-centered appreciation of God wherein the divine demand of faith is the beginning of salvation. Thus, concerning the doctrine of salvation, Pesch understood Aquinas's "faith formed by love" to be a statement about faith and not meritorious works since love *(caritas)* shows that a person's faith is more than mere intellectual assent. Thomas conceptualized metaphorically in order to explore human responsibility for the creator's order. For Luther, on the other hand, faith was probed in an existential perspective as the confession of total personal dependence upon God as savior rather than the demonstration of one's movement toward God (1970, 61–81).[62]

Similarly, Pesch has argued that Luther stands completely within the tradition when he argues for the simultaneity of sin and salvation in the believer. While Luther differed from Aquinas conceptually, Pesch stated, reminiscent of Lortz, that "the representatives of the church, involved as they were in a practice of piety that issued in financial and political practices seriously lacking theological foundation, refused to acknowledge an essential part of their own tradition which Luther, and his friends, has rediscovered and intensified by solid academic research" (1985, 47).

Pesch's assertion that Luther is truly Catholic stemmed from the recognition that the reformer's teachings, while novel, reflect much of the classic Catholic tradition before the sixteenth century. Given that many of the differences between Luther and Catholicism have dissipated in light of the Second Vatican Council and postconciliar developments (e.g., the decline of scholasticism and Neo-scholasticism, the implementation of liturgical reforms, the reform of the Curia), Pesch has called for a predenominational study of Luther (1984a, 17). He claimed that Luther is a "Catholic possibility" and that the historical reclamation of Luther by Catholics is secondary to the Catholic engagement of Luther's thought on a systematic level. Overall Pesch concluded that Catholic theology "has to ask in a more unbiased manner about the *contemporary* consensus with the Luther *of that time* who has already formulated, sometimes in an uncanny way, so much of what is also today self-evident to the Catholic sense of faith" (1984b, 40).

This has promoted an acrimonious relationship between Pesch and Manns. In October 1982 their fundamental differences were expressed at a conference celebrating the 450th anniversary of the Augsburg Confession at Maria Rosenberg Academy in Speyer, Germany. Manns acknowledged the validity of some criticisms of Lortz's original position, especially regarding Ockhamism and subjectivism, but argued that some unconvincing conclusions of the historical Catholic Luther-hermeneutic do not invalidate the entire approach. He contended subsequently that the value of Lortz's conception of Luther as holy and heretical can be demonstrated by pursuing Luther's understandings of love as well as ministry, eucharist, and church. Therein, he believes, the full ecumenical value of the historical hermeneutic can be realized. Manns further argued that the precise value of the historical approach is not only in overcoming the distortions of Catholic controversialists but also in redefining Luther as a "father in faith" (Manns 1984, 16–22).[63]

Pesch responded by acknowledging the necessary interplay of the historical and the contemporary in Catholic ecumenical endeavors. Thus, he asserted that the precise difference between the two schools of Catholic Luther-studies really concerns the question whether what was "un-Catholic" in the sixteenth century can be considered "Catholic" today. One should view Luther's theology as an innovative translation of the Catholic tradition that anticipated much of Catholic postconciliar understanding. Pesch concluded that certain elements of faith that Luther articulated are readily admitted now, for example, transubstantiation in existentialist categories and the principle that persons are simultaneously holy and sinful *(simul iustis et peccator)* (1984b, 32–39).[64]

Finally, this survey of twentieth-century Catholic theologians who evaluate Luther must recognize a non-German theologian who ranks as the pre-eminent Catholic ecumenist of the twentieth century (Stacpoole 1988, 502+). Yves M.-J. Congar, OP, (1904–95), who taught fundamental theology and ecclesiology at Le Saulchoir, a Dominican house of studies, and served as an expert for the Second Vatican Council, incorporated both historical and systematic methods in his assessment of Luther. Congar had realized a personal ecumenical vocation long before the publication of his *Divided Christendom* in 1937, which established fundamental principles of Catholic ecumenical thought, many of which were incorporated into the Second Vatican Council, (Congar 1988, 77–82). Of his ecumenical research, he stated, "I looked into the question of Luther, whose writings I turn to, in one way or another, almost monthly" (Congar 1963, 74; 1964, 62).

While cognizant of German Luther-scholarship, and accepting the Lortzian conclusions as to Luther's profound religious motivations Congar has assessed the reformer predominantly from an ecclesiological perspective.[65] Generally, he argued that ongoing reformation is vital for the church and that Luther's opportunity for reformation, historically justifiable and authentically inspired, was less than able given the reduction of Luther's insights by theological and operational mistakes.

Divided Christendom (*Chrétiens désunis*) was the first systematic attempt by a Catholic scholar since Möhler to define the theological characteristics of the Protestant churches. Congar presented a basic plan for Christian unity after examining the theological grounding for Roman Catholic unity and catholicity as well as the situation of non–Roman Catholic churches. Christian unity in the Catholic church is based, he argued, on the common Christian participation in triune divine life; the actual incarnation of the church, however imperfect, is the single avenue by which God communicates divine life to persons. The Catholic Christian, and by extension the church

is therefore one who interiorly lives in faith and charity, knows himself to be by grace the son of the Father, and radiates the likeness of God in sufficient measure to be recognized as a member incorporate with those who are also of the family of God and bear the stamp of Christ's likeness. He is one in whom the sense of unity is strong enough to enable him to honor in others, under their diverse forms of experience and expression, the same life of Christ in whom we are universally brethren. (Congar 1939, 113–114)

All authentic Christian experiences of God, including the authentic *vestigia Ecclesiae* of Protestant churches, find a place in the Roman Catholic church. Translations of the book were forbidden by Roman authorities who contended that the Roman Catholic church could not merit from dissident Christians (Minus 1976, 105).

Congar acknowledged Luther's legitimate criticism of the sixteenth-century church but faults the reformer for a lack of theological balance that resulted primarily from myopia regarding the nature of the church and the role of tradition. He also contended that Catholic reaction promoted a Catholic imbalance, evident in hierarchical and ecclesio-political developments during the Catholic Reformation (*Divided Christendom*, 24–39). Congar's claim for Luther's ecclesiological shortsightedness is further explicated in *Vraie et fausse réforme dans l'Église* of 1950. He contended that Luther's reformation is a false reformation because it failed to honor four basic criteria: (1) love of concretely existing church and contact with parish life; (2) intent to remain within church; (3) patience and power to wait for meaningful opportunities for reform; and, (4) return to the church tradition as a whole (Persson 1963, 27–29).[66] Luther's overemphasis of scripture and especially the denial of the radical sacramentality of a visible church, concluded Congar, are the unfortunate foundations of the Protestant Reformation.

Congar's most definitive assessment of Luther is *Martin Luther, sa foi, sa réforme: Études de théologie historique* of 1983. He considered Luther to be a profound spiritual teacher whose doctrinal oversights and invitation of ecclesial divisions do not fundamentally undermine his legitimate reformational values. Thus Luther's theological acumen regarding justification by faith alone, Christology, and the eucharist were affirmed. Congar stated

> It is here that, while recognizing the greatness of Luther and the soundness of his intention, we cannot follow him in the way in which he exercised it. The intention was to establish as the principle of reform the sovereignty of the Word of God. The application was made in the sense of a *sola Scriptura* which we believe we must reject. We cannot accept the break which an extreme pessimism made between nature (creation) and grace (redemption). And Scripture—we may even say here the *Word*—is it the only gift which God has given us that there might be a Church-body of Christ? The Church as a sacrament of Christ, a sacrament of salvation, is made up of gifts, instituted means of grace, which have been placed in position as such without their institution being necessarily attested in Scripture. (Congar 1983b, 75)[67]

In the final analysis, Congar views contemporary Protestant churches, the heirs of Luther's testament to faith, as legitimate interim churches whose final status vis-à-vis Roman Catholicism is as yet unimaginable (1982, 161–177).

CONCLUSION

Catholic theological opinion about Luther and his work in the twentieth century has changed in substance and style from that of previous generations. A generally appreciative understanding of the reformer has been forged from scholarly attention to primary sources concerning Luther as well as from the practice and cross-pollination of various historical and systematic hermeneutics. Those few who would perpetuate the denial of Luther's religious insight and genuine contributions to Christianity find little hearing in academe.[68]

Catholic theologians recognize a fundamentally religious motivation in the reformer, dismissing the psychobiographical approach of their predecessors by investigating Luther's writings as they evolved in ecclesial, social, and political circumstances most often not under Luther's control and very often inspired by the Catholic church. This religious motivation is most often evident in Luther's tenable theological reinterpretation of the Pauline-Augustinian tradition of grace and his profound pastoral sensibilities. In displacing the polemics of centuries of theologians, contemporary Catholic scholars have not disregarded the significant factor of Luther's personality, especially notable in discussions of Luther's attitudes toward the papacy.

If an authentic reformer in the sixteenth century, theologians continue to explore the future for Luther in Catholic life. Generally, the historical interpretation of Luther identifies perspectives that are common with the Catholic tradition. The systematic interpretation seeks to discover implicit connections between Luther's theology and the Catholic tradition as well as explicit correlations between Luther's innovative theology and subsequent developments within the tradition, especially in the postconciliar era.[69] Throughout these investigations Luther appeared less and less as a foreigner to Catholics, who discovered their own evangelical heritage in the return to doctrinal sources at the Second Vatican Council and who pledged their turn to revitalize the world afterward.

To understand the future of Luther within the Roman Catholic community one must consider the magisterial rehabilitation of the reformer, a newly observed phenomenon in the postconciliar decades.[70] One notes, in the words of Walther von Loewenich, that

> The Catholic portrait of Luther at the present time is not uniform. Real advances have been made, and we must be thankful for them, but, over and above this, we must never forget the evidence we have adduced for real change of attitude toward the Reformation represents the individual opinions of certain theologians, and therefore cannot bear the weight of official pronouncements. They can contribute fruitfully to the discussion only as long as, and in so far as, they have the sanction of the Teaching Office. We must still hope that this revised view of history will be spared the fate of Modernism and the New Theology. (1959, 292)

3

LUTHER AND THE ROMAN CATHOLIC MAGISTERIUM IN THE SIXTEENTH CENTURY

> The books of those heresiarchs, who after the aforesaid year [1521] originated or revived heresies, as well as those who are or have been the heads or leaders of heretics, as Luther, Zwingli, Calvin, Balthasar Friedberg, Schwenkfeld, and others like these, whatever may be their name, title or nature of their heresy, are absolutely forbidden.
> —Tridentine Index of Books, 1564[1]

> But if we are to speak the truth we cannot do otherwise than confess that we are conscious of having been greatly wanting in fulfilling the duties imposed on us; and indeed of having in no small part been the cause of the very evils we have been summoned to mend.
> —Cardinal Pole's *Admonitio* to the Council of Trent, 1546[2]

Sixteenth-century magisterial assessments of Martin Luther can be divided into two areas: his person and his teachings. Given the indisputable charisma of the Wittenberg reformer, the rapid escalation of Catholic polemics against him, and the uneven coalescence of official Roman reaction to the events in Saxon Germany between 1517 and 1530, these two aspects are not always neatly divided. Thus the papal bull that sought Luther's recantation and proposed his excommunication, *Exsurge Domine* (1520), introduced both evaluations while the canons and decrees of the Council of Trent (1545–63) produced no explicit reference to Luther personally in their judgments against his theology. Nonetheless, these twin verdicts promoted an initially decisive and later probative locomotion of official Catholic teaching against the professor of Bible from the young University at Wittenberg.

In contending that Catholic magisterial statements of the twentieth century project an understanding of Luther as a prophetic reformer rather than a misguided renegade, I have introduced a spectrum of Catholic theological studies in order to appreciate any claim of a Catholic reconsideration of Luther, to establish current ecumenical parameters, and to document the need for this study itself. In this segment my investigation of the Catholic Luther-image is recalibrated to show magisterial perspectives at the initiation of the Protestant Reformation. A determination of the essential reasons for Catholic teachings and disciplinary actions against him will illuminate what remains, has been discarded, or is pending in the Catholic magisterial regard of Martin Luther. This sixteenth-century Roman magisterial assessment of Luther is considered in three aspects: papal pronouncements, papal theologians, and the Council of Trent.

PAPAL PRONOUNCEMENTS

Pope Leo X's bulls of excommunication represent the first explicit magisterial rejection of Luther and his thought. *Exsurge Domine* (1520) and *Decet Romanum Pontificem* (1521) respectively declared and condemned him as a heretic. While Pope Adrian VI's instruction to Chieregati in 1522 at Nürnberg is often quoted as a frank admission of the church's need for reform, and thereby construed as tacit toleration of Luther by Leo X's successor, the fact that the bulls of excommunication deserve strict priority is evidenced by Pope Adrian's additional remarks: "What concerns faith is to be believed on account of divine authority and is not to be questioned. . . . You may add that almost everything in which Luther departs from the consensus is already condemned by various councils. What general councils and the universal Church have approved as matters of faith must not be called into question" (Adrian VI 1969, 124–125).

Luther's Challenge

Luther's departure from the consensus determined by the curia was typified in his *Disputation on the Power and Efficacy of Indulgences* (*Disputatio pro declaratione virtutis indulgentiarum*) of 17 October 1517, commonly known as the *Ninety-five Theses*. Acting according to an evangelical theology that had emerged from his lectures in Bible at Wittenberg since 1513 and reacting to the recent indulgence-preaching of John Tetzel, OP, (1465–1519) in Jüterborg and Zerbst near Wittenberg, Luther submitted the theses to Archbishop Albrecht of Mainz (1490–1545). The archbishop had authorized this preaching to finance curial fees for the multiple episcopal offices that made him the most powerful churchman in the Holy Roman Empire.[3] Intended to begin an academic disputation, Luther's theses, as stated in a companion letter to Albrecht, were to remedy a gross misunderstanding of the Catholic faith among the people that the indulgence-preachers promoted. By that preaching, Luther emoted to Albrecht, "O great God! The souls committed to your care, excellent Father, are thus directed to death" (Luther 1963, 46).

Luther never received an answer directly from Albrecht who had received them on 17 November 1517 and, after consultation with his advisors, mapped a three-pronged circuitous reply. On a local level Albrecht moved to establish a consultation with theologians about substantive issues. Further, he directed the North German bishops who were meeting at Halle to restrain Luther. Finally, after silence from the theological faculty at Mainz and inaction by the German bishops, he directed a dossier to Pope Leo X (1475–1521; pope from 11 March 1513) in mid-December for the more authoritative *processus inhibitorius*. The theological faculty of Mainz had declined an opinion on the increasingly popular theses, writing to Albrecht on December 17 that to debate the extent of papal power was forbidden by canon law (Hendrix 1981, 33).

Luther's theses are understood essentially by focusing on his inter-related judgments concerning salvation, the papacy, and pastoral practices. As demonstrated clearly in his *Lectures on Romans of 1515–16* and in the *Disputation against Scholastic Theology* of September 1517, Luther's nascent evangelical theology proceeded from the assertions that faith alone was the sole way for a Christian to participate in God's salvation for persons and that all faith proceeded from the believer's recognition of the cross as the key to God's gift of faith. This theology of the cross is traditionally associated with the Heidelberg Disputation of April 1518 when Luther presented his theology to the Augustinian order upon the request of the German Augustinian vicar, John von Staupitz. Luther contended that the church preaches the gospel to announce God's promise of salvation to which faith responds and that theology explores the absurdity of the cross which vexes reason but gives faith. Correspondingly, the *Ninety-five Theses* challenge any idea of salvation that subverts faith by emphasizing a believer's moral performance; delimit the authority of the pope to the canonical realm, excluding control of a living or deceased sinner's actual status before God; and berate preachers and theologians who "say that a man is absolved from every penalty and saved by papal indulgences" (Luther 1957d, 27).

Luther's positions were amplified in his *Explanations of the Ninety-five Theses* (*Resolutiones disputationem de indulgentiarum virtute*), published in August 1518 after the Roman proceedings against him had begun in the curia but before he received the summons to appear at Rome. Copies were sent to his ecclesiastical superiors, namely,

Bishop Jerome Schultz, Staupitz, and Pope Leo X (Böhmer 1946, 199; Iserloh 1980, 50).

In terms of salvation, Luther stated that "Indeed, I believe there is a big difference between redeeming souls and the remission of punishments" (1957a, 186). Thus he asserted that indulgences, as the remission of temporal punishment due sins, are an ecclesiastically valid but inferior gift of the church. They inhibit the progress of the soul by increasing fear of God rather than love of God; they exist for those who are lazy in faith rather than those who would receive a faith that more clearly knows God. As mere remediation of the punishments of sin, Luther concluded that the preaching of indulgences had actually displaced the preaching of the gospel by obscuring the promise of God in Christ which is the true beginning of faith. This promise is particularly clouded, he asserted, with the teaching that indulgences are funded by the merits of Christ and the saints. In thesis 58 he denied this *thesaurus ecclesiae*, developed in medieval theology and defined in Pope Clement VI's *Unigenitus Dei filius* (27 January 1343).[4] Insofar as the saints could not have adequately fulfilled God's commandments, Luther argued, they have no superabundance to allocate. Moreover, the desire to escape suffering for sin contradicts the example of the saints and martyrs whose own suffering promoted faith in the church (Ibid., 212–213). Insofar as Christ's merit is coterminous with everyone's grace of contrition, there is nothing to distribute. Luther's soteriological argument posited a contradiction between indulgences and genuine Christian faith.

The emphasis on the moral performance of believers is also obscene to Luther because it is prompted by Albrecht's financial interests as well as Rome's capitalization of Saint Peter's Basilica (Ibid., 187). Coordinately, Luther affirmed purgatory as a place of suffering in emulation of Jesus at Calvary—it exists for the growth in the love of God. The promotion of vicarious indulgences for the dead thus undermined the biblical teaching that some suffering is necessary for sinners and profitable for growth in love of God which is necessary for eternal salvation (Ibid., 90–92).

Luther's *Explanations* are ambivalent regarding the papacy. While he believed that Pope Leo X must be deceived by the indulgence-preachers he also asserted that papal power regarding indulgences is restricted to the canonical realm. Luther observed the value of the papacy as a pastoral office and did not at this point deride individual popes. He stated diplomatically that "we now have a very good Pope, Leo X, whose integrity and learning are a delight to all upright persons.

... He is worthy of having become pope in better times, or of having better times during his pontificate" (Ibid., 155).

While Luther distinguished Leo from the "hucksters" who preach indulgences, his strict separation of papal from divine prerogatives regarding souls in purgatory became the most contentious point at Rome. Luther argued that the pope may intercede for sinners who have died in grace but may not command remission of their suffering.[5] As seen above, Luther emphasized faith as the response of every individual, one which ecclesial authority may not preempt. Additionally, he argued that the pope would be exceedingly cruel if he *could* empty purgatory by virtue of the papal keys but *would* not do so because of desire for profit or other motives. Insofar as no pope has ever bound souls in purgatory, he asserted, no pope may ever loose them (Luther 1957a, 158–159). His denial of papal intercession for souls in purgatory challenges Pope Sixtus IV's *Salvator noster* (3 August 1476) which stated that "it is then our will that plenary remission should avail by intercession for the said souls in purgatory, to win them relief from their punishments—the souls, that is, for whose sakes the stated quantity or value of money has been paid in the manner declared" (1970, 14). Correction of Sixtus's excess, Luther argued, would restore the papacy from false honor (Bagchi 1991, 17–20).

In the *Ninety-five Theses* and the *Explanations* Luther excoriated indulgence-preachers and theologians as "ingrafters of heretical perversity" (1957a, 88). He claimed that they produce tormented consciences rather than promote the peace that is evident with authentic faith. Among the most passionate remarks in the *Explanations* is a theme which would soon emerge more completely in the Heidelberg Disputation (1518): "A theologian of glory does not recognize, along with the Apostle [Paul] the crucified and hidden God alone. . . . for there is no harm that is greater than that of taking away from men the image of the Son of God and robbing them of those inestimable treasures [the freely given merits of Christ]" (Luther 1957a, 227). Notably, the kind regard for Albrecht in the *Ninety-five Theses* is excluded in the *Explanations* where he is considered among those who act out of ignorance and consequently produce great harm among believers. Luther here refers to Albrecht as a 'herdsman', diminishing the biblical 'shepherd' for polemical purposes (Ibid., 183–184).

With remarkable speed Luther's call for theological debate and pastoral reform became the refrain of both common-folk and cultured-folk who protested the indulgence seller's invocation, "When the money in the coffer rings, then the soul from purging fire springs."[6] Albrecht, interested in maintaining harmonious relations with Frederick of Saxony and having failed to secure a theological rejoinder to Luther's theses, requested Rome's action on 13 December 1517 so "that his Holiness would grasp the situation so as to meet the error at once, as occasion offers and as the exigency requires, and not lay the responsibility on us" (McNally 1967, 463).[7] Luther's commitment to stand by the church, however "wretchedly it operated", was soon tested.

Initial Roman Assessment

While Albrecht's complete dossier to Rome is not extant, it is commonly held that the curia possessed the documents from Mainz in early January 1518 (Wicks 1983b, 521–523). By the time Tetzel was refuting Luther with 106 theses supplied by Konrad Wimpina at the Dominican assembly at Frankfurt-on-Oder on 20 January, Luther's dossier had been forwarded to a three-member commission formed by Pope Leo X which would begin the *processus ordinarius*, a preliminary investigation of heresy. The commission was not designed to engage the theological complexities of the case; Mario de Perusco was bishop of Ascoli and a curial finance chief while Girolamo Ghinucci was a canon lawyer whose responsibilities were mainly confined to administration in the papal court. Only Sylvester Mazzolini, a Dominican more frequently known as Prierias, carried credentials as the pope's theologian, censor of books, and a well-published scholastic theologian (Scionti 1967, 61–64). While this commission and its successors eventually decided the case with their publications of *Exsurge Domine* and *Decet Romanum Pontificem*, Rome's first two admonitions to Luther were executed on a local level.

On 3 February 1518 Gabriele della Volta, the new Vicar General of the Augustinians was told by Cardinal Gulio de Medici, cousin of Leo X, to compel Luther both to cease the attack on the indulgence to build Saint Peter's and to withdraw or recant his statements regarding the papacy within four months (Wicks 1983b, 523). In April Luther's response to Tetzel, Lenten sermons on penance and grace, which successfully popularized his positions, were published. About the same time Staupitz, Luther's regional superior, advised him of the order to della Volta and that a disciplinary procedure was scheduled for the triennial Augustinian convention at Heidelberg in April.

Frederick, the elector of Saxony, protected Luther from Augustinian censure in April by guaranteeing his safe return to Wittenberg.

When Frederick's effort, apparently motivated by the desire to guarantee the rising star of his university at Wittenberg with its increasingly popular biblical professor, became known in Rome in May, the Luther case was formalized into the canonical *processus ordinarius*, that is, an investigation with suspicion of heresy. Oddly, Bishop Jerome Schultz of Brandenburg approved publication of the *Explanations* in April although he had forbidden publication in February (McNally 1967, 465).

Rome's second local admonition developed around the person of Cajetan (Thomas de Vio), a notable Dominican scholar of Thomas Aquinas who had been appointed papal legate to the Diet of Worms and the Emperor Maximillian in late April 1518. Luther's meeting with Cajetan the following October was the single and most substantive magisterial debate with the reformer, muted though it was. In terms of magisterial assessment, it later spawned Pope Leo X's bull *Cum postquam*, a clear denial of Luther's position on indulgences which, while leaving Luther unnamed, provided the canonical grounds for the formal *processus summarius* which eventually condemned him as a heretic (Wicks 1983b, 558).

Cajetan had no indication of his impending role in the Luther issue when he traveled to Germany in early May; by July he had received the summons for Luther to appear in Rome within sixty days from de Perusco of the Roman commission.[8] On 8 August, the day after he received the summons together with a scathing assessment of his ideas by Prierias of the same curial commission, Luther appealed to Frederick for a hearing in Germany. With Dominican sentiment against him, as displayed in a collective denunciation from a Dominican convocation at Saxony in March as well as in the persons of Tetzel and Prierias, Luther anticipated a prejudicial hearing in the curia which was thoroughly staffed and advised by Dominicans. Pope Leo responded favorably to Frederick's request for a local hearing and on 11 September 1518 moderated earlier instructions to Cajetan, now authorizing the legate to meet with Luther and to pardon him if he recanted or arrest him if he did not.[9] By this time the case had escalated to a formal condemnation at Rome, apparently due to Emperor Maximillian's pledge for cooperative action due to his concern over Luther's capacity to arouse popular unrest (Wicks 1983b, 537–538).

By the end of September 1518 Cajetan had completed a study of Luther's *Ninety-five Theses*, *Explanations*, and his sermons on penance and grace from the previous March. Now delegated with the formal authority of the pope in regard to Luther, he advised Rome that the case was more complex than the proscribed format could resolve insofar as Luther's teachings produced serious theological divergences from the Catholic faith and merited more significant discussion (Ibid., 540). For his part, Luther continued to pledge a type of docility to Rome, writing to his friend Spalatin on 28 August: "I am still ready to present myself, as I have previously . . . I shall never be a heretic. I can err in a debate, but I do not desire to settle anything, nor am I, on the other hand, bound by human opinions" (Luther 1963, 74). On the other hand, Luther's tenacity, not to say obstinacy, in the early stages of the dispute is seen in his *Explanations*: "Speaking boldly, I declare that I have no doubt about those things I have just now said, rather I am prepared to endure death by fire for them, and I maintain that everyone who holds the contrary is a heretic" (Luther 1957a, 215).

When Cajetan and Luther first met at Augsburg on 12 October 1518, the papal legate presented Luther with three demands: to recant his errors and repent of them, to cease teaching associated positions, and to avoid activities which would disturb public order (Peter 1986, 250–271). Cajetan specified two errors in particular. First, Luther's denial of the *thesaurus ecclesiae* in thesis 58 was seen as a dismissal of Pope Clement VI's *Unigenitus Dei filius* (1343), the classic doctrinal locus (Wicks 1978, 72–74). Second, the former Dominican vicar general rejected Luther's assertion in thesis 7 of the *Explanations* that "God's remission effects grace, but the priest's remission brings peace, which is both the grace and gift of God, since it is faith in actual remission and grace" (Luther 1957a, 102). Thereby, he stated, Luther denied the notion of sacraments as efficacious signs, restricting their effectiveness to the quieting of the individual's conscience through a certitude of forgiveness. The subjunction of contrition to faith was, Cajetan argued, contrary to the faith of the church which presented no concept of the certitude of grace (Wicks 1978, 63–67).

On the following day, Luther submitted a written statement of fidelity to the Catholic faith in the matters at hand and a pledge to recant his positions if shown his errors; on 14 October he submitted a written reaffirmation of his positions on indulgences and sacramental faith. An impasse resulted. In a conciliatory gesture Cajetan informed Luther that the sacramental issue was temporarily suspended; Luther pledged silence on indulgences, contingent to the reciprocity of the other principal parties and pending the papal clarification that he requested in a notarized appeal to the pope. In the same appeal, Luther protested the pressuring tactics of Cajetan and the propriety of Prierias's role on the curial commission, given the latter's strong attacks in the *Dialogue against the Presumptuous Theses of Martin Luther* (Iserloh 1980, 57–58).[10]

Written by Cajetan, Pope Leo X's *Cum postquam* replied to Luther on 9 November 1518:

> And lest anyone in the future should plead ignorance of the Roman Church with regard to indulgences of this sort and their efficacy, or excuse himself under the pretext of such ignorance, or have recourse to protests that are insincere. . . . the Vicar of Jesus Christ on earth, by the power of the keys, can for reasonable causes grant to the faithful who are members of Christ . . . indulgences from the superabundance of the merits of Christ and the Saints. (Palmer 1959, 360–361)

Luther rejected the teaching in a letter to Elector Frederick in January 1519, reiterating his primary contention that no coordination of scripture, the fathers, and canon law overturned his own assertions. Luther's docility to the magisterium had ended (1963, 105).

The year 1519 was a quiet one in Rome's deliberation of Luther. The selection of a new emperor after the death of Maximillian I on 12 January had major implications for the Medicis, the papal family, and the papacy that courted Frederick's vote. Rome favored the election of the more cooperative Francis I of France rather than the eventual successor, Charles V of Spain. Charles already possessed Naples and, if elected, would gain the northern regions and would virtually surround the papal territories. Thus Rome sought to mollify Frederick, who had rejected Cajetan's request for the extradition of Luther in December 1518, by promising a distinguished papal award, the Golden Rose of Virtue. In addition to personal prestige, the Golden Rose also offered Frederick added indulgences to those already totaling 1,902,202 years and 270 days that were associated with the collection at Castle Church, Wittenberg. In this quid pro quo, he was encouraged to secure his own election should Francis I become an unlikely successor to Maximillian and, in a gesture with possible implications for Luther, Rome promised the outstanding papal favor of the cardinalate for one of Frederick's friends. This delay in the Roman condemnation contributed to the rapid growth of the protest in Germany and to the disregard of Rome by Luther and the imperial estates.

The role of Karl von Miltitz, papal nuncio for the Golden Rose who was a subordinate to Cajetan, deserves mention because he bargained with Luther on behalf of Rome amid the judgments of Cajetan at Augsburg and Leo X in *Cum postquam* and in the midst of the suspended *processus*. Deputed to Augsburg in November 1518, Miltitz arrived to find that Cajetan was traveling with the emperor in Austria. In an audacious move, Miltitz traveled to Altenberg and attempted to forge a reconciliation between Rome and Luther. In January 1519 he met with Luther to suggest a conciliatory letter to Leo X that Luther composed but did not send. In May Cajetan agreed to mediation by the Archbishop Richard Greiffenklau of Trier. Luther declined, preferring the upcoming academic debate of his case at Leipzig. He also resented Cajetan for his utter disregard of Luther's evangelical theology which Luther argued by showing a biblical consensus (Brecht 1985, 265–273). After Frederick had received the Golden Rose in September, Miltitz facilitated another unsuccessful effort to reconcile Luther and Rome at Liebenwerda on 9 October. For his part, Luther left the meeting with no clear understanding of the next step (1963, 126–128). Finally, on 11 October 1520, the nuncio succeeded in prompting Luther to write the *Open Letter to Pope Leo X* which was sent to the pope in November along with Luther's most succinct statement of evangelical theology, *Freedom of a Christian*.

Rome reinvigorated its case against Luther in December 1519 when Miltitz, ordered by Rome, requested Frederick's cooperation in the proceedings against Luther in order to avoid papal interdict of Saxony and other ecclesiastical punishments. After months of Miltitz's optimistic reports, which had inspired a fraternal letter from Pope Leo X to Luther in March, and the election of Charles V as Holy Roman Emperor in June, the third and decisive phase of Roman magisterial judgment of Luther began in February 1520 with the formation of a new commission to produce the required canonical instrument of excommunication.

Excommunication

The commission to reject Luther's theology and to introduce his excommunication, chaired by Cajetan and the canonist Cardinal Pietro Accolti, was reconstituted twice after its initial organization on February 1 and each meeting produced a harsher judgment. Consistent with Pope Leo X's instructions to Cajetan at Augsburg in August 1518 that had ordered the detainment of Luther as a heretic, the commission's particular work was now to establish detailed objections to Luther. The first commission proceeded quickly, condemning Luther's positions as known from the Basel edition of his works and the recent condemnations from the faculties of Louvain and Cologne (Brecht 1985, 348–349). Concerned that more serious theological investigation was needed, Cajetan prompted the pope to enhance the commission with more theologians, including representation from major religious orders. With the addition of three Dominicans, Cajetan was able to forge the opinions of this second committee into a more moderate and nuanced statement that spoke of errors rather than heresies. Correspondingly, it recommended in mid-March that a papal declaration reproving Luther be issued and that proceedings condemning him as a heretic proceed contingent upon Luther's expressed failure to recant (Fife 1957, 494–495).

This plan was scuttled by the influence of John Eck of Ingolstadt who gained Pope Leo X's ear after coming to Rome, by the pope's request, to report on Luther. A third committee, composed of Cajetan, Accolti, Eck, and a certain John Hispanus convened at the end of April 1520. By most accounts Eck's vigorous denunciations of Luther, begun at the Leipzig Disputation in July 1519 and accelerated by the mixed decisions regarding the dispute and increasingly polemical exchanges with Luther, displaced the previous moderation of Cajetan (Böhmer 1946, 349–350; Iserloh 1980, 72).[11] *Exsurge Domine*, the condemnatory papal document, was discussed in four consistories from 21 May to 1 June with Pope Leo X issuing the document on 15 June 1520. In compliance with the bull, Luther's books were later burned at Rome's Piazza Navona.

Exsurge Domine, which was posted at Saint Peter's in Rome on 24 July has a tripartite structure. An introduction summarily condemned Luther and his errors which are "either heretical, false, scandalous, and offensive to pious ears or seductive of simple minds." A specific listing of forty-one errors that included five of the *Ninety-five Theses* was facilitated by judgments from the universities of Cologne and Louvain in February 1520 which were therein described as "most devoted and religious cultivators of the Lord's field."[12] A conclusion generally described the adjudication that produced the bull, the consequent sanctions, and a lamentation concerning Luther's intransigence.

Roman Catholic ecclesiological emphasis on the organic unity of the church was a dominant factor in both the introduction and the conclusion. The four-fold invocation of the Lord, Peter, Paul, and the saints to arise with the universal church and to serve judgment on Luther indicates the ferverous opposition which the curia presented to him and indicated the power associated with the pope in the sixteenth century.[13] This appeal to the unity of the church is further evident in the extended reference to the history of German participation in the universal church, particularly in the condemnations of Wyclif and Huss. Finally, the claim that Luther is breaking with the body of Christ known in the church of Rome is emphasized often with images of defilement. His teachings are a "pernicious poison" *(virus pestiferum ulterius)* which seek "to destroy the vineyard whose winepress you [Christ] alone have trod." This defilement is focused in consideration of "the Roman pontiffs, our predecessors, whom he injuriously attacks beyond all decency." The concluding lamentation of Luther's "obstinacy and contumacy" emphasized the disobedience to the pope, Peter's successor in caring for, ruling, and administering the church:

> No one of sound mind is ignorant how destructive, pernicious, scandalous, and seductive to pious and simple minds these various errors are, how opposed to all charity and reverence for the holy Roman Church which is the mother of all the faithful and teacher of the faith; how destructive they are of the vigor of ecclesiastical discipline, namely obedience. This virtue is the font and origin of all virtues and without it anyone is readily convicted of being unfaithful.

The principle of ecclesial unity both interpreted and judged Luther. By appeal to this catholicity Rome judges Luther to be personally ambitious and doctrinally perverse, whose evangelical theology is blinded by Satan (Leo X 1985, 635–638).

The forty-one errors listed in *Exsurge Domine* are brief denunciations of Luther's teachings and contain almost no theological explication, listing the points of Luther's threat to the faith rather than counterarguing the substance of those threats. The primary doctrinal issue is salvation in terms of sin, penance, contrition, and indulgences. A second concern is Luther's diminishment of the authority of the papacy and church councils. Finally, diverse issues such as Luther's advocacy of communion in both species and concerns about mendicancy are addressed.

As a legal document *Exsurge Domine* presumed the theological refutations provided by Prierias, Cajetan, and, most demonstrably, Eck. The brief denunciations and an incomplete statement of Luther's teachings provide little opportunity for determining the finer points of magisterial objections to the reformer (Hillerbrand 1969, 108–112). The document contains no hierarchy of condemnation, never distinguishing which of the forty-one errors are heretical doctrinally and which are merely "offensive to pious ears." The second part of this chapter considers the commentaries of Prierias, Cajetan, and Eck to illuminate the magisterial assessment in *Exsurge Domine*. The effect of the bull was clear: Luther was to recant or merit automatic excommunication. *Exsurge Domine* effectively ended all serious consideration of Luther's theology by his Italian detractors (Gleason 1969, 166). Eck and Jerome Aleander (1480–1542), Pope Leo X's librarian, were charged with disseminating the bull throughout the empire. Aleander was generally more successful in the Netherlands and later at Cologne and Mainz, where Luther's books were publicly burned, than Eck was in eastern Germany. There, for example, citizens of Leipzig thought he continued his anger toward Luther from the Leipzig Disputation by means of the bull (Brecht 1985, 400–416; Fife 1957, 565–567). At one point Eck apparently feared for his life as he secreted away to a convent (Bagchi 1991, 94). The effects of the bull in Germany were almost nil, despite Eck's categorical summons for all bishops to publish the document to all clergy and to promote burning of Luther's books. Secular authorities left matters to the bishops who remained unenthusiastic about particular immediate actions. More important, the polarization of the church and the common people accelerated to a new level while Luther remained at Wittenberg to produce major treatises in the latter half of 1520 that consolidated his evangelical theology into a call for secular and ecclesiastical reform (Atkinson 1971, 92).

Luther's personal response to the papal document occurred on 10 December 1520 (six days after its delivery to Wittenberg) at Holy Cross Chapel where he burned copies of the bull, canon law, Angelus de Clavisio's *Summa de casibus conscientiae* (the "Angelica"), and some books by Eck. The affront to Rome was absolute, no less in the burning of canon law than in the burning of the bull of condemnation. Shortly after that, Luther defended his actions with the popular work *Why the Books of the Pope and His Disciples Were Burned by Doctor Martin Luther*. In the apocalyptic tone that was to dominate his considerations of the papacy until death, Luther wrote that "I now wish to embrace all the articles as Christian and true which were damned and burned in the last bull by the nuncio [Aleander] of Antichrist now come from Rome and on the other hand to charge just as many articles of the pope with being antichristian and unchristian as the number of my articles which have been condemned" (1957e, 394).

Pope Leo X's *Decet Romanum Pontificem* formally excommunicated Luther on 3 January 1521 and the pope wrote Charles V, requesting enforcement of the excommunication according to imperial law. In declaring Luther to be a heretic, the bull listed no additional errors to those specified in *Exsurge*. As a juridical exercise it opened with a preamble recounting the responsibility of the pope to administer spiritual and temporal punishments for the

> repression of the wicked designs of misguided men, who have been so captivated by the debased impulse of their evil purposes as to forget fear of the Lord, to set aside with contempt canonical decrees and apostolic commandments, and to dare to formulate new and false dogmas and to introduce the evil of schism into the Church of God—or to support, help, and adhere to such schismatics, who make it their business to cleave asunder the seamless robe of our Redeemer and the unity of the orthodox faith. (Leo X 1970, 63)

By extending excommunication to those who adhered to Luther's teachings the scope of curial concern was formally broadened to include the rising tide of 'Lutheran' sentiment. The growth of the protest was explicitly recognized in the procedure for publicizing the bull which stated that "since it would be difficult to deliver the present missive, with its declarations and announcements, to Martin and the other declared excommunicates in person, because of the strength of their faction, our wish is that a public nailing of this missive [occur] on the doors of two cathedrals." The bull was to be announced in all major congregations of worship in accord with Paul's practice in Titus 3:10–11: "After a first and second admonition, have nothing more to do with anyone who causes divisions, since you know that such a person is perverted and sinful, being self-condemned" (NRSV). Two days were allotted for warning the faithful of the errors they might hold and the third day for confirming the excommunication of those who believe, engage, or in any way harbor Luther and his confreres. In the same appeal to the biblical image of the body of Christ, *Decet* outlines various strictures, including loss of civil honors, property titles, and social standing, to "protect the herd from one infectious animal, lest its infection spread to the healthy ones" (Leo X 1970, 66–67).

In November, Frederick the Wise had refused to turn Luther over to Aleander at Cologne. By February 1521 Aleander had reported to Rome that "All Germany is in an uproar. For nine-tenths 'Luther' is the warcry; for the rest, if they are indifferent to Luther, it is at least 'Death to the Roman Curia,' and everyone demands and shouts for a council" (Iserloh 1980, 76).[14] With the expiration of the sixty-day interim of *Exsurge Domine* and the inaction of secular authority, particularly Frederick, Aleander called for the suppression of Luther and full enforcement of the civil penalties consequent to excommunication at the Diet of Worms on 13 February. He emphasized that continued delay in dealing with Luther would dishonor the pope and allow the heresies to rampage the empire (Hendrix 1981, 131).

For their part the imperial estates had no compelling reason to act decisively especially when their own solidarity might weaken in the midst of a struggle to win more local autonomy from the emperor. They rejected Aleander's drafted mandate against Luther on 19 February and prompted Charles V to guarantee Luther's safe conduct to Worms for a hearing. While Aleander rejected this development, which reduced the authority of the pope and encouraged attitudes of ambivalence and laissez faire about Luther, the reformer appeared before the emperor and estates on 17 April (Brecht 1985, 433–452). He responded to two formal questions of John von Eck, jurist and public orator for Charles V, that the books in question were indeed his and that he needed time to consider the request for recantation. On the evening of 18 April, Luther refused to recant, in the often quoted appeal to conscience: "I am bound by the Scriptures I have quoted and my conscience is captive to the Word of God. I cannot and will not retract anything since it is neither safe nor right to go against conscience. I cannot do otherwise, here I stand, may God help me, Amen." (1958b, 112–113).

In response, Charles V spoke of his religious responsibilities to enforce the bull and the estates' electoral council voted to support Charles while the full assembly voted to abstain, forming a commission to instruct Luther on his errors. Charles regretted having delayed prosecution of Luther and now "resolved to act and proceed against him as a notorious heretic, asking you to state your opinion as good Christians and to keep the vow given me" (Hillerbrand 1978, 94). Negotiations with imperial lawyers, Archbishop Richard Greiffenklau of Trier (whom Miltitz had proposed earlier as a mediator), and others on 24 and 25 April were unproductive. Luther left Worms on 26 April to live in hideaway at Wartburg, after a prearranged "abduction" on 4 May, until March 1522. The Edict of Worms, composed primarily by Aleander and strongly reminiscent of *Exsurge Domine*, was signed by Charles V on 26 May 1521 (Iserloh 1980, 77–82; Hillerbrand 1978, 95–100).

While the spiritual judgment of Rome against Martin Luther was complemented by imperial sanctions, secular action against Luther never achieved momentum. *Exsurge Domine* determined the outcome of the stalled deliberation of Luther's positions in the theological faculty at the Sorbonne and had begun to circle the theological wagons of Catholic controversialists (Hempsall 1973, 39; Bagchi 1991, 265–266). However, Frederick continued to protect Luther well after the death of Pope Leo X on 1 December 1521 (from malaria) and the enthronement of his successor, Adrian VI (1459–1523; pope from 9 January 1522) (Bornkamm 1983, 295–316). Magisterial activity against the reformer waned after 1524 as Popes Clement VII and Paul III became more concerned with curial affairs (Hendrix 1981, 146).

Luther himself became engaged in the spectrum of issues that emerged as Protestantism grew: church structure and discipline, the enthusiasts, and Zwingli's doctrine on the eucharist. In the 1520s his attitude toward Roman magisterial judgment was succinctly expressed in his frequent and increasingly acrimonious assertion that the papacy was governed by the antichrist. While earlier reformers used the epithet to criticize the moral lapses of popes, Luther so criticized each pope because they opposed Christ's gospel of forgiveness of sin by grace alone, free from observance of divine or human law. His expectation that history was nearly over compelled Luther to see the popes' judgments as opposed to the Word of God, a disregard animated by the devil himself (Russell 1994). By 1541 Luther referred to Tetzel and Pope Leo X as the real progenitors of Lutheranism, a place where the gospel was preached and the sacraments properly administered (1966a, 231–235).

PAPAL THEOLOGIANS

Explaining theologically the magisterial judgment of Luther is satisfactorily achieved by investigating three prominent theologians who informed and shaped these statements. We here consider Prierias, who began theological assessment for the magisterium; Cajetan, who exercised the first direct engagement with Luther and who championed the deliberative and conciliatory route in the events immediately before the papal pronouncements; and, Eck, whose influence is found especially in *Exsurge Domine* and whose reflections in the mid-1520s provide significant insight into the earlier and decisive Roman documents.

Sylvester Prierias, OP (1456–1523)

Prierias wrote the first official magisterial words about Luther in his capacity as Master of the Sacred Palace, the pope's theologian who wrote ad hoc theological opinions and censored books in Rome. Prierias, who was sixty-one when he engaged Luther, had been summoned from Venice to Rome by Pope Leo X in 1514 to teach Thomism in the Roman Curial School, whose repristination was a special project for the humanist pontiff. Prierias had taught at Bologna and Padua and was a Thomist of considerable reputation, having codified his thought to aid confessors in the *Summa Silvestrina* of 1514–15. By the time he was deputed to the papal office in December 1515, Prierias's *Summa* was an established regional sourcebook, an encyclopedic consideration of every problem in canon law according to Thomistic principles (Lindberg 1972, 58). The work's comprehensiveness was its primary virtue as it provided an accessible and thorough rendering of the Angelic Doctor and his followers. When Albrecht's request for Roman intervention arrived, Prierias was a natural choice for Leo's committee of three investigators (Scionti 1967, 61–77; Tavuzzi 1997, 72–75).

Published in June 1518, Prierias's *Dialogue against the Presumptuous Theses of Martin Luther Concerning the Power of the Pope* (*R. p. fratris Silvestri Prieratis ordinis predicatorum: et sacre Theolgie professoris celeberrimi: sacrique palatii apostolici magistri: in presumptuosas Martini Lutheri conclusiones de potestate pape dialogus*) was the first, and most original, of four works written against Luther. Composed in three days, it countered Luther's theses (save the final three), delineating the terms of a debate as Luther had done rather than explaining theological assertions. Prierias pledged in the introduction to defend the truth of the church although he curiously understood his own participation in such a task to be a new one. Admitting a defense of the church to be a new task is somewhat strange insofar as he had previously worked on Rome's behalf in the controversy with John Reuchlin (1455–1522) in which the latter was accused of heresy for defending the value of Hebrew books. Moreover, Prierias was a member of the Dominican order which championed the restoration of the papacy after the conciliar controversies and had been the guardians of doctrine since the papacy of Gregory IX (1227–41) (Scionti 1967, 104–105). David V. N. Bagchi illustrates the polyvalent nature of Prierias's *Dialogue*, being both an individual's rational argument against Luther as well as a churchman's authoritative condemnation (1991, 202–204). Michael Tavuzzi argues that Prierias correctly perceived the ecclesiological problems in Luther even as he mishandled seriously the response, treating Luther's theses as heretical conclusions against the faith rather than debatable theological opinions (Tavuzzi 1997, 109–114).

The *Dialogue* considered the *Ninety-five Theses* to be heretical because they violate four fundamental norms which, in Prierias's strongly papal and anticonciliar ecclesiology, provided a concise and clear canon of orthodoxy (Hendrix 1981, 47).[15] Not untypical of Renaissance-Roman, and especially Dominican, ecclesiology, Prierias's four norms served as the philosophical basis for declarations against Luther:

> 1. Essentially the universal Church is the assembly in divine worship of all who believe in Christ. The true universal Church virtually is the Roman Church, the head of all Churches, and the sovereign pontiff. The Roman Church is represented by the College of Cardinals, however, virtually it is the pope who is head of the Church, though in another manner than Christ.

> 2. Accordingly, the Roman Church and the pope cannot err when he in his capacity as pope comes to a decision, i.e., when he comes to a decision in consequence of his office and thereby does his best to know the truth.

> 3. He who does not hold to the teaching of the Roman Church and the pope as an infallible rule of faith, from which even Scripture draws its power and authority, he is a heretic.

> 4. The Roman Church can establish something with regard to faith and ethics not only through word but through act. And there is no difference therein, except that the word is more suitable for this than the act. In this same sense custom acquires the power of law, for the will of the prince expresses itself in acts which he allows or puts into effect. And it follows that he is a heretic who wrongly interprets Scripture, so also is he a heretic who wrongly interprets the teaching and acts of the Church insofar as they relate to faith and ethics.

> Corollary: He who says in regard to indulgences that the Roman Church cannot do what she has actually done is a heretic. (Scionti 1967, 106)[16]

At the institution of proceedings against Luther one finds that the primary magisterial theological issue is ecclesiological, not soteriological, and that the Roman flashpoint for controversy is primarily papal authority and not indulgences. This fact is a bone of contention among historians, many of whom argue that Prierias's response is unconvincing, shallow, and inept as it dismisses Luther without considering his evangelical theology (Lindberg 1972, 47). Others argue that Prierias's ecclesiological focus anticipated the real

~ implications of Luther's work although in fact it did not engage Luther adequately (Scionti 1967, 209–212; Tavuzzi 1997, 108–110).

In the subsequent rejoinders to Luther's theses, the Dominican related these norms with frequent invocation of Thomas Aquinas. For example, against Luther's thesis 5 which asserted that "The pope neither desires nor is able to remit any penalties except those imposed by his own authority or that of the canons," Prierias stated that Luther thereby rejects both the practice of the church (norm 4) as well as the authority of Aquinas (Scionti 1967, 109–110). Again, when Luther considered papal authority regarding purgatory to be equivalent to that of a parish priest insofar as both can intercede but neither can displace divine authority, Prierias asserted that the pope's preeminence reserves the dispensation of Christ's superfluous satisfactory merits (Ibid., 114–115). This preeminence is not limited to spiritual affairs, Prierias argued, because the pope acts with singular authority for the temporal welfare of Christians as in the allocation of funds for the building of Saint Peter's Basilica (Ibid., 121). Prierias's zealously papal ecclesiology, consistent with late medieval scholasticism, reached its zenith in norm 3 which excoriates Luther's evangelical theology by asserting that scripture itself is dependent on the papacy for authority.[17]

While Luther's criticism of indulgences caused Prierias's assertion of papal prerogatives, soteriological concerns were secondary in the *Dialogue*. More definite than claims about how persons are saved is Prierias's positive anthropology. Typical of Catholic responses to the reformation in every age, Prierias rejected the self-loathing of Luther's thesis 4 which stated that "The penalty of sin remains as long as the hatred of self, that is, true inner repentance, until our entrance into the kingdom of heaven" (1957c, 26). Anyone who is imbued with grace, Prierias argued, cannot hate himself more than his neighbor whom he loves as himself (Scionti 1967, 108). Contrary to Luther's theses 30 and 31, which asserted that full contrition and real penance are rare, Prierias stated that nevertheless such persons acquire God's grace since they have posed no barrier to it. Persevering contrition is enough, stated Prierias, as God's mercy is only comprehended by God's judgment. Contrary to Luther's assertion that the dying person's fear of their future is punishment enough, Prierias stated that the souls in purgatory possess joy rather than fear insofar as they possess the hope of salvation whereby grace has driven out fear (Ibid., 112–118). In concert with Thomas, Prierias consistently presented a transformative
~ sense of grace over against Luther's emerging forensic sense.

The great chasm between Luther and Prierias is seen succinctly in the matter of indulgences. Prierias agreed that indulgences do not remove the guilt of sin but only its temporal punishments. However, he did not believe that the removal of guilt was being preached as "it must be clear even to the most ignorant that the obtaining of an indulgence demands a prior cleansing of guilt" (Ibid., 125). The Roman magisterium, in the person of the *magister sacrii palatii*, denied outright the fundamental grievance that spawned the *Ninety-five Theses*. Moreover, this denial occurred in the midst of an accelerated defense of the papacy which was absolutely intolerant of contrary points of view. Together with personal insults as caustic as Luther would ever inveigh, this initial magisterial assessment met with utter defiance from Luther.

The reformer received the summons from the Roman commission with the *Dialogue* on 7 August 1518. The next day he wrote to Spalatin:

> I am already replying to the *Dialogue of Sylvester*, which is exactly like a wild, entangled jungle. You will soon have the whole work, when it is completed. That "sweetest" man is simultaneously my accuser and my judge, as you can see from the *Summons*. (Luther 1963, 72)

His eighty-page *Responsio* appeared in late August and contained the theological principles evident in the *Explanations of the Ninety-five Theses*, unavailable to Prierias and now cast polemically. Luther denied Prierias's four fundamental norms, rejected the authority of Aquinas and scholasticism "with their excessive classifications," and asserted that God's grace is completely prior to contrition, thereby denying the sacramental efficacy which Prierias claimed for penance (Scionti 1967, 137–139). Clearly asserting the principle of *sola fide*, Luther contended Prierias's suggestion that the power of the keys can augment a believer's contrition or diminish punishment in purgatory, stating that "It is not in the hands of man to reconcile man to God, nor can the pope grant justifying grace of God, as the entire Church is aware, and the opposite of this no one has been so vile a heretic as to teach" (Ibid., 160).

In his second work, the *Replica* (*Replica fratris Silvestri prieriatis: Magistri sacri Palatii apostolici: ad Fratrem Martinum luther: ordinis heremitarum*) of November 1518, Prierias refuted Luther's personal attacks and promised a substantive theological response. He disparaged Luther for his denial of Aquinas, asserted that his biblical theology is erroneous, and reaffirmed papal primacy as a check against the chaos of opinions which Luther typified. He claimed that Luther's rejection of Aristotle and thus Aquinas is the fundamental source of his errors (Bagchi 1991, 76). Luther responded with a brief prologue to a reprinted version in Germany: "These replies of my Sylvester, best reader, I earnestly commend to you. For in a wonderful manner they are in need of commendation or this repute, that they bring to birth some kind of threats. I beg you, pray for them, lest they miscarry. Fare you well and take pity on theologians such as this" (Scionti 1967, 172).

The papal theologian's full refutation came in the *Summary of Sylvester Prierias's Responses to Luther* (*Silvestri Prieriatis Epithoma responsionis ad Lutherum*) of December 1519 which was Book III and an abridgment of a more extensive work, *The Errors and Arguments of Martin Luther Enumerated, Exposed, Repelled, and Fully Ground to Pieces* (*Errata et argumenta M. Luteris recitata, detecta, repulsa, et copiosissime trita*) that appeared in March 1520. The companion-works added no new arguments against the reformer but reiterated the positions of the *Dialogue*. In a hyperbolic restatement that in part was meant to counter Luther's antipapal thesis 13 proposed for the Leipzig Disputation with Eck, Prierias stated that the Roman Catholic church is the Kingdom of Christ and to attack the pope as head of the church by questioning indulgences is heresy.

Luther replied by reprinting the *Summary* in June 1520 with a forward, conclusion, and marginalia. Subtitled, "Wittenberg, to the praise and glory of all enemies of Christian truth," he stated that if Prierias is truly believed then the pope is the antichrist (Scionti 1967, 190–194). The first exchange between Luther and the magisterium had now devolved into shrill polemics. Pope Leo X declared Prierias's works "canonical" in July, praising the *Summary* in particular (Hendrix 1981, 185). By the time Luther received the full text of the *Errata* in Spring 1521 he had been formally condemned as a heretic and was soon to leave for the Diet of Worms. Carter Lindberg argues that Luther was influenced greatly by the engagement with Prierias. He states that Luther thereby (1) saw papal authority as the larger issue behind indulgences, (2) developed his theology more clearly for the impending "Tower Experience," (3) began conceptualization of the papacy as the antichrist, (4) was prepared for the confrontations with Cajetan and Eck, and (5) initiated rationale for an eventual appeal to German secular authority (1972, 57–64).

Prierias remained as Master of the Sacred Palace until his death, participating in the second stillborn pontifical commission which led to *Exsurge Domine*. He later publicized and explained the bull to Italian princes (Scionti 1967, 73). His narrow and long-distance rehearsal of Catholic curial positions against Luther contrasts with the second magisterial engagement by Cajetan, the papal legate to the Holy Roman Empire.

Thomas de Vio [Cajetan], OP (1469–1534)

Historians generally agree that Cardinal Cajetan at Augsburg (1518) and Cardinal Contarini at Regensburg (1541) were the two most theologically competent Catholic evaluators of Luther because they proceeded with theological and doctrinal criticisms and avoided the polemics characteristic of both their Catholic colleagues and Lutheran counterparts (Gleason 1969, 163; Wicks 1983b, 549). Cajetan's engagement of Luther occurred in two roles: as papal legate at Augsburg and as a theological consultant to Pope Clement VII (1479–1534; pope from 19 November 1523). The cardinal's encounter with Luther in the autumn of 1518 dwelled primarily on the issues of the merit and the interrelationship of faith and contrition regarding   --
the efficacy of the sacrament of penance. Consequently, Pope Leo X's *Cum postquam*, written by Cajetan, formulated the magisterial response that served as the immediate technical basis for the canonical condemnation of Luther. The legate's theological preparation for both the dialogue and the papal decree is found in the series of treatises written at Augsburg in September and October 1518 in response to Luther's *Ninety-five Theses*, *Explanations*, and Lenten sermons.

These "Augsburg Treatises" considered Luther's positions in a thematic fashion using the classic medieval *quaestio* to delineate, rebut, and refute Luther's positions. This style was natural for the Thomistic scholar but also facilitated the respectful and non-polemical tone of the assessment despite the often repeated overall conclusion that Luther's soteriological, sacramental, and ecclesiological positions were contrary to the common faith of the church. At the same time it spoke clearly of the intellectual and ecclesiastical framework which could neither appreciate nor be appreciated by Luther's evangelical theology, thus enabling the inevitable breakdown in discourse at Augsburg.

Cajetan offered significant analysis on the matter of indulgences, especially in response to Luther's assertions in *Ninety-five Theses* that (1) they are not applications of merits won by Christ and the saints, and (2) they are the remission of canonical penalties and not divine punishments (Luther 1957a, 27–30). Cajetan himself had appealed

to Cardinal Medici for a clearer magisterial explanation of indulgences in the autumn of 1517 and reasoned the opinions of Luther to
be contrary to the "ordinary understanding of the church," comprised
of scripture, fathers, theologians, and ecclesial tradition. In the
Dominican's eighth treatise, however, Pope Clement VI's *Unigenitus*
(1343) and Pope Gregory XI's *De haereticis* (1377) augment the
refutation with papal authority. The church's understanding of
indulgences is thus seen as doctrinally certain and in concert with
Gregory's teaching that dissent from sacramental doctrines is not
possible.

Cajetan appeals to reason to highlight Luther's departure from the
received teaching in the eighth treatise. He argued that the works of
Christ and the saints are simultaneously meritorious and satisfactory.
Christ and the saints alone merit from their works accomplished in
love because they were accomplished by their own free response to
God's grace. However, the body of Christ shares in the satisfactions
of punishment attached to these same works insofar as these satisfactions are superfluous to Christ and the saints. He contended that this
principle of vicarious participation is also evident in baptism where
believers share in the salvation won at Calvary.

Cajetan argued in the third treatise that indulgences remit the
temporal punishment of both sacramental and divine penalties according to the principle that the church's penalties are but the
determinate form of the indeterminate divine penalty. Similarly, as
God requires confession of sins in a general way the church mandates
confession once annually in a specific way. He claimed that one must
understand remission of penalties in indulgences as distinct from
remission of civil penalties by a secular governor. Secular rulers remit
penalties by virtue of the power of their office while the pope remits
punishments by virtue of the Petrine privilege which is directed to
eternal life (Wicks 1978, 56–78).

Sacramental efficacy was a second prominent theme at Augsburg
even though it receded into the background with the legate's attempt
to reconcile Luther to the teaching of the church on indulgences.
Luther had argued for the primacy of the individual's faith in
sacramental forgiveness in his *Sermon on the Sacrament of Penance* in
1518 and in the *Explanations of the Ninety-five Theses*, concluding that
grace comes from such faith and that peace of soul is subsequently
derived from the priest's sacramental declarations (Luther 1957a, 98–
99). In a perspicacious remark, Cajetan stated that "this asserts that
the sacrament of penance, which the church administers with the
requirement of confession, contrition, and satisfaction, leads to

damnation without a fourth element, namely, certain belief in the effect in the recipient. This is to construct a new Church."

Arguing that faith in sacramental effectiveness means that kind of faith which trusts in Christ's biblical promise for loosing and binding, the basis of sacramental penance, Cajetan considered the extension to certainty of faith in the recipient to be incorrect and "a hitherto unknown dogma" (Wicks 1978, 54–55). As distinct from the acquired faith wherein believers trust in particular phenomena, for example, the real presence of Christ in the host, Cajetan argued that infused faith, which trusts in the promises of Christ, cannot be diminished by merely human faith.

Cajetan's treatises consistently honored the ecclesiological doctrines of tradition and the primacy of the pope. These doctrines were assumed principles rather than ideas under debate. Conciliar and papal decrees are revered while novelty is eschewed. The ecclesiological chasm between Luther and Cajetan became evident in the actual meetings at Augsburg where Luther would shrink neither from denying the authority of popes to commute divine penalties for sin nor from denying the authority of Pope Clement VI's indulgence decree and subsequent practices. This ecclesiological issue was more evident in Cajetan's *Misuse of Scripture—Response to Charges Against the Holy See*, written in March 1519 in answer to Luther's account of the Augsburg encounter in the *Acta Augustana* of November 1518. Luther had been incensed especially by Cajetan's rejection of his own biblical arguments by means of papal decrees rather than scriptural interpretation. He contended that these decrees corrupted or at least obscured scripture (Luther 1957d, 276–278). In response, Cajetan defended "the dignity of the Apostolic authority" by interpreting scripture and cited the fathers and other magisterial decrees.

The second phase of Cajetan's engagement of Luther came in his capacity as theological advisor to Pope Clement VII from 1529 to 1534 where he produced biblical refutations of Luther's theology.[18] Four works are written against Lutherans in this period and collectively they responded to the Lutheran *Confessio Augustana* of summer 1530. None of them explicitly considered Luther's post-excommunication theology in itself.

In *Faith and Works—Against the Lutherans* of 1532, Cajetan responded to Melanchthon's *Apology of the Augsburg Confession* to assert the very same position of faith which he presented in the eighth Augsburg treatise. He considered Melanchthon (1497–1560), in imitation of Luther, to have enlarged the common faith by requiring the sinner's certainty of forgiveness. As in 1518, and upon citation of

Exsurge Domine's articles 10–12, he argued that Christian faith cannot grasp the state of the individual here and now but must abide in the faith of the church after a true contrition. Without reference to Luther's theology he argued against Melanchthon and the Augsburg Confession regarding condign (deserving) and congruent (undeserving) merit. Essentially, he invoked scripture to arrive at an understanding of merit as a legitimate increase in grace and heavenly beatitude, not to say justifying grace, by the believer (Wicks 1978, 223–238).

A year earlier Cajetan had argued against Lutheran positions on communion in two forms, the confession of mortal sins, penitential satisfaction, and the invocation of saints in his *Four Lutheran Errors*. This brief treatise clearly relied more upon a literal sense of the Bible rather than the syllogisms of Thomas. Interestingly, he linked Lutherans to Luther with the same appeal used in 1518: "Now that these answers have been given on the issues raised, let the reader recall that it is uneducated persons who demand the certitude of mathematical proof in matters of morality and the wider fields of our human actions" (Ibid., 217).

Cajetan's refutation of Luther's and his allies' quests for certitude in faith was more informed and yet more ignored than the work of any other principle player in the early magisterial assessment of the events in Saxon Germany. His *Guidelines for Concessions to Lutherans* of 1531, a response to Melanchthon's proposals regarding sacramental practices and clerical celibacy, was roundly defeated in consistory (Ibid., 41). Earlier, upon his return from the imperial legacy in September 1519 he remained in the background at the Holy See, giving up title to the diocese of Palermo for the minor diocese of Gaeta (his hometown), presumably for his failure to deliver Luther's recantation and an imperial resolution for a crusade against the Turks. In 1520 his attempt to discriminate problems in Luther's positions fell silent to the wholesale castigations of *Exsurge Domine* where John Eck of Ingolstadt was the dominant voice of the drafting committee.

John Eck (1486–1543)

John Eck's stinging condemnations of Martin Luther voiced in *Exsurge Domine* should be seen in stark contrast to the academic prescriptions in Eck's refutation of the *Ninety-five Theses* of early 1518.[19] A diocesan priest and professor at Ingolstadt in Bavaria, Eck, who was three years younger than Luther, wrote his *Adnotationes* in mid-February to assist Bishop Gabriel von Eyb of Eichstätt in determining Luther's errors. Unlike other Catholic opponents of Luther, he did not react with ecclesiastical sanctions in mind (Bagchi 1991, 22–23). Also known as the *Obelisci*, referring to the convention often used to note suspicious passages in an author's work, these private annotations were in Luther's hands by March (McNally 1967, 465). By the end of the next year, Eck would be the fiercest opponent of Luther, having determined Luther's heresy in the pugnacious Leipzig Disputation in the summer of 1519 and having his own ire at the Wittenberger reciprocated as often as it increased. His lobbying for Luther's condemnation and subsequent publicizing of Luther's errors make him the most important figure in the magisterial rejection of Luther from the current set of three papal theologians.

In the *Obelisci* Eck argued that Luther displayed a "Bohemian virus" when he undermined papal authority in the church by restriction of papal prerogatives regarding indulgences to the canonical realm. In applying this epithet, which conjured images of John Huss as well as the cultural disdain of Germans, a succinct characterization arose which many Catholic controversialists would reiterate (Bagchi 1991, 106). Luther's reply came in May 1518 with the *Asterisks*, a title referring to typographical marks placed before imperfect passages in an author's work. For the most part, Luther defended his theses consistent with remarks in his *Explanations of the Ninety-five Theses* which would appear in August but had been completed in March 1518. He encouraged Eck to a more astute theology, suggesting a reconsideration of Augustine's *On the Spirit and the Letter* regarding the powers of the will. Thus, the reformer dismissed Eck's defense of post-baptismal regeneration which Luther said "stinks again of his goat Aristotle" (Fife 1957, 336–337). Eck did not respond and the exchange lapsed until the debates at Leipzig publicized the essential ecclesiological difficulties which Eck found in Luther.

This normally private exchange between professors became public upon Andreas Karlstadt's (1480–1541) defense of Luther in 380 theses against Eck's *Obelisci*, published in summer 1518 as a prelude for a series of debates. By the time of the debate in summer 1519, Karlstadt's list had grown to 426 theses. Karlstadt, a senior colleague of Luther at the University of Wittenberg, asserted the primacy of scripture, the radical continuance of sin in the life of a Christian, denial of free will, and the impossibility of papal remission of divine punishment. Despite conciliatory letters in which Eck and Karlstadt sought to avoid public debate, the publication of Karlstadt's theses necessitated Eck's *Defense against Karlstadt* in August 1518, which produced a subsequent rebuttal from Karlstadt. In December, after a nonconfrontational meeting in October at Leipzig, Luther and Eck applied for Duke George's permission to debate. By the end of 1518 Eck had published twelve theses that included absolution, purgatory, and indulgences—topics which Karlstadt had not broached earlier. Moreover, Eck directly challenged Luther with his enumeration of the continuous historical evidence for superiority of the Roman see, a clear rebuttal of Luther's *Resolutiones*. An inflammatory spiral ensued in 1519 with (1) February's exchange of letters asserting Luther's disobedience to the pope and Eck's excessive ambition and blind hatred, (2) Eck's revised theses to include a discussion of freedom of the will, (3) Karlstadt's and Luther's counter-theses in April and May, and (4) Luther's staunch defense in June of his proposition thirteen:

> The very callous decrees of the Roman pontiffs which have appeared in the last four hundred years prove that the Roman church is superior to all others. Against them stand the history of eleven hundred years, the test of divine Scripture, and the decree of the council of Nicea, the most sacred of all councils. (1957b, 318)

The debates in July 1519 at Leipzig, a commercial center which joined five great German highways, illustrated conclusively that Luther and Rome were oriented in different directions. Karlstadt and Luther later would assess the event according to the evangelical insights which governed their preparation: Eck had rejected the primacy of biblical authority and was blinded by scholastic theology from seeing the biblical truth concerning the impotence of the human will regarding salvation. Eck's verve and flair were construed as grandstanding (Brecht 1985, 299–300).[20] Luther did not shrink from his assertion made in *Explanation of Proposition Thirteen on Papal Power* that the papacy enjoyed authority by human and not divine right. With the public ceremony of the debates, Luther's appeal increased together with public reaction against Rome. For many, Luther's use of scripture had established Leipzig as the model for future debates with papal Christians. On the other hand, Duke George now saw the dangerous ramifications of Luther's positions. Elector Frederick maintained Luther's freedom, even when the Roman lobby for secular justice increased after Emperor Charles V's election and the simultaneous end of Rome's soliciting kindness to the upstart professor (Ibid., 323).

Eck concluded that Luther and the reformers had rejected ecclesial authority, blinded by their own interpretation of the Bible over and against that of the fathers and councils, unable to construe the divine mandate which Peter and his successors enjoyed. While Luther's position regarding the source and extent of papal authority had not advanced beyond the positions laid out in his theses of May 1519, his opposition of biblical and conciliar authorities with the singular elevation of scripture over fallible councils was particularly striking for Eck. The reformer's distinctive ecclesiology conceived an invisible church with Christ as the only true head. His consequent rejection of the singular privileges granted to Peter and his successors in Matthew 16 and John 21, according to Eck, aligned Luther with Huss and Wyclif who were condemned by the Council of Constance for denying the superiority of the Roman church (Hendrix 1981, 85–89). In April 1520 Eck's *On the Primacy of Peter in Three Books Against Luther* reasserted his Leipzig positions and now called for quick imperial and ecclesiastical condemnations of Luther: "What else do they seem to do who seek to abolish the ministerial head, or assert that it was not established by divine right, than prepare and strew the way with heresies, schisms, rebellions, dissensions, and contentions?"[21]

On the Primacy of Peter was dedicated to Pope Leo X in Rome, where Eck had resided for a month upon a summons from the pope who would include him in the third commission to prepare an official condemnation. By the time Eck returned to German lands with Aleander to promulgate the bull in July 1520 the official verdict on the Leipzig Disputation from the Sorbonne was still pending but popular verdict had gone with Luther (Hempsall 1973, 32–38). In September 1520 Eck attacked Luther in his *Defense of the Sacred Council of Constance*, which excoriated him for appealing for a general reform council in his *Babylonian Captivity* of 1520 while denying the legitimacy of Constance at Leipzig in 1519. He concluded that this was an example of the general anarchy which could be expected from such cavalier dismissal of traditional authority (Bagchi 1991, 94). For his part, Luther recognized Eck's authorship of *Exsurge Domine* in a response to the condemnation in March 1521, *Defense and Explanation of all the Articles of Dr. Martin Luther* (1958a, 99).

Ironically, Eck and other Catholic controversialists would increasingly languish in relationship to magisterial authorities who preferred to support political and military enforcements against Luther rather than rational or propagandistic avenues (Bagchi 1991, 218–237). From January to April 1521 Cardinal-legate Aleander sought enforcement of *Decet Romanum Pontificem* by Emperor Charles V and the Diet of Worms. Meetings in April between Luther and the imperial estates, including Archbishop Greiffenklau of Trier, were his last formal contacts with a magisterium offering reconciliation. Imperial forces never pursued Luther because the resolve of the estates never matched that of Charles V who also needed their political solidarity more than he needed Rome's often-cavalier grasp of people's dedication to Luther and his own desire for a reforming council (Brecht 1985, 433–476; Iserloh 1980, 71–80).

By 1525 Eck's *Enchiridion of Commonplaces Against Luther and Other Enemies of the Church* would distill his thought and offer a dominant perspective for pastoral Catholic reactions to him. When Eck published the *Enchiridion* he was clearly not traveling in magisterial circles. In October 1521 the legate Aleander had written to Cochläus, who wished to defend Roman condemnations of Luther in debates, that "it would be wrong to permit or conduct such an untimely disputation. Had our friend Eck followed such advice at the outset, perhaps this disaster would never have overtaken the Church" (Bagchi 1991, 221). Consultations between Pope Adrian VI and Catholic controversialists, including Eck who presented his case personally to the pope in March 1523, regarding the correction of abuses and public refutations of new heretical developments ended upon the pope's death later that year (Iserloh 1980, 111). The *Enchiridion*, however, was revised nine times before Eck's death in 1543, translated into German, Flemish, and French, and reprinted about ninety times before the end of the century. This catalog of Protestant errors, mirroring Melanchthon's *Loci communes* of 1521, was produced at the request of many Catholics (including papal legate-cardinal Lorenzo Compeggio) who expressed the need to Eck for a concise refutation of the Protestants. It was dedicated to King Henry VIII of England whose own defense of Catholicism, the *Assertion of the Seven Sacraments* (1521), Eck had defended in 1523 and whose patronage he was now seeking.[22]

The most effective and widely read of Eck's works, the *Enchiridion* was organized into brief considerations of disputed doctrines and practices which emphasized biblical and patristic commentaries rather than theological speculation. It did not refute any particular work of Luther but his evangelical theology as a whole. Each chapter presented Eck's thesis which was followed by authoritative support from scripture and the fathers, allegedly heretical rejoinders, and finally, refutations of Protestant positions. Pierre Fraenkel has shown that Eck is generally faithful to Luther's positions. At the same time the style of the work makes the reformer appear to be more direct, systematic, and less cautious than he actually was in these early years. Eck's readers would see the general historical and exegetical outlines of the issues rather than the arguments surrounding the divine-human basis of the papacy, the free-bound human will, and the relation of Luther to Huss and Wyclif (Fraenkel 1967, 110–163).

For Eck, Luther is the heretic par excellence, often referred to as the 'new Mani' or the 'patriarch of heretics' (1979, 11). The clear presumption in the work was that Luther's interpretation of scripture, ✓ the basis for his teachings, violated the fathers and the whole received tradition, thus separating him from the church. This emphasis is generally free from *argumenta ad hominem*, although Luther was occasionally described as lazy, insane, and tolerant of immorality. Interestingly, Luther was seen to be a correct judge of Zwingli. Followers of Luther were said to derive weak and corrupted faith from their founder (Ibid., 81).

Eck's basic contention that Luther was alienated from the full tradition of the church is seen in the ordering of chapters as well as their common internal structure. After opening the work with a chapter on the church's authority, he continued with chapters on councils, primacy of the Roman see, scriptures, and faith and works. The followers of Luther were thus seen to misconstrue scripture, the relationship of faith and works and dozens of other doctrine and practices against the context of an authority established on the "consummate harmony between the Holy Scriptures, the Church, and her councils" (Ibid., 27). Eck stated "Thus the Lutherans, leaving the true and living fountain of the Church, dig leaky cisterns of heretics, of Wyclif, Huss, the Albigenses and others" (Ibid., 11).

Consistent with his previous efforts, Eck asserted the singular and divine privilege of Peter and his successors to rule the church, the necessity of faith formed by love, and the absurdity of an unfree will. As in other chapters that included indulgences, monastic vows, and sacramental character, Eck asserted that the reformers' teachings subverted the faith of the whole church as exemplified in councils, popes, and saints.

As a group, the three papal theologians most associated with the magisterial response to Luther evinced a fundamental concern that Luther departed radically from the Catholic faith. Whether the reflexive assertions of absolute papal authority by Prierias, the considered opinions of the scholastic Cajetan, or the pugnacious retrenchments of Eck, the subversion of papal authority at Wittenberg overshadowed Luther's evangelical concerns regarding salvation, whether theological or practical, to a remarkable degree. In time, Luther would mirror this Roman judgment in his counter-indictments of the papal antichrist.[23]

COUNCIL OF TRENT (1545–63)

Cajetan's premonition of 1518, which saw the foundations of a new church arising out of Luther's teaching certainty of faith, was a social reality in 1531. Papal excommunication and subsequent denunciation of Luther proved to be insufficient weapons against the reformer and subsequent ecclesial fracture as the failure to implement decisive imperial sanctions at Worms in 1521 and Augsburg in 1530 demonstrated. Protestants, as the imperial Diet of Speyer had named them in 1529, had inked increasingly collective statements of faith. Luther's *Schwabach Articles* (1529) prepared the Wittenberg theologians for the Marburg Colloquy against Zwingli and the *Articles of Torgau* (1530) readied them for the Diet of Augsburg; together these would influence the *Confessio Augustana* which emerged as the fundamental Protestant creed at Augsburg, signed by Elector John Frederick and Lutheran estates outside Saxony (Iserloh 1980, 230–237).[24]

Increasing Protestant cohesion was not complemented by a collectively compelling Catholic response. Continually frustrated reliance on secular enforcement rather than pastoral reforms was complemented by Pope Clement VII's decided reluctance to convene a reforming council. The episcopacy outside Rome was left in the unappealing stance of invoking authority to defend a tradition that seemed as incapable of changing the reformers as it was passionate about their offenses. Moreover, local bishops were habituated to their own parochial responsibilities rather than the policies of Rome.

Common people often perceived Luther as a prophet and saint, as his teachings on the freedom and condemnation of the pope were effectively distributed in the mass-distributed pamphlets and broadsides of printing presses. Ecclesiastical authorities did not aid Catholic pamphleteers against Luther and pamphleteers themselves responded with typically Catholic emphasis on hierarchical authority and moral rigor. Unable to correct Luther politically, the magisterium was unable to connect with popular rejection of law-and-order Catholicism. Thus, enhancing the scholarly opinions of Johannes Hessen, Daniel Olivier, and Jared Wicks mentioned in chapter two, Mark U. Edwards writes that "As people came increasingly to see the contest between Luther and the papacy in apocalyptic terms, Luther's public persona took on many attributes of the biblical prophet" (1994, 170).

The Council of Trent provided the broad magisterial refutation of the reformers and effective implementation of disciplinary reforms. It reclaimed and clarified Catholic tradition and inseminated new doctrinal developments into the Catholic faith. The fear of a council dominating the pope that haunted the Roman curia evaporated as bishops enhanced the church's unity that the papal responses to Luther had invoked repeatedly. Throughout, Luther was absent and his theology was forgotten.

Prelude

Ironically, the significance of the collective magisterial teachings of Trent can first be seen in light of notable magisterial inaction at the Diet of Augsburg in 1530 and the conversations between Catholics and Lutherans at the Diet of Regensburg in 1541. On 21 January 1530 Charles V summoned the imperial diet to Augsburg, a city founded by the Romans in the time of Caesar Augustus, in order to promote defense of the realm against the Turks and to inhibit religious acrimony. On the heels of peaceful accords with Francis I of France and Pope Clement VII, the emperor's invitation was highly conciliatory although he was no less loyal to Rome than when the Diet of Worms ended in 1521. His frustration with papal comings-and-goings about a council and a fear of the consequences of an internal religious war fostered a restrained and constructive tone (Misner 1980, 485). This conciliatory posture was paramount in his rejection of two drafts of the *Confutatio Romano*, which had been submitted on June 25 by twenty Catholic controversialists, led by the papal legate Lorenzo Compeggio and John Eck. The *Confutatio* was a rejoinder to the Lutherans' articles of faith in the *Confessio Augustana*, the Lutheran response to Eck's explosive *404 Articles for the Diet of Augsburg*. Authored by Philip Melanchthon, the *Confessio* reflected much of Luther's Smalcaldic Articles in the doctrinal section and much of the *Articles of Torgau*, produced in the spring of 1530 by the Wittenberg theologians, including Luther at the request of Elector John Frederick. This latter document was incorporated especially in a section that illustrated how Luther's evangelical theology had remedied significant Roman pastoral abuses. Consistent with Eck's earlier tone in the *Enchiridion*, the *404 Articles* had claimed that over three thousand heresies could actually be enumerated in the evangelical theology (Brecht 1991, 369–410). The emperor finally accepted the draft of late July which softened the Catholic polemic with a moderate tone and did not call for the enforcement of the Edict of Worms against Luther.

Retaining a focus on Luther's stature in Rome, we consider the papal legate Compeggio who was engaged in private conciliatory conversations with Melanchthon while the commission of Catholic theologians reworked the response in July 1530.[25] Commanding greater attention from Compeggio than the formal response to the *Confessio*, these conversations anticipated similarly irenic conversations between the committee and the Wittenbergers which achieved broad reconciliation of doctrinal matters in August.[26] While these talks foundered on the issues of communion in the chalice for the laity and priestly celibacy, Compeggio's fruitful advances with Melanchthon were stopped when the legate received word from the papal secretary Salviati that a papal consistory in mid-July had mandated that no concessions be made to the Lutherans (Wicks 1980a, 293–297). Rome's position was complemented by Charles V in late September when, after the negotiations between Catholics and Lutherans in August lapsed, the Recess of Augsburg directed the religious question to a council and stayed the terms of the Edict of Worms until that time. Unlike Rome, Charles would pursue a vigorous policy of reconciliation with Protestants, anticipated at Augsburg by the six-month grace period for compliance that was extended to Lutherans.

Thus, while local representatives of the Roman perspective saw room for reconciliation, Rome itself inhibited any progress. The definitive condemnation of Luther was no less applicable to his followers. While possible outcomes are purely speculative, the fact that such ardent defenders of Rome had become inclined to Charles's reconciliatory posture is fascinating. For example, Compeggio had begun the diet assured that force would be the single effective option (Iserloh 1980, 254). He anticipated the work of the diet to reiterate condemnation of Luther's errors enumerated in *Exsurge Domine*, specification of new errors, and a definitive imperial statement against these errors (Wicks 1980a, 294).

More important here is the fact that progress was made when discussion of the papacy was explicitly absent. Lutherans had viewed inclusion of the papacy into the *Confessio* as too explosive, an issue that might turn Charles's hand decidedly against them. However, it seems that the Lutheran strategy was to accept some form of Roman jurisdiction in return for freedoms in evangelical preaching (Ibid., 276). In fact, this complemented the ecclesiological concerns of Eck and the drafting committee which asserted faith held by a hierarchical church to be greater than interpretations of an individual. Only in February 1537 did the Smalcaldic League add Melanchthon's *Treatise on the Power and Primacy of the Pope* to the confessional statement of Augsburg, concluding that "all the godly have weighty, compelling, and evident reasons for not submitting to the pope and these urgent reasons are a comfort to the godly when, as often happens, they are reproached for scandal, schism, and discord" (Tappert 1959, 330).

Augsburg had demonstrated a mixed magisterial reaction to Luther's teachings, if not Luther himself. This ambivalence disappeared at the Council of Trent and it was foreshadowed in the activity of papal legate Gasparo Contarini (1483–1542) at the imperial Diet of Regensburg and its theological colloquy in 1541.

Sandwiched within escalating tensions between Francis I to the west and the Turks to the east and south, Emperor Charles V vigorously pursued a policy of reconciliation to promote imperial unity. Engineered by Nicholas Granvelle, this policy achieved special impetus from the realization in 1538 that Lutherans would not attend a general council and the pope would provide no real commitment to convening one (Jedin 1957–61, 1:355–356). The Diet of Regensburg was intended to promote solidarity among the estates and their religious collocutors who had maintained the confrontational status quo previously at Frankfurt (1539) and Worms (1540). The allied theological colloquy was especially important because no true political union could occur without a precedent of religious peace. To this end, the colloquy considered the Regensburg Book, a compilation of articles which the Catholic John Gropper (1503–59) and Lutheran Martin Bucer (1491–1551) had secretly developed under Granvelle's sponsorship at the Diet of Worms (Matheson 1972, 4–32).

Cardinal Contarini was an ideal representative for Pope Paul III (1468–1549; pope from 13 October 1534) as he evinced a strong appreciation of the doctrine of justification by faith alone, which he saw in Paul and Augustine along with Luther, and an optimistic commitment to church unity that was clearly more compatible with Charles V's desires than the defensive posture evident in Giovanni Morone, a previous cardinal-legate to the emperor. Contarini was a fresh magisterial face whom the Germans too would recognize as a sign of Rome's hopes for the return of Catholic unity. Having studied Luther and participated in a circle of "evangelical Catholics" in the 1530s, Contarini's loyalty to Rome was also secure.[27] This was important as magisterial anxiety about Charles's policy of reconciliation was exceedingly high insofar as there were repeated indications that the emperor would forego Roman approval of agreements in the interests of national harmony. This was especially evident in the Respite of Frankfurt and the proposed meeting of Catholic estates at Speyer in 1540 (Matheson 1972, 9).

Contarini's evangelical yet loyal Catholicism was evident as the diet and colloquy opened in April 1541. John Eck's tenacious opposition to discussing the Regensburg Book was quelled by the legate and imperial efforts to minimize papal authority in the religious matters discussed there were also thwarted (Matheson 1972, 90–92).[28] Contarini's personal approval of the Regensburg Book moved the Catholic side (Eck, Gropper, and Julius Pflug) to approve a revised article five on justification, a development which subdued the suspicious Lutheran negotiators (Melanchthon, Bucer, and John Pistorius the Elder) as much as it excited the Catholics. Positing a double justice grounded solely in the merits of Christ on the cross yet found inherently in the believer, the article asserted that faith was efficacious in love. Contarini's support of a compromise which favored the position of the Augsburg Confession had clearly raised the level of discussions to an unprecedented importance.

Dissolution of this momentous event soon occurred in both proximate and remote ways. At Regensburg, the dialogue crashed first on the issue of authoritative ecclesial interpretations of scripture and decisively on the issue of transubstantiation. On 4 May Melanchthon objected vigorously to the assertion of infallible conciliar authority stated in articles six to nine, arguing for the polarity of divine will and human traditions as a fundamental element in evangelical theology. Contarini, who met with the Catholic negotiators daily although he was not a formal negotiator, advised postponement of the issue which he rightly perceived as incapable of clear Catholic theological resolution and capable of ending the talks with the politically damaging onus of Roman authority. After obtaining consensus on articles concerning ordination, baptism, and confirmation, Melanchthon stated that article fourteen on the doctrine of transubstantiation could not be tolerated. Contarini's defense of this Catholic doctrine defined at Lateran Council IV (1215) was unyielding. Rejecting theological amendments of Gropper and the postponement of the issue offered by Granvelle, the legate requested the authoritative correction of the Lutherans by Charles V on 15 May (Matheson 1972, 122–144). Lapsing into the pattern of magisterial reliance on civil reversal of heresy, Contarini's resolve was further accelerated by the Lutherans' rejection of article nineteen on the hierarchical order of the church.

At a distance, dissolution of the talks was precipitated by both Luther and the Roman curia. Luther's rejection of the agreement on justification due to its ambiguity was reinforced by the directive of Elector John Frederick of Saxony to Melanchthon— Lutheran negotiators were to receive prior approval from Wittenberg for all agreements.[29] Even Luther's qualified agreement to the article on justification on 9 June 1541, brought about by Granvelle's secret delegation to

Wittenberg, could not reverse the stiffening of Lutheran resolve. On 8 June a dispatch from Cardinal Alessandro Farnese at Rome reached Contarini. It too rejected the article on justification as ambiguous and encouraged serious review of all future developments by Contarini. As important, it chastised Contarini for his waffling on conciliar authority and papal primacy. Contarini's diminishment was further compounded with great praise for Eck's learning and knowledge of the German situation (Ibid., 149–153).

By the Recess of Regensburg on 29 July Catholics estates had rejected the Regensburg Book and called for attention to the general council which Contarini had promised on behalf of Paul III to Charles on 10 July. With this major assault on Charles's reunion policy, Contarini "found himself regarded as a nonentity, uninformed by the Emperor, ignored by the estates, the target of vicious abuse from the Protestants" (Ibid., 169–170). Moreover, the ecumenical evangelical parties in the Catholic magisterium, associated with Contarini and Cardinal Reginald Pole (1500–58), suffered a decisive setback that paved the way for defensive curial forces to dominate the Council of Trent (Fenlon 1972, 62–68). Hubert Jedin concludes, "Only the failure of the Ratisbon [Regensburg] attempt at reunion could justify the drawing of the Tridentine line of demarcation" (Jedin 1957–61, 1:391).

It is important to note that decisive magisterial rejections of both Luther and his work had now occurred before the Council of Trent began. Condemned as a heretic for antipapal and antitraditional ecclesiology in *Exsurge Domine*, Regensburg revealed further that his teaching regarding justification by faith alone, the most likely connection to Rome in 1541 as it had not been at Augsburg in 1530, was unacceptable. As before, Lutheran rejection of ecclesiastical authority, both in rejection of the church's interpretive authority concerning scriptures and her definition of eucharistic presence with the scholastic doctrine of transubstantiation, was intolerable. The very limited magisterial encounter with Luther and his work disappeared. Trent would provide full collective magisterial rejection of Luther and Lutheran teaching with its statements of Catholic doctrinal boundaries. The exhortative dialogues that had followed the initial condemnation of Luther in *Exsurge Domine*, with Lutherans in the foreground and Luther in the background, ended.

Teaching against Luther and His Theology

The ineffective condemnation of Luther at the imperial Diet of Worms in 1521 had not diminished the ecclesiastical resolution against him but had shifted magisterial concern to the political and social ramifications of his teachings. The movement overshadowed its creator by endlessly complicating the church's relationships with Valois France and Habsburg Germany and, together with the diminishment of social authority of local clergy, by disassembling medieval Christendom. Consequently, the council at Trent was anticipated in various ways by the three Christian parties. Luther and German Protestants no longer believed that a "free general and Christian council" was possible and summarily dismissed the event.[30] Emperor Charles V had functional expectations as he saw the council as a means for resolving the social conflicts that the schism introduced. His design at the council's convocation was to promote reform of abuses within the church and to force the Protestants to submit to magisterial judgment, presuming his military victory over the Smalcaldic League. Finally, Pope Paul III expected doctrinal clarity to counter the heretics and the increasing quasi-Lutheran understandings of the Catholic faith (Jedin 1967b, 5–7; O'Malley 1979, 262–273).

The fact that a personal assessment of Luther is of little importance to the conciliar fathers is evident by the fact that the legates' report to the council on 20 March 1546 of Luther's death had little impact on the proceedings or the bishops (Jedin 1957–61, 2:208). More important, Luther and other reformers are not mentioned by name in any of the conciliar documents. While Joachim of Fiore was condemned at the Fourth Lateran Council (1215) and Wyclif and Huss were condemned at the Council of Constance (1414–17), Luther is not condemned specifically until the Tridentine Index of Books which was promulgated after the council on 24 March 1564 by Pope Pius IV's *Dominici gregis* (Barry 1985, 705). Luther's fate had already been established irreversibly in the excommunication of 1521 and the presiding legates at Trent did not want to change the character of the proceedings, which were focused with significant effort on the twin goals of doctrinal clarity and disciplinary reform, into a personal inquisition (Jedin 1962, 6).

Rather, Luther's teachings were anathematized, especially documents from the first session on the Bible and tradition, original sin, justification, and the sacraments. Bishops and theologians at Trent knew Luther's teachings accurately, however incompletely, by consulting various lists and catalogs of errors provided by conciliar theologians and Catholic controversialists (Iserloh 1983, 570–573).

Trent's decree on the biblical canon and apostolic tradition emerged on 8 April 1546 and asserted implicitly that Luther's theological vision was myopic due to his rejection of apostolic traditions authorized by the magisterium. In contrast to Luther's principle of *sola Scriptura*, Trent stated that "this truth and rule [of the gospel] are contained in written books and unwritten traditions" and that the church "accepts and venerates with a like feeling of piety and reverence *(pari pietatis affectu ac reverentia suscipit et veneratur)* all the books of the old and new Testament, since the one God is author of both, as well as the traditions concerning faith and conduct, as either directly spoken by Christ or dictated by the holy Spirit, which have been preserved in unbroken sequence in the catholic church" (Tanner 1990, 663).[31] The unbroken sequence emphatically distinguished the Catholic faith from that held by various heretics across the centuries.

Trent's decree on original sin proceeded from session five on 17 June 1546 and rejected Luther's view that concupiscence inherent in persons ought to be regarded as sin per se. While Luther's personal stature as a Catholic heretic is not explicitly mentioned in the documents, the debate on original sin revealed that the animosity toward the reformer is clearly not absent from the mind of the bishops. Some of them argued that extracts from Luther's writings on original sin should be condemned word for word (Jedin 1957–61, 2:143). While both Luther and Trent saw the guilt of original sin removed at baptism, the reformer had interpreted Paul and Augustine to conclude that persons remain inherently corrupt because concupiscence fully opposes God by imprisoning the human will which would seek God. In sharp relief, the council stated that

> God hates nothing in the reborn, because there is no condemnation for those who are truly buried with Christ by baptism into death, who do not walk according to the flesh but, putting off the old person and putting on the new person created according to God, become innocent, stainless, pure, blameless and beloved children of God. . . . the council confesses and perceives that in the baptized concupiscence or a tendency to sin remains; since this is left as a form of testing, it cannot harm those who do not give consent but, by the grace of Christ, offer strong resistance. (Tanner 1990, 667)

Thus the magisterium dismissed the anthropological axiom which undergirded Luther's rejection of indulgences. While Luther's totally corrupt person was unable de facto to merit spiritual benefits, Trent taught that personally salvific activity is possible within a partial spiritual corruption. The bishops taught that persons are truly wounded spiritually but also that believers wrestle with this tendency to sin as a genuine exercise of faith.

Issued on 13 January 1547, the decree on justification provided the first magisterial determination on the great issue posed by Luther's evangelical theology to the Catholic faith. In asserting that persons are reconciled to God through faith alone, Luther contrasted the Word of God with the word of philosophers, especially Aristotle. In his *Lectures on Romans* (1515) he had determined from that

> Only in the Gospel is the righteousness of God revealed (that is, who is and becomes righteous before God and how this takes place) by faith alone, by which the Word of God is believed. . . . according to God, righteousness precedes works, and thus works are the result of righteousness, just as no person can do the works of a bishop or priest unless he is first consecrated and has been set apart for this. Righteous works of people who are not yet righteous are like the works of a person who performs the functions of a priest and bishop without being a priest; in other words, such works are foolish and tricky and are to be compared with the antics of hucksters in the marketplace. (Luther 1972, 151–152)

While Trent's decree was also replete with biblical authorities, it was scholastic philosophy that articulated the manner in which the Catholic faithful likewise depended on God's grace but also expected that salvific faith was enhanced by personal fulfillment of divine law. Thus, baptism was seen as the instrumental cause which transmits the merciful justice of God, the formal cause, won by the merits of Christ on the cross.[32] In contrast to Luther's emphasis on personal faith, Trent emphasized an explicitly sacramental and therefore ecclesial justification, "which consists not only in the forgiveness of sins but also in the sanctification and renewal of the inward being by a willing acceptance of the grace and gifts whereby someone from being unjust becomes just, from being an enemy becomes a friend, so that he is an heir in hope of eternal life" (Tanner 1990, 673). Thus the council could move from a description of persons' sinful incapacity to achieve justification and the welcome gratuitousness of God's grace in chapters one through nine, to discuss the increase of justifying grace by personal merit in chapters ten through thirteen, and conclude with a similarly ecclesial emphasis on the recovery of justifying grace through the sacrament of penance in chapters fourteen through sixteen. Personal animosity toward Luther is evident again in this debate on justification. Diego Laynez, SJ, argued that the notion of double justification (*duplex iustitia*), which posited our right relationship with God due to both God's grace and our good works, ought to be rejected. It was, he stated, a novelty introduced by John Gropper at Regensburg which was ultimately founded upon the work of the ignoble professor from Wittenberg (Maxcey 1979, 276). In the most significant doctrinal development of the council, Luther's evangelical theology was rejected from the Catholic faith.[33]

Issued on 3 March 1547, the first decree on sacraments continued this ecclesial and transformative sense of justification with its regard of the church's sacraments "by means of which all true justice either begins, or once received gains strength, or if lost restored" (Tanner 1990, 684). In contrast to Luther's conception of a sacrament as a sign requiring faith and operating through faith, Trent understood the sacraments to be ecclesially efficacious signs that convey grace. However, Trent's emphasis on sacramental efficacy in this document, mainly containing condemnatory canons, was not matched by significant elucidation of their ecclesial context. As has been shown earlier in this study, the ecclesial nature of faith was the prime catalyst in magisterial reaction against Luther. The ecclesial nature of sacraments was restricted to canons delineating efficacy and numbers because, in the judgment of Hubert Jedin, "the doctrine of the Church . . . still needed so many further elucidations and deeper foundations that the council preferred not to oppose a definition of the Catholic conception of the Church to that of Protestants" (Jedin 1962, 12).

Insofar as Trent taught that sacraments are effective *ex opere operato*, thereby emphasizing the activity of God's grace more than the church's mediation, the absence of an explicit ecclesiological component in Trent's teachings seems merely odd. Indulgences, on the other hand, remit temporal punishment for sin *ex opere operantis*, emphasizing the church's authority to judge and to reward, a contrite penitent. It is puzzling, to say the least, that this specific challenge to episcopal and papal authority which spawned the evangelical movement was not extensively answered at the council.[34]

This inability to develop deeper ecclesiological foundations at Trent was further evident in the third session when gridlock developed over the specific nature of episcopal authority. Specifically, the bishops considered whether they possessed authority by divine right (*de iure divino*) or by deputation of the pope. Trent stated delicately that bishops existed by "divine appointment" and by virtue of elevation by the pope. However, while bishops were determined to have universal and not merely a jurisdictional parochial authority, the issues of papal primacy, conciliar authority, and ecclesial infallibility were never resolved (Jedin 1967b, 80–137). In effect, the Council of

Trent was able to demarcate significant aspects of Luther's theology from Catholic doctrine but did not provide compelling answers to the reformer's fundamental theological questions about how scripture and tradition are mediated authoritatively in Christian life. Luther was excommunicated for placing himself outside the authoritatively interpreted tradition of the church yet Trent was little able to encourage profound appreciation of ecclesial authority.

Postlude

The extensive influence of the Council of Trent in subsequent Catholicism resulted from the complete systematization and codification of the faith by the papal curia following closure of the council on 4 December 1563. Pope Pius IV (1499–1565; pope from 25 December 1559) put the curia at the forefront of conciliar interpretation in 1564 by confirming the council in January, mandating enforcement of the doctrinal and reform decrees in Italy throughout the summer, and proscribing the Tridentine Profession of Faith to be sworn by all bishops in November. Widespread uniformity of faith was achieved further by Pius V (1504–72; pope from 7 January 1566), who published the Roman Catechism in 1566, the Roman Breviary in 1568, and the Roman Missal in 1570. He established the Congregation of the Index in March 1571 in order to enforce the revised Index of Forbidden Books. In contrast to the diversity of faith evident in the conciliar debates, Trent's postlude spawned a more passive Catholicism with a Catholic society led by a strong and defensive hierarchy that had accepted the spiritual and temporal divisions within Christianity (Alberigo 1988, 219).

The catechism was the primary instrument by which most Catholics were apprised of the reconfigured faith.[35] Instruction in knowledge of the faith was a concern at Trent from the beginning, as a formal catechism of the council was anticipated as early as April 1546 and a writing commission was in place by November 1547. Significant work was not achieved, however, until a commission headed by Cardinal Girolamo Seripando, OSA, (1492–1563) convened in March 1563. In October the commission, chaired by Charles Borromeo (1538–84) after Seripando's death on 17 March, was given the specific charge of providing a catechism for parish priests. Published in October 1566, the *Catechism of the Council of Trent for Parish Priests* (*Catechismus ex decreto Ss. Concilii Tridentini ad Parochos Pii V. Pont. Max. iussu editus*) contained sections on the creed, sacraments, decalogue, and prayer (Bradley 1990, 110–120). This first-ever magisterial catechism was a manual of doctrine that integrated scriptural and traditional authorities in a largely scholastic fashion, with few polemical overtones. While the catechism never mentioned the reformers or their subsequent communities by name, its preface refuted non-Catholic catechetics where

> To such extremes has their impiety, practiced in all the arts of Satan, been carried, that it would seem almost impossible to confine it within any bounds. . . . For those who intended to corrupt the minds of the faithful, knowing that they could not hold immediate personal intercourse with all, and thus pour into their ears their poisonous doctrines, adopted another plan which enabled them to disseminate error and impiety more easily and extensively. (McHugh and Callan, 3–4)

The ecclesio-sacramental focus of the Trent's decrees continued in its catechism, evident in the fact that section two on sacraments is twice as long as any other section. There one finds this kernel of Tridentine faith:

> Since the ministers of the Sacraments represent in their discharge of their sacred functions, not their own, but the person of Christ, be they good or bad, they validly perform and confer the Sacraments, provided they make use of the matter and form always observed in the Catholic Church according to the institution of Christ, and provided they intend to do what the Church does in their administration. Hence, unless the recipients wish to deprive themselves of so great a good and resist the Holy Ghost, nothing can prevent them from receiving (through the Sacraments) the fruit of grace. (Ibid., 155)

Likewise, the catechism's commentary on the forgiveness of sins, article ten of the creed, emphasized the church's mediation of God's forgiveness "which absolves from sin and restores the unjust to a state of justification" (Ibid., 116).

The Roman Catechism penetrated the Catholic anima in ways that the decrees could not.[36] With it, priests often fulfilled the council's mandate to study and preach the Tridentine faith as is remarkably evident in the diocese of Milan where Borromeo, the catechism's overseer, succeeded in implementing profound reforms. The *Catechismus ad parochos* was the cornerstone of Borromeo's new catechetical agency, the Confraternity of Christian Doctrine (Tomaro 1988, 67–84).[37] Testimony to the enduring effectiveness of the Roman catechism is found in the 1985 Roman Synod of Bishops that commemorated the anniversary of the Second Vatican Council (1962–65) by calling for a universal catechism. The appeal to Trent's successful model of catechesis in the midst of widespread Catholic illiteracy about the faith was echoed by many twentieth-century bishops for both nostalgic and pedagogical reasons (Wrenn 1991, 75–138).

While the Roman catechism was the outstanding magisterial transmission of the Tridentine teaching to parishes, the council's doctrines were also woven into the fabric of Catholicism with significant contributions by two Jesuits, Peter Canisius (1521–97) and Robert Bellarmine (1542–1621). Canisius, who coedited the first German translation of the Roman Catechism in 1568, had produced a tripartite series of catechisms from 1555 to 1558 that refuted the *sola fide* of Luther with emphasis on Christian wisdom and justice. The *summa, minor,* and *minima* were addressed in question-and-answer format respectively to catechists, adolescents, and beginners and were the most popular catechisms in Germany, also circulating internationally (Brodrick 1935, 241–252). Commissioned by King Ferdinand of Austria (Emperor Charles V's brother), Canisius arranged the *summa* to emphasize the complementarity of the creed, prayer, and sacraments (wisdom) with the virtues and beatitudes (justice). The revised and definitive *summa* of 1566 incorporated the teachings of Trent regarding original sin and justification and presented a full treatment on the primacy of the pope.[38] Canisius, whose name became a synonym for catechism, so influenced the Catholic Reformation that in May 1925 *L'Osservatore Romano* spoke of Luther and Canisius, stating that "these two names are to one another as light is to the shadow, as heresy to the rope which hangs it, as rebellion to obedience, as the athlete of God to one who has already been laid low by the darts of Erasmus" (Loewenich 1959, 272).

Bellarmine produced two widely-circulated catechisms in 1597 and 1598 but is more generally recognized for the more thoughtful *Disputations on Controversies of the Christian Faith Against Contemporary Heretics* (*Disputationes de controversiis Christianae fidei adversus huius temporis haereticos*) published in four volumes from 1586 to 1593 and definitively revised in 1596.[39] The work systematized Roman Catholic arguments against Protestantism and remained at the forefront of Catholic apologetic literature until the First Vatican Council in 1869–70 (Brodrick 1961, 87). In steady defense of Tridentine doctrine, Bellarmine, professor of controversial theology at the Roman College from 1576 to 1588, refuted Reformed and Lutheran positions by juxtaposing Catholic teachings with positions derived directly from Protestant sources. Although he was concerned more with the Lutherans than the Reformed, he cited John Calvin more than Luther, who is supplanted as the primary Lutheran target by Martin Chemnitz (1522–86), the great Lutheran critic of the Council of Trent in his *Examination of the Council of Trent* (1565–74). As the chief apologist for Catholicism at the end of the sixteenth century, a role which has evoked comparison with Athanasius of Alexandria for some, Bellarmine placed the eucharist, papacy, and sacraments ("the true and direct causes of justification") as prominent themes (Richgels 1980, 3–15).[40] Echoing the doctrinal declarations of Trent's first session, he considered the primary problems posed by the Protestant heretics to be those concerning the church and forgiveness of sins.

CONCLUSION

Luther was excommunicated and his evangelical theology was anathematized by the magisterium in the sixteenth century because the professor of Bible broke faith with the church and because the magisterium was immunized against his theological novelty with entrenched political and theological expectations. Luther's earliest thoughts to correct pastoral abuses regarding indulgences and to reemphasize the biblical compass for theology were received without reflection by Archbishop Albrecht of Mainz or understanding by Rome where the Saxon problem appeared to need swift fraternal correction. Luther's fervor for pure preaching of the gospel and for administration of the sacraments according to biblical standards was perceived in Rome as an outright denial of papal prerogatives to guide the church according to the course which tradition had already delineated and generations of popes had steered.

Prierias's curt defense of the pope as infallible legislator, Cajetan's thoughtful exposition of the pope as mediator of the apostolic tradition, and Eck's pugnacious claims for the pope as arbiter of doctrine all presupposed the united visible society of faith which was, in their judgment, hopelessly absent from Luther's teachings. The bishops at Trent judged the dire warnings in the papal bulls of excommunication to be true: Luther had not only denied papal preeminence in the society of believers but had displaced sacramental faith with a merely individualistic belief that was elevated to the supreme criterion for surety of God's forgiving love. They perceived that the reformer mocked other divinely instituted structures which enervated the body of Christ—indulgences of the church, which were the gift of God from the meritorious legacy of the saints, and meritorious works of the faithful, gifts to God in personal appreciation of the singular achievement of Jesus Christ.

Luther's separation from Roman Catholicism, caused freely and deliberately by his own thought and activity, was authorized by the magisterium with a tenacious sense of a hierarchically-constituted, sacramental, and visible church. Cajetan and Contarini, the two most thoughtful representatives of the magisterium in dialogue with Luther, both stiffened their resolve when Luther and his followers became intractable opponents of papal primacy and established sacramental doctrines. While the Council of Trent could not develop a doctrine of papal primacy with episcopal corollaries, it clearly embraced a sense of papal primacy that became fully evident in its implementation. Further, Trent defined the Catholic doctrine of justification by integrating throughout an emphasis on the sacraments of baptism and penance. It maintained the practice of indulgences while revising their administration. The magisterial mind could not appreciate Luther because its ecclesiology permitted no room for him in the church.

To a lesser degree, magisterial revulsion was fostered when Luther rejected bitterly the scholastic theological authorities who informed most curial thought. The opinions of Prierias and Cajetan as well as the teachings of Trent on justification, considered by the conciliar fathers to be the crown of the doctrinal decrees, demonstrate the value of scholastic thought for the church's leaders. Even as Cajetan, Eck, and Trent saw the need for more explicitly biblical theology, the scholastic style remained in marked difference to the popular personalized discourse of Luther and other reformers.

Ironically, the ecclesiological component that is fundamental to Roman Catholic rejection of Luther in the sixteenth century will be essential for understanding Catholic magisterial appreciation of Luther in the twentieth century when its understanding of the church would become more explicitly biblical.

4

LUTHER AND THE ROMAN CATHOLIC MAGISTERIUM IN THE TWENTIETH CENTURY

> Wasn't it perhaps even necessary, we might ask here at Augsburg, in accordance with God's unfathomable wisdom, for religious schisms and religious wars to occur in order to lead the Church to reflect on and renew her original values?
>
> —Pope John Paul II, May 1987[1]

Pope John Paul II issued the first papal statement focused on Luther since his excommunication in 1521 when the pontiff appreciatively noted the five-hundredth birthday of the reformer in 1983. During the interval, the magisterium observed the precedent established by the Council of Trent; it avoided assessments of individuals in order to teach emphatically the traditional and complete faith of the one, holy, catholic, and apostolic church that the Roman hierarchy protected and heretics eschewed.

Roman Catholic emphasis on *unity* within the hierarchically-constituted, sacramental, visible church of Rome dominated all magisterial perspectives on non-Catholics until the Second Vatican Council (1962–65). In contrast to Protestant emphasis on ecclesial *purity* evidenced from strict attention to the Bible and corresponding apostolic traditions together with proper administration of sacraments, magisterial pronouncements regarding non-Catholics, few though they were, firmly taught that repatriation to Roman Catholicism was the solution to the sixteenth-century schism. Magisterial opinion of Luther was subsumed by the church's ecclesiological assessment of Christian divisions that appreciated deeply the security provided by the church's universal adherence to doctrine rather than reformers' innovations to the common faith. Luther's excommunication became merely the foundational event among more obvious and far-reaching threats to Catholic unity that had evolved in the sixteenth century. Secular divorce from ecclesiastical policies had undermined episcopal and papal authority, evident in the ability of Luther to ignore the sanctions at Worms in 1521. The perpetuation of a dissenting society with an increasingly unified Lutheran community after the Diet of Augsburg in 1530 diminished the Catholic worldview through parochial, intellectual, and pastoral competition. Superceding the regional problem posed by Luther, the threat of Protestantism to Roman catholicity provided the primary target that the Council of Trent exposed, diagnosed, and intended to rectify.

The magisterium's decidedly negative opinion of Luther in the sixteenth century was reinforced by these developments that extended the un-Catholic teachings of Martin Luther even while generations of adherents modified many of them. As heresiarch extraordinaire, Luther was vilified as one who began an atrocious dissembling of the sacred order typified in the church under papal authority. Characteristically, in 1565 the Jesuit Pedro Juan Perpiña (1530–66), master of rhetoric at the Collegio Romano, decried Luther and other reformers: "You plagues of the human race, furies of the Church, destroyers of the *patria*, enemies of religion, robbers of the *sacra*, destruction and ruin of the world; you, I say, who from the stables and piggeries have suddenly been made teachers and doctors of the people" (McGinness 1995, 130). Magisterial reappraisal of the reformer in the twentieth century can be understood as a progressive reconfiguration of such ironclad sentiments and their corresponding ecclesiological motivation with a relocation of Luther to the spectrum of inspired believers. Official Roman Catholic appreciation of Luther as a legitimate Catholic prophet and reformer occurred in three incremental developments: (1) recognition before the Second Vatican Council of the ecumenical movement and concession of a legitimate non-Catholic Christianity; (2) commitment at the Second Vatican Council to the ecumenical enterprise and affirmation of the Christian authenticity of Protestants; and, (3) significant magisterial gestures demonstrating a revaluation of Luther in postconciliar decades.

Catholic Magisterium and Ecumenism Before Vatican II

The interval from Trent until Catholic recognition of the validity of the twentieth-century ecumenical movement is described as a period of "rigid and intractable opposition" in which Catholics saw Protestant sects as "doctrinally and spiritually impoverished imitations of the true church" and individual Protestants as "pitifully and dangerously benighted perpetrators of heresy" (McNeill 1967, 35; Minus 1976, 74). Similarly, on the eve of the Second Vatican

Council, Lutheran scholar Wilhelm Pauck stated that "The difference between Protestantism and Roman Catholicism is so profound that it almost seems impossible to recognize them as two forms of one Christianity" (1961, 231).

Pauck's sentiments reciprocate the magisterial opinion of Protestants before Pope Leo XIII (1810–1903, pope from 20 February 1878). In November 1742, for example, Pope Benedict XIV (1675–1758, pope from 17 August 1740) defended the validity of sole communion by priests at Mass by construing Trent to have explicitly condemned Luther's opposite opinion (Pius XII 1981b, 4: 138). In May 1844, Pope Gregory XVI (1765–1846, pope from 3 February 1831) condemned Protestant biblical societies, even naming the Christian League of New York City among "special schemes which non-Catholics plot against the adherents of Catholic truth to turn their minds away from faith." The pope determined that the Protestant practice of private interpretation promoted modern religious indifferentism just as it had rooted the turn from the magisterium in the sixteenth century (Gregory XVI 1981, 1: 267).

In contrast, the fundamental magisterial assessment of schismatic Eastern churches was much more positive and welcoming than its appraisal of Luther as a heretic and Lutherans as malevolent dissenters. In the preparations for the First Vatican Council (1869–70), for example, Pope Pius IX (1792–1878, pope from 16 June 1846) invited Eastern bishops not in communion with the Holy See to attend the council so "the serene radiance of the desired union may begin to shine on all after a long period of dark sorrow and the black, depressing gloom of longstanding discord" (Brodrick 1971, 21). The pope's tone was noticeably distant toward Protestants; in contrast to Eastern non-Catholics communities, *Iam vos omnes* of 13 September 1868 did not define Protestant communities as churches. After asserting the fundamental spiritual deficiency of Protestant sects, in contrast to the one Roman church, and the clear civic liability posed by Protestants who are prone to social disorders by virtue of their habit of rejecting legitimate authority, the pope encouraged their return to Catholicism. Enunciating the return motif that would anchor the Catholic ecumenical posture until the Second Vatican Council, Pius IX stated:

> And since we, although unworthy, function as His vicar here on earth, we ardently await with outstretched arms the return to the Catholic church of her wandering children so that we can lovingly receive them into the home of the heavenly Father, and enrich them with its unexhausted treasures. For the salvation of both individu-

als and of all Christian society depends to a very great extent on this
ardently desired return to the truth and to communion with the
Catholic Church; and the whole world cannot enjoy true peace
unless there be one fold and one shepherd. (Brodrick 1971, 23–
27)[2]

While the First Vatican Council never presented a complete
ecclesiology and is noted most often for its definitions of papal
primacy and papal infallibility, the first draft version of the constitution *On the Church* stated that there was no true religion of Christ
outside the Roman Catholic church, a spiritual society with visible
bonds in the "magisterial, ministerial, and regiminal power" of the
magisterium. A subsequent draft by Joseph Kleutgen, SJ, (1811–83)
did nuance the assertion regarding true religion by allowing for a
membership-by-desire for the non-Catholic Christian who "through
no fault of his own does not enter the Church and who obeys the
natural law." The council ended before some bishops could extend
this idea further, opining that certain vestiges of the religion of Christ
exist outside Catholicism (Ahern 1966, 275–283).

Pope Leo XIII, Pius IX's successor, established the priority of
Christian unity for the twentieth-century magisterium, compiling a
corpus of thirty-five documents dedicated to the issue. In contrast to
Pius IX, Leo XIII promoted a more positive relationship between the
church and civilization and he believed that Christian unity was an
essential demand of the changing world as well as of the gospel itself.
Leo's *Praeclara gratulationis* of 20 June 1894 was the first papal
document specifically dedicated to modern Christian unity and was
issued on the fiftieth anniversary of the pope's episcopal installation.
In appreciation of the vitality of the Catholic church the pope
encouraged non-Christians, Orthodox, and Protestants, and Catholics to more fully acknowledge the definitive way of truth that
Catholicism presents. Regarding Protestants, Pope Leo XIII re-
marked that "with no less affection [than for Orthodox Christians] do
We now look upon the nations, who at a more recent date, were
separated from the Roman Church by an extraordinary revolution of
things and circumstances." The pope encouraged the return of
Protestants to the Catholic church "with brotherly love" while maintaining the opinion that the Protestant rejection of authority by
private interpretation of scripture caused both a spiritual malady and
a civic liability. With a veiled reference to Luther he stated that

If they will but compare that [Catholic] Church with their own communions, and consider what the actual state of religion is in these, they will easily acknowledge that, forgetful of their early history, they have drifted away, on many and important points, into the novelty of various errors; nor will they deny that of what may be called the patrimony of truth, which the authors of these innovations carried away with them in their desertion, there now scarcely remains to them any article of belief that is really certain and supported by authority. (Leo XIII 1903, 310)

Pope Leo XIII's characterization of the reformers as whimsical purveyors of diverse errors of faith typified the Tridentine evaluation of Luther that would remain until the bold initiatives of the Secretariat for Christian Unity and Pope John Paul II after the Second Vatican Council. In August 1879 Leo XIII reinforced the image of the reformers as breezy innovators when he called for the restoration of Thomas Aquinas's philosophy to preeminence in Catholic intellectual pursuits with the encyclical *Aeterni Patris*, stating that "It pleased the struggling innovators of the sixteenth century to philosophize without any respect for faith, the power of inventing in accordance with his own pleasure and bent being asked and given in turn by each one" (1981, 2: 24).

While *Praeclara* was more appreciative of Orthodox Christianity than Protestantism, with the papal guarantee to preserve Orthodox rites and practices upon reentry to the Catholic church, the pope's *Amantissima voluntatis* of 14 April 1895 was noticeably cordial to Protestants. Written to the English on the thirteen-hundredth anniversary of Christianity in the British Isles, Leo XIII established magisterial precedent with the irenic and prayerful use of "separated brethren" rather than the term "dissenters" that characterized Protestants in *Praeclara* and *Longinqua*, his encyclical of 6 January 1895 on Catholicism in the United States.[3] Further, *Amantissima* contained no reference to Protestant defections from the church or infections of society. It encouraged English Catholics, "Uniting your prayer with Ours, your great desire may now be that God will grant you to welcome your fellow-citizens and brethren in the bond of perfect charity" (Leo XII 1903, 347).

While Pope Leo XIII's reference to "brethren in the bond of perfect charity" hinted at some restricted kind of legitimate Christianity among Protestants, his second major encyclical on Christian unity, *Satis cognitum* of 29 June 1896, clearly explained the ecclesiological basis for authentic Christianity available to non-Catholics upon their return to the Catholic church. In arguing for the essentially visible nature of Christ's church, Leo denied any non-Catholic conceptualization of an invisible church or federation of individual churches. The hierarchical and sacramental communion of Catholicism was explored according to the image of the mystical body of Christ in Ephesians and in patristic testimony. The pope stated that "For this reason, as the unity of the faith is of necessity required for the unity of the church, inasmuch as it is the *body of the faithful,* so also for this same unity, inasmuch as the Church is the divinely constituted society, unity of government, which effects and involves *unity of communion,* is necessary de jure divino" (Leo XIII 1981, 2: 396). Thus, as asserted with Luther and sixteenth-century Protestants, recognition of the biblical and traditional ordination of apostolic succession and papal primacy remained the key to Christian unity. Accordingly, *Satis* and other pronouncements by Pope Leo XIII operated on the assumption that a clear delineation of Catholic teaching will dispel non-Catholic prejudices and the "essential beauty and comeliness of the Church ought to influence the minds of those who consider it" (Ibid., 2: 387).

In a review of his nearly twenty-year pontificate in 1897, the pope stated that the restoration of Christian principles in civil life and the promotion of Christian unity were his two main aims (Ibid., 2: 409–410).[4] Pope Leo XIII, who authorized the annual prayer for Christian unity among Catholics, had displayed a welcoming and cordial attitude to non-Catholics that was complemented with the firm and constant requirement that they embrace the full Catholic tradition with its emphasis on apostolic succession.[5] In *Caritatis studium* of 25 July 1898, he wrote to Scottish Catholics that

> The ardent charity which renders Us solicitous of Our separated brethren, in no wise permits Us to cease Our efforts to bring back to the embrace of the Good Shepherd those whom manifold error causes to stand aloof from the one Fold of Christ. Day after day We deplore the unhappy lot of those who are deprived of the fullness of the Christian Faith. (Ibid., 2: 433)[6]

Pope Pius X (1835–1914, pope from 4 August 1903) succeeded Leo XIII and froze his predecessor's now-modest ecumenical initiatives. Pius X's worry about modernism, a derogatory term for the Catholic scholarly movement that strove to reconcile traditional Catholic theology with modern developments in philosophical, historical, and other social sciences, disabled ecumenical progress until the very end of his papacy. Then, in 1914, Cardinal Enrico Gasparri, Secretary of

State, began a series of letters with Robert Gardiner (1855–1924), an organizer for the World Conference on Faith and Order (Tatlow 1967, 412–414). Pius X's *Pascendi Dominici gregis* of 8 September 1907 had likened the "unchecked passion for novelty" of the modernists to the reformers of the sixteenth century. Pius stated that "Acting on the principle that science in no way depends on faith, when they treat of philosophy, history, criticism, feeling no horror at treading in the footsteps of Luther, they are wont to display a certain contempt for Catholic doctrine, or the Holy Fathers, for the Ecumenical Councils, for the ecclesiastical magisterium" (1981, 3: 78). Further, the pope determined that Protestantism had been the first step toward the annihilation of religion; now, modernism placed civilization on the very brink of atheism (Ibid., 3:90). Modernism, which Pius termed the "synthesis of all heresies," was perceived to imitate the reformers' apotheosis of individual antirational experience (Ibid., 3:89). In a summary of modernism that could serve as a sixteenth-century magisterial appraisal of Luther and Protestantism, Pius stated that modernists "recognize that the three difficulties for them are scholastic philosophy, the authority of the fathers and tradition, and the magisterium of the Church, and on these they wage unrelenting war" (Ibid., 3:91).

Pius X recapitulated magisterial wrath for Luther and Protestantism when honoring Saint Charles Borromeo on the third centennial of his death in the encyclical, *Editae saepe* of 26 May 1910. The vilification of modernism continued by comparison to the sixteenth century's dissenters but the pope found the modernists to be more pernicious than Protestants as "The wild innovators of former times generally preserved some fragments of the treasury of revealed doctrine, these moderns act as if they will not rest until they completely destroy it" (Ibid., 3:119). The pope contrasted Charles Borromeo with the false reformers of his age by extolling Borromeo's faithfulness to the church and his denial of self-interest (Ibid., 3: 122–123). Earlier, Pius X's maintenance of the magisterial ecumenism-of-return was symbolized by his blessing of Rev. Paul Wattson and the Society of the Atonement on 27 December 1909 after their entry into the Roman Catholic church from Anglicanism on 30 October (Minus 1976, 38–41).[7]

During the pontificate of Benedict XV (1854–1922, pope from 3 September 1914) the ecumenical movement among non-Catholics coalesced because of the World Conference of the Protestant Missionary Society at Edinburgh in 1910. Recognizing the impediments posed to the spread of Christianity by the fact of separate and competitive churches, non-Catholics established a World Alliance for

Promoting International Friendship through Churches in 1915 and were planning the first Life and Work Conference for Stockholm (19–30 August 1925) when Benedict XV died (Tatlow 1967, 407–416). The pope had maintained a strict separation between Catholic ecumenical designs and those of non-Catholics. He declined participation in the World Alliance and in the Uppsala Conference that planned for an international unity conference, which eventually convened as the Life and Work Conference at Stockholm in 1925 without Roman Catholic participation. Regarding the World Alliance, Benedict XV stated, through Cardinal-Secretary of State Enrico Gasparri, that he approved of the effort for unity "and He asks the same of Jesus Christ with fervent prayers, all the more because, with the voice of Christ Himself sounding before and bidding Him, He knows that He Himself, as the one to whom all men have been given over to be fed, is the source and cause of the unity of the Church" (Ibid., 413). Benedict also reiterated the policy of prohibiting Catholic participation in ecumenical meetings that the Holy Office under Pius IX had established. Thus, in the Holy Office's *De participatione catholicorum societatis* of 4 July 1919, Catholic involvement in the English Association for the Promotion of the Unity of Christendom was forbidden.[8]

The pope sustained Catholic ecumenical efforts by extending to the universal Church the Chair of Unity Octave (18–25 January), a period of prayer for Christian unity established by Rev. Paul Wattson in 1908 at Graymoor, New York. He also established the Pontifical Oriental Institute at Rome, dedicating it to the study of the doctrine and history of Eastern non-Catholic churches in order to foster eventual reunion.[9]

Pope Pius XI (1857–1939, pope from 6 February 1922) succeeded Benedict XV and began his pontificate as the world attempted to recover from the devastation of World War I. The pope's encyclical *Ubi arcano Dei consilio* of 23 December 1922 considered the "peace of Christ in the Kingdom of Christ." A meditative exploration of the debilitating effects of materialism in the postwar era, the encyclical directed humanity's attention to the peace of Christ evident in the church that "alone possesses in any complete and true sense the power effectively to combat that materialistic philosophy which has already done and, still threatens, such tremendous harm to the home and to the state." Pius XI enunciated firmly that non-Catholics must return to the Roman Catholic church because their separation from visible unity keeps them outside the church (Pius XI 1981c, 3: 233–235).

Pius XI intensified the concern of Leo XIII and Benedict XV for the reunion of Eastern non-Catholic churches. His exhortation for their return in *Ecclesiam Dei* (12 November 1923) was given on the third centenary of the death of Saint Josaphat of the Eastern Slavic Rite and was followed on 21 March 1924 with the inauguration of Oriental studies among Belgian Benedictines who established a new monastery for that purpose at Amay-sur-Meuse in December 1925 (Pius XI 1981c, 3: 259–264; Minus 1976, 58–60).

Pius XI's magnanimity was not extended to Protestant Christians. The Holy Office's prohibition in 1927 of Catholic involvement in the ecumenical work of the High Church Ecumenical Federation in Germany and in the first Faith and Order Conference at Lausanne was explained in encyclical *Mortalium animos* (6 January 1928) (Bell 1955, 187–188). It began by stating that "some are more easily deceived by the outward appearance of good when there is question of fostering unity among Christians" (Pius XI 1981b, 3: 313).

The Lausanne Conference of August 1927 had raised the issue of the nature of the Christian church and debated whether the church was one in visible unity or one invisibly and diverse temporally. *Mortalium animos*, while resolute in the desire for Christian unity, adamantly rejected any "pan-Christian" notion that "the unity of faith and government, which is a note of the one true Church of Christ, has hardly up to the present time existed, and does not to-day exist" (Ibid., 3: 315). Repeatedly, Pius XI asserted that indifferentism regarding the ecclesiological doctrines of the Roman Catholic church placed believers on the slippery slope that trails into atheism. The pope asserted that the only way to restore the union of Christ's mystical body is the submission of all "separated children" to the teaching and government of the Catholic church (Ibid., 3: 318).

In sustained defense of a hierarchical, sacramental, and visible church, Pius XI acknowledged the noble ecumenical purpose of non-Catholics but diagnosed their fault according to the typical disdain for private judgment that rooted Catholic criticisms of Protestantism since the sixteenth century. Stated the pontiff, "it is clear why this Apostolic See has never allowed its subjects to take part in the assemblies of non-Catholics: for the union of Christians can only be promoted by promoting the return to the one true Church of Christ of those who are separated from it, for in the past they have unhappily left it" (Ibid., 3: 317).[10] Pius XI affirmed prayer as the chief ecumenical tool in *Caritate Christi compulsi* of 3 May 1932. The pope exhorted Catholics to pray and do penance for the world which faced universal economic depression and an increasing appeal for atheistic communism: "Let them pray for their brethren who believe, for their brethren who err, for believers, for infidels, even for the enemies of God and the Church, that they may be converted, and let them pray for the whole of poor mankind" (Pius XI 1981c, 3: 482).

Pius XI had shown that the magisterial refrain for non-Catholic return to the Roman Catholic church harbored especially strict consideration for Protestants whose very existence defied the Catholic tradition of ecclesial unity in apostolic succession. His successor, Pius XII (1876–1958, pope from 2 March 1939), inaugurated a new attitude in magisterial regard of Protestants, as symbolized by this remark in his first encyclical of 20 October 1939: "Nor can We pass over in silence the profound impression of heartfelt gratitude made on Us by the good wishes of those who, though not belonging to the visible body of the Catholic Church, have given noble and sincere expression to their appreciation of all that unites them to Us in love for the Person of Christ or in belief in God" (1981d, 4: 7). Like a few bishops at Vatican I, Pius XII's pontificate demonstrated elasticity in Catholic ecclesiology by positing visible traces of the Church (*vestigia ecclesiae*) outside Roman Catholicism.[11]

While Leo XIII and his successors authorized Catholic ecumenism based on the premise that reunion with the visible Catholic church is essential, Pius XII's *Mystici corporis Christi* of 29 June 1943 introduced the possibility that unity need not strictly be conceived according to the criterion of submission to Rome. In concert with his predecessors, Pius XII stated that "how grievously they err who arbitrarily claim that the Church is something hidden and invisible, as they also do who look upon her as a mere human institution possessing a certain disciplinary code and external ritual, but lacking power to communicate supernatural life" (1981c, 4: 50).[12] Likewise, the pope asserted that the "visible and normal" government of the church occurred in communion with the Bishop of Rome (Ibid., 4: 44). With frequent reference to Pope Leo XIII, Pius XII concluded in the constancy and vigor of his predecessors that "[Jesus Christ] refuses to dwell through sanctifying grace in those members that are wholly severed from the Body" (Ibid., 4:48).

Unlike his predecessors and in a highly nuanced way, Pius XII posited a definite link between non-Catholics and the mystical body of Christ evident in the Roman Catholic church:

> We have proclaimed the "great and glorious Body of Christ," and from a heart overflowing with love We ask each and every one of them [separated brethren] to correspond to the interior move-

ments of grace, and to seek to withdraw from that state in which they cannot be sure of their salvation. For even though by an unconscious desire and longing they have a certain relationship with the Mystical Body of the Redeemer, they still remain deprived of those many heavenly gifts and helps which can only be enjoyed in the Catholic Church. (Ibid., 4:58)

In effect, Pius XII had distinguished the mystical body of Christ from the visible Catholic church, emphasizing in the encyclical that the body was essentially visible but that it somehow also transcended the visible, that is, the hierarchical, sacramental communion with the Bishop of Rome. The pope began with two presuppositions of his predecessors who spoke of non-Catholics returning to the Catholic church and taught that heresy was not hereditary. Recognizing the basic elements of faith evident among non-Catholics, baptism and the profession of faith in Christ, Pius XII then concluded that even Protestants were part of, although imperfectly, the mystical body of Christ. While the relationship of Catholics and non-Catholics within the body of Christ was not clarified, the ambiguity could not diminish the fact that the magisterium had defined the relationship of non-Catholic Christians to Catholicism in a new manner. This was evident in two statements of policy from the Holy Office in 1949.

On 8 August, *Suprema haec sacra* informed Archbishop Richard J. Cushing (1895–1970) of Boston that Rev. Leonard Feeney, SJ, (1897–1978) was erroneous in teaching at Harvard's Saint Benedict Center that "outside the church there is no salvation." With reference to *Mystici corporis*, the letter stated that

One may obtain eternal salvation, it is not always required that he be incorporated into the Church *actually* as a member, but it is necessary that at least he be united to her by *desire* and *longing*… when a person is involved in invincible ignorance, God accepts also an *implicit desire*, so called because it is included in that good disposition of soul whereby a person wishes his will to be conformed to the will of God. (Holy Office 1952, 313)

On 20 December, *Ecclesia Catholica* advised diocesan bishops that they were especially responsible for monitoring and promoting ecumenical developments that the instruction termed "inspired" (Holy Office 1950, 207).[13] In a muted acknowledgment of Catholic complicity for the Reformation, the instruction stated that bishops

should scrupulously take precautions and firmly insist that, in rehearsing the history of the Reformation or the Reformers, the

faults and foibles of Catholics are not overemphasized, whilst the
blame and defects of the Reformers are dissimulated; nor that
rather accidental circumstances be placed in such a light that the
main fact, consisting in the defection from Catholic Faith, is
allowed to dwindle from sight and mind. (Ibid., 209)

For the first time, Catholics were encouraged by the magisterium to
study Protestantism.

Pope Pius XII promoted a significant yet restrained Catholic
ecumenical posture toward Protestants. His subtly inclusive notion of
the mystical body of Christ quieted any notion that Western schis-
matics were quasi-atheistic or at least antagonistic to authentic
Christianity. His frequent appeals for Christian unity in face of threats
posed to all Christian believers by the increasingly atheistic, materialistic, and changing modern world indicate that the magisterium
now saw more common faith with Protestant Christianity than ever
before.

Nevertheless, Pius XII maintained a fervent and sustained defense
of the hierarchical and sacramental ecclesiology of his predecessors,
including its ecumenical mandate for the return of non-Catholics. In
Wie hätten Wir, a radio address to the Mainz Catholic Congress on 5
September 1948, for example, the Pope stated that "If the Church is
inflexible before all that could have even the appearance of compromise or an adjustment of the Catholic faith with other confessions, or
its mixture or confusion with them, it is because she knows that there
has always been and always will be one sole and infallible sure rock of
truth and of the fullness of grace come to her from Christ, and that this
rock, according to the explicit will of the Divine Founder, is herself
and simply herself" (Pius XII 1948, 1). *Humani generis* of 12 August
1950 placed a gloss on his teaching regarding the mystical body of
Christ and the Roman Catholic church by asserting that the two
entities were synonymous if not coterminous (Pius XII 1981a, 4:
179). Strict ecclesiastical supervision of Catholic participation in
ecumenical meetings remained the norm. This latter emphasis was
especially clear in *Humani generis* that warned of a false irenicism
based on the diminution of basic Catholic doctrines "with the tenets
of dissidents" (Ibid., 4:177).[14] The pope had earlier included among
these Luther's teachings on the priesthood of believers and the
eucharist (Pius XII 1981b, 4:133–138). Pius XII's contribution to the
Catholic embrace of Christian ecumenism and the dawn of new
relations to Protestants is symbolized in his remark to Cardinal
Francis Spellman of New York on the fiftieth anniversary of the Unity

Octave: "Especially by His divine light can the minds of men be illumined—minds to whom it often happens that they are drawn from the bosom of the Church, not through perversity; it also happens that through this heart-softening grace even perverse and stubborn wills may be changed and moved to embrace the full Christian truth" (1957, 260).

In summary, the Catholic magisterium on the eve of the Second Vatican Council reiterated the clarion sounded since Trent: heretics had torn the seamless robe of faith but their successors were capable of a greater realization of Christian belief by returning to the societal confines of the Catholic church. Luther remained a misguided scoundrel who was always associated with the darkest side of the Reformation and continued as the archetypal heretic reemerging in modern departures from the faith. Although careful admissions to magisterial culpability were slightly extended, the Roman Catholic church saw itself as the single authorized defender of the faith that could rally Christians in the modern world. Pius XII's brief letter commemorating the fourth centenary of the Council of Trent clearly articulates this scarcely relaxed and confident posture:

> If they [non-Catholic Christians] consider what supernatural truths have flowed from it [Trent] to the Church and civil society, and finally note how all the truths held in common by the reformers and the Church in the sixteenth century have been preserved by her alone in their integrity, despite the chilling religious doubt which has settled on so many so many souls . . . let those separated from the Church form, as it is hoped they will, a sound judgment, in accordance with history, on the event the commemoration recalls, and they will surely feel a desire of that necessary union with Peter and his successors so unhappily broken by the circumstances of four centuries ago. (Pius XII 1945, 297)

CATHOLIC MAGISTERIUM AND PROTESTANTISM AT VATICAN II

Remarkably, the Second Vatican Council (1962–65) developed Pius XII's concession of nascent, authentic, non-Catholic Christianity into a fundamental assertion of Protestant holiness. The council probed Pius XII's notion of the mystical body of Christ to teach that the church "is joined to those who, though baptized and so honored with the Christian name, do not profess the faith in its entirety or do not preserve the unity of communion under the successor of Peter" (*Lumen gentium* § 15). Through an ecclesiology of communion the council radically widened Catholicism's embrace of Christianity and thereby paved the way for magisterial appreciation and relocation of

Luther that would come in the immediate postconciliar decades. The considered and extensive revaluation of Protestantism at Vatican II dissipated Catholic resentment of the "separated brethren" by means of both historical and theological reconsiderations that were evident in the gestures of the popes as well as the documents of the council.[15]

While quite different in temperament and style, Popes John XXIII (1881–1963; pope from 28 October 1959) and Paul VI (1897–1978, pope from 21 June 1963) displayed significant solidarity in conducting Vatican II, a fact that Pope Paul VI established in his opening speech for the second conciliar session which began three months after John XXIII's death in June 1963:

> Dear revered Pope John! What gratitude, what recognition is not due you for having been inspired to call this Council, implementing your resolve to open out new pathways for the Church, and to water the earth with the teaching and grace of Jesus Christ in new, fair-flowing, still uncharted streams! . . . May this coming second session of the ecumenical council, which you organized and inaugurated, faithfully follow the direction you have given it, and be enabled, with God's help, to achieve those aims which you most ardently desired and prayed for. . . . We will summarize these aims under four headings: (1) The notion, or, if you prefer it, the awareness of the Church; (2) Her renewal; (3) The restoration of unity among all Christians; (4) The Church's dialogue with the men of our own day. (Paul VI 1963b, 127–130)[16]

Pope John XXIII's inspiration for the council was sudden, by his own admission, and resulted in his announcement of the council on 25 January 1959, the first of a series of gestures that sparked considerable ecumenical interest in both Catholic and Protestants.[17] The pope anticipated that internal Catholic renewal would provide a significant testimony to the wonder of Catholic unity for non-Catholic Christians and during his initial announcement prayed for "a friendly and renewed invitation to our brothers of the separated Christian Churches to share with us in this banquet of grace and brotherhood." Reminiscent of the traditional Catholic ecumenism-of-return, these words were later officially transcribed as "the inducement of the faithful of the separated communities to follow us amicably in this quest for unity and for grace."[18] While John XXIII clearly operated under the paradigm of Protestant return to the Catholic church like his predecessors, the novel linkage of Catholic renewal to Christian unity was to be followed by other gestures that alerted onlookers to the ecumenical leap that the Catholic church was taking.[19] Thus, *Ad Petri Cathedram* (29 June 1959), Pope John XXIII's first encyclical, stated:

> May this wonderful spectacle of unity, by which the Catholic Church is set apart and distinguished, as well as the prayers and entreaties with which she begs God for unity, stir your [non-Catholic Christian] hearts and awaken you to what is really in your best interest. May we, in fond anticipation, address you as sons and brethren? May we hope with a father's love for your return? (1981, 5:12)[20]

Significantly, the pope's address to the conciliar preparatory commissions on 14 November 1960 anticipated vaguely the ecclesiology of the subsequent conciliar documents by referring to an incomplete ecclesial faith of non-Catholic Christians rather than a defective faith characterized by his predecessors. Concerning "those who do not share Our full profession of faith," he stated: "This is the important point that every baptized person must bear in mind: belonging to the Church of Christ is not just something of an individual nature for each person but it is an eminently social nature for everybody. . . . Hence each of the faithful belongs to the whole entire catholicity" (John XXIII 1960, 379). Minimally, Christian unity for Pope John XXIII did not involve a mere return *from* Christian alienation but a return *to* Catholicism, the Christian homeland (1981, 5:13).

Pope John XXIII's council was to promote Christian unity insofar as the entire body of bishops in union with the pope would dedicate the church to a more profound awareness of herself for the age. Two of the pope's gestures toward the ecumenical movement itself were particularly encouraging to Protestants. The appointment of non-Catholic observers to the council and the creation of the Secretariat for Promoting Christian Unity showed that attitudes of the Counter-Reformation were evaporating quickly.

In the summer of 1962 twelve non-Catholic churches were invited to send observers to witness the deliberations of the bishops at Saint Peter's Basilica where they would have access to all documents that circulated. In October 1962 the pope stated to observers that "Without wishing to encroach on the future, let us content ourselves today with stating the fact: *Benedictus Deus per singulos dies!* [Bless the Lord day after day.] Yet, if you would read my heart, you would perhaps understand much more than words can say" (John XXIII 1962–63, 226). For the conciliar Fathers, the presence of observers sustained a keen ecumenical awareness throughout the council (Bea 1969, 34).

Dr. Heiko Oberman of Harvard Divinity School, a representative of the International Congregational Council, said: "All this respect that has been shown to us is a symbol, but a symbol that goes well beyond a mere gesture" (1963, 101).

Creating the Secretariat for Promoting Christian Unity under the presidency of Cardinal Agostino Bea, SJ, (1881–1968) during the establishment of the council's preparatory commissions signaled the pope's fundamental commitment toward non-Catholic Christians in another dramatic way. Bea, who had termed the pope's speech to the observers "a miracle," and his secretariat were to provide a direct link between non-Catholics and the Holy See for the first time since the Council of Trent (Bea 1969, 49). While the secretariat was to have significant influence on the conciliar documents concerning the church, ecumenism, and revelation, its constant meetings with non-Catholic Christians, officially and through the first instances of magisterial interviews in popular media, helped convince Protestants by the opening of the council that Rome was no longer unchangeable (Marty 1968, 205–215). Cardinal Bea wrote during the council what he reiterated on his speaking tours:

> All these things [faith, prayer, charity], and most especially the precious gift of baptism, which joins the baptized to Christ in his mystical body, unite Christians. It is true—and must be admitted with deep grief—that there have been periods when these principles and facts of unity seemed to be forgotten amid the bitterness and resentments which followed breaches among Christians. But in these last decades, Christians seem almost to be awakening, as if from a long and heavy sleep, and to be realizing how much there is that unites them in spite of their divisions. (Bea 1964, 142)

When Pope John XXIII convoked the council on 25 December 1961 he envisioned humanity to be engaged by a renewed Catholic church that would display how it is suited to solve the problems of the age. Essential to that renewal was the healing of Christian divisions by the reintegration of those separated from the Catholic church (John XXIII 1961, 353–361). Consistent with the teachings of Pius XII, Pope John XXIII had nevertheless introduced possibilities for Christian unity that startled all participants and effected a new posture in Catholic doctrine that would materialize distinctive ecclesiological teachings with profound ecumenical implications. Notably, John XXIII's dying prayer was "That all may be one!" (Hebblethwaite 1985, 501–502).

Pope Paul VI's reaffirmation of his predecessor's goals at the opening of the second session of Vatican II was also matched by a series of outstanding ecumenical gestures. Earlier, in his coronation homily in June 1963, Paul had stated that "In this regard [Christian unity] we embrace the heritage of our unforgettable predecessor. . . . Moved by the Holy Spirit, he brought into being in this domain great hopes which We consider it a duty and an honor not to disappoint" (Paul VI 1963a, 9). The pope would meet Patriarch Athenagoras I of Constantinople in a trip to the Holy Land in January 1964 and together in December 1965 they would "erase from memory" the excommunications of 1054 that had separated the churches.

Paul VI's most significant gesture to Protestants during the council is found in the opening speech of the second session. The pope indicated that the recomposition of Christian unity in faith, sacraments, and hierarchical discipline did not mean that particular "traditional rites and customs, local prerogatives, different schools of spirituality, legitimate institutions" of non-Catholic communities would be necessarily preempted (Paul VI 1963b, 135). This theme of diversity within unity would occupy a considerable place in Paul VI's encouragement of ecumenical dialogues, a hallmark of the ecumenical movement in his pontificate. More significant for the council and the evaporation of Protestant mistrust of Catholics was the pope's remarkably affectionate recognition of Catholic responsibility for Christian divisions, the first confession since Pope Adrian VI to Chieregati in 1522. Paul VI stated:

> If we are in any way to blame for this separation, we humbly beg God's forgiveness, and ask our brothers' pardon for any injuries they feel they have sustained from us. For our part, we willingly forgive whatever injuries the Catholic Church has suffered, and forget the grief she has long endured, as a result of the long years of dissension and separation. (Ibid., 134)

On 13 October 1963, in an address to non-Catholic observers at the council, the pope reiterated these remarks, adding that this attitude contained no hidden trap and no minimalization of differences but that "It seems wiser not to look to the past, but to the present and to the future" (Paul VI 1964a, 231).[21] On 8 March 1964 he repeated this expectant orientation to pilgrims celebrating the fourth centenary of the Council of Trent (Paul VI 1964b, 493–494).

Lumen gentium and *Unitatis redintegratio* were approved by the council and Pope Paul VI on 21 November 1964. Their teachings on the church and ecumenism fulfilled the anticipatory gestures of the council's popes who preferred to teach with constant commitment to Pius XII's conceptualization of the church but, as Pope Paul VI stated in his first encyclical *Ecclesiam Suam* (6 August 1964), "with a view to infusing fresh spiritual vigor into Christ's Mystical Body considered as a visible society, and to purifying it from the defects of many of its members and urging it on to the attainment of new virtue" (Paul VI 1981, 5: 144). Regarding Protestants, and with considerable importance for the Roman view of Martin Luther, it was clear that their relegation to the extremities of that mystical body was now surpassed, a fact of preconciliar Catholicism.

The Dogmatic Constitution on the Church (*Lumen gentium*) neither conceived the corporate church simply as the Roman Catholic church nor did it understand membership in the Catholic church to be the sole determinant of individual Christian authenticity. The remarkable paragraph eight asserted that

> This church, set up and organized in this world as a society, subsists in the catholic church [*subsistet in ecclesia catholica*], governed by the successor of Peter and the bishops in communion with him, although outside its structure many elements of sanctification and of truth are to be found which, as proper gifts to the church of Christ, impel towards catholic unity. (*Lumen gentium* § 8.2)

This extraordinary enhancement of Pope Pius XII's *Mystici corporis* recognized various communities in the body of Christ that together and apart participate legitimately in the outpouring of the Holy Spirit while it maintained the preeminence of Rome in that communion. Thus all Christians are linked by "elements of sanctification" and not merely by the desire for the Catholic membership (*votum Ecclesiae*) as Pius XII had proposed.

This extension of the teaching on the mystical body should be seen as a fundamental development in Catholic ecclesiology and also as a critical moment in the evolution of the council itself. The council broadened the juridical and societal model of Catholicism cemented after the Council of Trent, particularly in the work of Cardinal Robert Bellarmine, SJ, whose *Controversies*, a multi-volume apologetic, had defined the church as those united under the bond of the same profession of faith and participation in sacraments as well as the authority of their pastor, especially the pope (Brodrick 1961, 51–90). Thus the council recovered an emphasis of Thomas Aquinas who taught that one is a member of the church through the grace of Christ (*Summa theologiae* I–II.89.6). *Lumen gentium* § 14 consequently recast Pius XII's concern for "real" membership by speaking of Roman Catholics as "fully incorporated" members who acknowledge faith and sacraments in communion with the hierarchy. The next paragraph stated that "for several reasons the church recognizes that it is joined to those who, though baptised and so honoured with the Christian name, do not profess the faith in its entirety or do not preserve the unity of communion under the successor of Peter." In this view, an incomplete but real communion exists on the basis of baptism, love of scripture, prayer, and some variously shared elements of faith.

The shift in conceptualizing an ecclesiology of communion rather than one of society, along with the use of the verb "subsists" rather than "is" to link the mystical body of the baptised to the Roman Catholic church, is a meaningful illustration of how the entire council itself evolved, if you will, the spirit of Vatican II. The initial draft *On the Church* presented by the Theological Commission had entitled the opening chapter "Nature of the church militant" and was officially presented by Bishop Franic of Split (Croatia) with the sentiment that "The purpose of chapter 1 is to show clearly . . . that there is no real distinction between the Mystical Body of Christ and the visible Church, but that the two names only point to different aspects of one and the same reality" (Kloppenburg 1974, 63–64). In prompting the conciliar modification of the notion of the mystical body in the Theological Commission's text in 1962 and 1963, Cardinals Giovanni Battista Montini of Milan (later, Pope Paul VI) and Giacomo Lercaro of Bologna would express views similar to Cardinal Achille Liénart of Lille, France: "I grieve that those outside the Roman Church do not share with us all the supernatural gifts which she dispenses; but I would not dare to say that they in no way belong to the Mystical Body of Christ, despite their not being incorporated into the Catholic Church" (Ibid., 64–65).[22]

Vatican II's ecclesiology of communion had evolved from Pius XII's teaching on the mystical body of Christ because the bishops and Paul VI could reconcile the institutional integrity of the Catholic church with the holiness of other churches and ecclesial communities according to a profound appreciation of the work of the Holy Spirit. The council saw the origins, perseverance, and the future of the faith according to the providential grace that baptizes, renews, and concludes all activities of all individual believers whose communities are necessarily defined in some way by the Holy Spirit. With multiple references to both Pius XII and to the New Testament, *Lumen gentium* stated that "In order that we may be continually renewed in him (see Eph 4,23), he gave us a share in his Spirit, who is one and the same in head and members. This Spirit gives life, unity and movement to the body, so that the fathers of the church could compare his task to that which is exercised by the life-principle, the soul, in the human body" (§ 7.7). This pneumatological emphasis reduced the institutional preoccupation of Catholic ecclesiology significantly while providing the hierarchical nature of Catholicism with a more charismatic foundation. Thus, the search for Christian unity was conceived as a properly magisterial enterprise according to Catholicism's own definition of faithful Christianity. Catholicism now recognized the authentic holiness in non-Catholic churches and ecclesial communities that, while not in communion with Rome, are nevertheless animated by the single Holy Spirit who wills Christian unity. For the first time since the Reformation, the Catholic church officially recognized holiness in Protestant communities as well as that of individual non-Catholics. While *Unitatis redintegratio* would provide the ecumenical charter for this ecclesiology, *Lumen gentium* presented a most remarkably succinct and zealous ecumenical principle when it stated:

> Until, therefore, the Lord comes in his majesty and all his angels with him (see Mt 25,31) and, when death has been destroyed, all things will have been made subject to him (see 1 Cor 15, 26–27), some of his disciples are pilgrims on earth, others who have departed this life are being purified, while others are in glory gazing "clearsighted on God himself as he is, three in one"; all of us, however, though in a different degree and manner, communicate in the same love of God and our neighbor and sing the same hymn of glory to our God. For all who are in Christ, possessing his Spirit, are joined together into one church and united with each other in him (see Eph 4,16). (§ 49)

In assessing the Second Vatican Council's Decree on Ecumenism, *Unitatis redintegratio*, Professor Edmund Schlink of the University of Heidelberg, a designated observer for the Evangelical church in Germany, stated that "in this decree the Roman Church with whom we have tried for a long time to enter into dialogue has finally decided to reach out to us and to give us her hand" (1965, 229). Similarly, Cardinal Bea of the Secretariat for Christian Unity summed up the events of the decree's advance by stating that the first sessions were most notable for the bishops' deep impressions of the divisions of Christianity and the legitimacy of the ecumenical impulse for all Christians. Further, Bea stated that he had never dreamed that the bishops would become so enthusiastic about the decree in the second session (1969, 165). Accordingly, the promulgated decree stated that "[Christian division] is a scandal to the world and damages the sacred cause of preaching the gospel to every creature" (*Unitatis redintegratio* § 1.1).

A significant demonstration of the inclusive ecclesiology of *Lumen gentium* is found in the fact that the decree's first chapter is entitled "Catholic Principles of Ecumenism" rather than the earlier drafts' "Principles of Catholic Ecumenism" (Feiner 1968, 2: 63). Thus the authentic movement of the Holy Spirit in the ecumenical movement before the council was recognized no less so than in paragraph four that stated "Today, in many parts of the world under the inspiring grace of the holy Spirit, many efforts are being made in prayer, word and action to attain that fullness of unity which Jesus Christ desires" (*Unitatis redintegratio* § 1.1). Reminiscent of the Dogmatic Constitution on the Church, the decree stated that while Christian unity "subsists" in the Catholic church, the church lacks catholicity due to Christian divisions (*Unitatis redintegratio* § 4.3).

An essential link to *Lumen gentium* is found in paragraph three that reaffirmed the baptismal communion of all Christians and the saving effects of non-Catholic Christian communities with their various customs. Scripture, the life of grace, and other interior gifts of the Holy Spirit give life to the church outside the visible confines of the Catholic church and "coming from Christ and leading back to Christ, properly belong to the one church of Christ," not to say the Roman Catholic church (*Unitatis redintegratio* § 3.2). Vatican II did not specify the submissive return of non-Catholics to Roman Catholicism as the fundamental prescription for Christian unity but foresaw that the restoration of full ecclesiastical communion is sought by which Christians find a unity within "various forms of spiritual life and discipline, in their different liturgical rites, and even in their theological elaborations of revealed truth" (*Unitatis redintegratio* § 4.5). As a model of such *communio* the trinity itself is invoked (*Unitatis redintegratio* § 2.6).

Consistent with the remarks of Pope Paul VI, the decree acknowledged the mutual complicity of Catholics in the sins of the sixteenth-century schism (*Unitatis redintegratio* §§ 3.1, 7.2). It accepted a history where "large communities came to be separated from the full communion of the Catholic Church" rather than an earlier draft's customary reference to a "separation from the communion of the Catholic Church" (Feiner 1968, 69–70). Moreover, the council's linkage of penitence for sins against Christian unity and recognition

of an imperfect Christian communion promoted the essential characteristics of magisterial ecumenical engagement for the postconciliar
decades: the Catholic church would pursue dialogues with non-
Catholic communities and would entrust Christian unity to the
impulses of the Holy Spirit. Committed in *Unitatis redintegratio* § 6
to "continual reformation" of the Church, the council encouraged
Catholic theologians to an ecumenical dialogue characterized by a
profound appreciation of Catholic doctrine *[doctrinae ecclesiae
inhaerentes]* as well as the awareness that these doctrines exist in a
hierarchy of truth relative to the foundations of Christian faith
(*Unitatis redintegratio* § 11.3). The decree's embrace of the Christian
unity yet-to-come elicited a positive Protestant commitment.[23] The
decree concluded with the admonition that

> It is the urgent wish of this holy synod that the measures under-
> taken by the sons and daughters of the catholic church should in
> practice develop in conjunction with those of our separated sisters
> and brothers, so as to place no obstacle to the ways of divine
> providence and to avoid prejudging the future inspirations of the
> holy Spirit. The synod moreover professes its awareness that
> human powers and capacities cannot achieve this holy objective—
> the reconciling of all Christians in the unity of the one and only
> Church of Christ. It is because of this that the synod grounds its
> hope deeply on Christ's prayer for the Church, on the Father's love
> for us, and on the power of the holy Spirit. (*Unitatis redintegratio*
> § 24.2)

Specific magisterial revaluation of Martin Luther would not substantially begin until six years after the promulgation of *Unitatis
redintegratio* in November 1964. However, conciliar repentance for
Catholic sins against Christian unity, affirmation of authentic Christian customs and theological perspectives outside Catholic purview,
and the reorientation of Catholic regard for non-Christians toward
future reconciliation rather than past divisions were decisively significant steps in permitting and promoting the revision of the magisterial
Luther-image. An ecclesiology of communion thus recognized Christian faith where Tridentine ecclesiology had not and was enacted to
build a greater community of faith in Christ than it had left behind.

Magisterial Revaluation of Luther after Vatican II

Outstanding magisterial statements regarding Martin Luther came
about during Cardinal Jan Willebrands's address to the fifth assembly

of the Lutheran World Federation at Évians-les-Bains, France, in 1970, the first global assembly after the Second Vatican Council, and in 1983 when Pope John Paul II contemplated Luther in a letter to Cardinal Willebrands on the quincentennial of the reformer's birth. Linked with other related gestures and statements, these fresh magisterial initiatives on the reformer present both symbolic and substantive revisions of the previous polemical and theological disregard of Luther. While preliminary and often ponderous, these statements also establish a footing for future considerations of Luther's Catholicity that the magisterium itself anticipates to occur in a consensual, if not canonical, fashion.

Pontificate of Pope Paul VI (1963–78)

Consistent with a manner established by the council's popes, innovative postconciliar statements on Luther honor Pope Paul's last will and testament, written in 1972 and released after his death in the summer of 1978: "Regarding ecumenism: May the work of bringing together separated brothers proceed with much understanding, patience and great love, but without defecting from true Catholic doctrine" (Paul VI 1978b, 176). Defined to a large degree by a constant and passionate yearning for the restoration of Christian unity, Paul VI's pontificate established an environment of reconciliation in which Cardinal Willebrands was to call Luther a "common teacher" of all Christians. Immediately after Vatican II the pope repeatedly affirmed that the Catholic commitment to Christian unity and ecumenical progress was unshakable, given the church's recognition of a divine imperative for unity. He stated that "the Council was imbued with this ecumenical spirit which tended to delate the heart of the Catholic Church beyond the limits of its actual hierarchical communion in order to give it the universal dimensions of the design of God and the character of Christ" (Paul VI 1966a, 42). In the same affective fashion he stated in April 1967 that "Various conciliar documents treat the question of Christian union explicitly or in passing. They are so clear-cut and authoritative, so explicit and binding, that they provide Catholic ecumenism with a doctrinal and pastoral foundation which it has never before enjoyed" (Paul VI 1967, 98).

The pope's frequent reiteration of the importance of individual and ecclesial conversion in accord with the movement of the Holy Spirit was especially meaningful for issues regarding the Reformation since the pope urged Catholics not to linger on the causes of Christian divisions but to understand them, insofar as they point the way to future healing.[24] In a general audience of 24 January 1968 he stated that "charity, which is necessary but not by itself sufficient to reestablish unity, often remains timid and uncertain in its ecumenical expression toward the brethren with whom we would want to restore sincere, integrated and complete relations" (Paul VI 1968, 59). Thus the pope encouraged formal theological dialogues, which began in a bilateral dialogue with the Lutheran World Federation in 1965 and continued to expand through the efforts of the Secretariat for Promoting Christian Unity. For his part, Paul VI continued the increasingly wide range of meetings with non-Catholic ecclesial leaders that had begun during the council.[25]

In the self-effacing manner that led the pope to assume Catholic coresponsibility for Christian divisions, Paul VI was especially moved by the impediments that the divisions had created for contemporary Christian evangelization. Thus, he stated at an ecumenical service in January 1973 that

> The historical mishaps which have split Christendom during the centuries reveal themselves today to reflection and experience as intolerable and as disproportionate, in the light of faith, to the causes that generated them; they are revealed as ruinous to the cause of religion in the modern world and as insupportable in view of the divine plan. (Paul VI 1973, 329)

Near the end of his pontificate he would say despondently, "The ruptures that have taken place have ossified, solidified, and organized themselves in such a way as to characterize as Utopian all attempts to reconstruct a dependency on the head, which is Christ" (Paul VI 1978a, 1).

Pope Paul VI's pontificate showed convincingly that the Second Vatican Council had turned Catholic polemics for non-Catholic Christians into dialogues with them. The pope's affirmation of Catholic commitment to Christian unity, promotion of ecumenical endeavors including dialogues and practical service to humanity, and an acute sense of the Christian vocation to promote a "civilization of love" cemented the ecumenical aspects of the Catholic ecclesiology of communion. The implantation of this ecclesiology's focus on Christian unity by Paul VI is remarkably demonstrated by Cardinal Jan Willebrands's statement on Martin Luther to the Lutheran World Federation on 15 July 1970.

Cardinal Willebrands (b.1909) began his ecumenical work while teaching philosophy at a seminary in Warmond, Holland in the 1940s. In 1951 he cofounded with Frans Thijssen the Catholic Conference on Ecumenical Questions that intended largely to follow the work of the World Council of Churches. This conference produced many original members of the Secretariat for Promoting Christian Unity, including Willebrands who was the first secretary at its founding in 1960 (Minus 1976, 179; Scrutator 1985, 976). A veritable Catholic ecumenical pioneer, Cardinal Willebrands served as president of the Secretariat after Cardinal Bea from 1969 to 1989 when he became president emeritus.

Willebrands introduced specific magisterial appreciation of Martin Luther when he spoke of the reformer before the Lutheran World Federation as a "deeply religious person" who "profoundly realized [faith's] value [whereby] many people in your churches, indeed far beyond your churches have since learned to live through it" (Willebrands 1970a, 208–209). Invoking the ecumenical prospectus mandated by Vatican II and reiterated by Paul VI, the cardinal cited Luther's *Freedom of a Christian* (1520) to speak of the complementarity of Christian religious traditions which are to evangelize the world.

Thus providing a specific recognition of a different "theological elaboration" which the council saw as a legitimate aspect of Christianity, Willebrands stated further that the new commitment to dialogue requires Catholics to understand Luther correctly (*Unitatis redintegratio* § 4.5). Noting that contemporary scholarship has provided a "scientifically more correct understanding of the Reformation . . . and of the figure of Martin Luther and his theology," he indicated that a "certain reserve" regarding Luther continues among Catholics due to the forceful personality of the reformer as well as his theological positions. Therefore, a correct Catholic appreciation of Luther is deemed essential to the restoration of Christian unity (Willebrands 1970a, 207–208).

Willebrands noted that many Lutherans join Catholics in lamenting the "particularly sharp attacks that Luther made against the Roman Pontiff," but that the reformer retained a considerable share of the "old Catholic faith." Willebrands also noted that the Second Vatican Council had implemented many of the reformers' requests of the sixteenth century, especially regarding the authority of the Bible. In a significant doctrinal assessment, the cardinal stated that "Luther's concept of faith, when taken in its full meaning, might not really mean anything other than what we designate by the word love in the Catholic church," thus not excluding good works (Ibid., 209).

While brief and tentative, Willebrands's remarks indicated a decisive shift in the magisterial view of Luther and a decided reversal of Catholic polemics regarding the reformer. Results of continued dialogue were clearly anticipated before further magisterial assessment could occur; nevertheless he stated remarkably that Luther serves as a "common teacher" for Christians insofar as the reformer asserted the absolute confidence and adoration of God required of all believers.[26]

The fact that remarks about Luther fall in the shortest and last section of Willebrands's speech that addressed the federation's theme of "Mission to the World" should not belie their outstanding importance. The Catholic church in the authority of the Roman curia reversed the direction of Catholic regard of Luther and established that the route of dialogue and collaborative theological investigation is reconfiguring the magisterial image of Luther. The ecclesiology of communion that had rooted the gestures of the council's popes and promoted the agenda of postconciliar conversations now projected an historically distinctive impulse for Christian unity. As Willebrands stated, "Who would not agree that a correct appreciation of the person and the work of Martin Luther forms part of this endeavor?" (Ibid., 207).

The fact that Pope Paul VI never repeated these positions personally does not undermine their magnitude. This is demonstrated by the pope's response to the "Memorandum of Worms" (18 April 1971) which was addressed to him by Rudolf Knecht, president of the Katholischer Dekanatsausschuss Worms, an organization of priests and laity at Worms that sought establishment of a commission to formally reexamine the Catholic position on Luther and to consider lifting Luther's excommunication. Written on the 450th anniversary of Luther's famous declaration of conscience before Emperor Charles V in 1521, the memorandum symbolized a general interest in lifting the excommunication by both Catholics and Lutherans. Rev. Bernard Häring, CSsR,(1912–98), had urged such reconsideration in Toronto in the fall of 1967 (1967, 10).[27] Wilhelm Michaelis, a Lutheran layperson and judge, had campaigned for the action since 1963 and had appealed to the bishops of United Evangelical Lutheran Church in Germany (VELKD) in January 1970 to urge Rome's lifting of Luther's excommunication.[28] In response to the Worms initiative, the pope stated through Cardinal Willebrands on 14 July 1971 that it did not seem desirable to go beyond the standard established by Willebrands himself at Évian. The results of further dialogues and historical research were anticipated (Willebrands 1972, 7). Earlier in Stockholm,

Willebrands had stated that "Excommunication considers a living person. After a person's death nothing can be done. We believe that Luther is now in the community of saints. Thus a revocation would be a meaningless act" (No Canonization 1968, 11).

When Pope Paul VI died on 6 August 1978 at Castel Gandolfo, the papal summer residence, the magisterial commitment to the restoration of Christian unity was already questioned by many who felt that the magisterium was betraying the inheritance of the council through tardiness (Hebblethwaite 1993, 96). When reviewing 450 years of Catholic invective against Luther from the perspective of Évian, one may not deny that Paul VI's pontificate had taken radical steps. After all, it had been Don Battista-Montini, the future Paul VI, who had translated and written an approving foreward in the late 1920s to Jacques Maritain's *Three Reformers* that castigated Luther for initiating modern individualism, the apotheosis of affectivity at the expense of reason, and the rejection in principle of church authority.

Pontificate of Pope John Paul II (1978–)

One criterion for determining the actual authority of a magisterial statement is the frequency of its repetition. Thus, the fact that Luther is not spoken of as a heretic but as a theologian by Cardinal Willebrands both at Évian in 1970 and at the quincentennial celebration of Luther's birth at Leipzig, Germany on 11 November 1983 is noteworthy. Speaking on the reputed date of Luther's baptism, the cardinal asserted that by baptism Luther was added to the body of Christ, a fact not erased by his excommunication from the terrestrial church (Willebrands 1983, 92). Stating that Luther was excommunicated for errors and mistakes in his teaching and personal attitudes, Willebrands asserted as he did at Évian that the consensus of historical scholarship adds "a more comprehensive appreciation" of the events surrounding the excommunication and that continued efforts at rereading Luther's theological legacy must continue. Echoing Évian, Willebrands adverts to Luther as a religious genius, "the standard bearer of the majesty, the honour and the judgeship of God and, at the same time, as the spokesman of man, who—mortal and turned inwards on himself—can rely on nothing other than God's mercy." Additionally, the president of the Secretariat for Promoting Christian Unity outlined a connection between Luther's theology of the cross and Vatican II's conception of an eschatological pilgrim church whose repentance and conversion in weakness are its ultimate source of strength (Ibid., 93–94).

Beyond frequency of repetition, a magisterial position is authoritative relative to the ecclesiastical status of its various spokesmen. The magisterial appreciation of Luther as theologian and reformer thus is most determined by the assessments of Pope John Paul II (b.1920; pope from 16 October 1978).[29] As with Willebrands, Pope John Paul II's statements on Luther have occurred on occasions of great mutual interest for Lutherans and Catholics. On 31 October 1983, the pope issued a statement to Cardinal Willebrands commemorating the quincentennial of the reformer's birth. Therein the pope characterized Luther as a reformer by appealing to a convergence of scholarship where "there is clearly outlined the deep religious feeling of Luther, who was driven with burning passion by the question of eternal salvation." He located Luther into an era where "the breach of Church unity cannot be traced back either to a lack of understanding on the part of the authorities of the Catholic church, or solely to Luther's lack of understanding of true Catholicism, even if both factors played their role." Additionally, the pope regarded Luther as a theologian whose work is to be considered in ongoing historical research that must be applied to the contemporary quest for ecclesial unity. The honest assigning of fault and greater attention to the common faith from scripture, the creeds, and the ancient councils are advised (John Paul II 1983b, 83).

On 11 December 1983 the pope addressed the Lutheran church in Rome, displaying the increasingly less-exceptional magisterial relocation of Luther into the body of Christ. With the eschatological expectancy normally associated with Advent, the pope emphasized further that "from afar there seems to arise like a dawn, on this 500th anniversary of the birth of Martin Luther, the Advent of a restoration of our unity and community" (1983a, 95). This grand expectation of Christian reconciliation is deeply rooted in an eschatological awareness that pervades the pope's full ecumenical aspiration (Williams 1982, 144–152). Roman preparations for the Jubilee year of 2000, a self-described hermeneutical key of John Paul II's pontificate, prompted the pope to reiterate and strengthen Pope Paul VI's confessions of Catholic complicity in breaking Christian unity (Accattoli 1998, 21–28). In *Tertio Millennio Advenienete,* the pope's millennial agenda, he states that "the approaching end of the second millennium demands of everyone an examination of conscience and the promotion of fitting ecumenical initiatives so that we can celebrate the Great Jubilee, if not completely united, at least much closer to overcoming the divisions of the second millennium (John Paul II 1994, 403, 410–411).

The pope's exhortation for healing based on sound historical research and steadfast dialogue between Lutherans and Catholics is an essential aspect of this ecumenical program. Canon 755, issued by Pope John Paul II in 1983, suppressed Canon 1325, § 3 of the 1917 code which forbade discussions about Christianity with non-Catholics. The new canon states, in part, that "It is within the special competence of the entire college of bishops and of the Apostolic See to promote and direct the participation of Catholics in the ecumenical movement, whose purpose is the restoration of Christian unity among all Christians, which the Church is bound by the will of Christ to promote" (Coriden 1985, 549). John Paul II's prepapal commentary on the Second Vatican Council, *Sources of Renewal*, stated that the ecumenical attitude is comprised of (1) full respect for human beings, (2) readiness to cooperate, and (3) dialogue with basic exposition of respective doctrines (Wojtyla 1980, 318). Throughout his pontificate, the pope has linked contemporary Christian ecumenism to healing of past conflicts, whether the fracturing events themselves or the subsequent polemics. In *Ut Unum Sint,* his hallmark encyclical on ecumenism, John Paul II succinctly expressed Vatican II's ecclesiology of communion that undergirds this dialogue, stating that "elements of this already-given church exist, found in their fullness in the Catholic Church and, without this fullness, in other communities, where certain features of the Christian mystery have at times been more effectively emphasized" (John Paul II 1995, 53).

Outstanding among various reiterations of dialogue in relationship to Luther are the pope's remarks to members of the Evangelical Church of Germany during a trip there in November 1980, to Lutherans of Scandinavia during his visit in June 1989, and to an ecumenical service in Paderborn during his third pastoral trip to Germany in June 1996.[30]

The pope's visit to Germany in the 450th anniversary-year of the Augsburg Confession provided no specific delineations of a new papal position on Luther as occurred later on Luther's birthday in 1983 but it did demonstrate the vital necessity of interconfessional historical research for the church's unity. Regarding the Augsburg Confession, the pope stated that "through numerous exchanges, we have realized anew that we believe and profess together all this." Further, he quoted approvingly the pastoral letter on the confession by the German bishops, "Thy Kingdom Come" (20 January 1980): "We are happy to discover not simply a partial consensus on some truths but rather a full accord on fundamental and partial truths" (John Paul II 1980a, 27).[31]

While papal approval of consensus on the Augsburg Confession does not imply any judgment about Luther explicitly, it does signify that Catholic evaluation of Luther's work has moved beyond the focus on the early Luther and his conflict with Rome that dominated so much of the prior Catholic conception. In contrast to simply derogatory polemics, Catholics now consider Luther as a theologian of considerable merit who had significant responsibility for the confession of 1530. Interestingly, the pope's speech referred explicitly to Luther's lectures on Romans twice, first to highlight the Gospel's demand for conversion to the ways of the Kingdom of God and, second, to accentuate a basic problem to be broached by Catholics and Lutherans in continued dialogue, "in believing that which is of Christ," that is, the church.

This ecclesiological focus is a central theme in current magisterial reflections on Luther. The reformer is spoken of as a theologian and a reformer but the issues of his theological compatibility with Catholic tradition, allowing for diverse expressions of piety and spirituality, and the constructive nature of his reforms are two key aspects of continuing magisterial concern. This ecclesiological concern about Luther is most evident in the pope's visit to predominantly Lutheran Scandinavia in June 1989.

The pope's speeches from June 1 to June 9 are replete with references to the "real but imperfect" communion that exists currently between Catholics and Lutherans. Echoes of the pope's eschatological reading of the ecumenical imperative are evident when he said that "before us lies the duty of opening a new Christian chapter in history in response to the many challenges of a changing world" (John Paul II 1989, 89). The pope's reiteration that "deep wounds were inflicted on the western Christian world, wounds which are still in need of healing" was complemented by the recognition of profound divisions between Catholicism and Lutheranism posed by unusually frank Scandinavian Lutheran bishops. Bishop Aarflot of Oslo stated in an ecumenical prayer service, for example, that "Today it is proper to say about the church that once brought about the condemnation of men like Galileo: The church itself is moving. . . . But we look forward to the day when your Holiness clearly and unequivocally expresses the ecclesial character of the Lutheran and other Protestant churches" (Ibid., 84).

Lutheran Bishop Ole Bertelsen reinforced Bishop Aarflot's comments more directly during a meeting with Danish Lutheran bishops at the Lutheran Cathedral of Roskilde on June 6:

> The condemnation of evangelical doctrine has not been annulled, which shows clearly and precisely that differences in doctrine are being taken seriously, and that they are decisive; and this they really are. Even from the Catholic side it has been said that the churches of the Reformation have moved the centre of gravity from the church's faith in Christ to God's faithfulness to his covenant of grace with us. Yes, exactly. Thus the church can become a counterpart in relation to the gospel. Visibility is not the truth. The institution does not guarantee anything. (Ibid., 99–100)

The pope's preprepared response contained a significant statement of the Catholic position on Luther. First, the pope affirmed the theological importance of Luther by repeating the sentiments of 1983 that highlighted Luther's passion for the question of Christian salvation but also by saying that "what we need today most of all is a joint new evaluation of many questions which were raised by Luther and his preaching." As he had in many speeches of the trip, the pope praised the work of the Roman Catholic–Lutheran Joint Commission that inaugurated Catholic bilateral dialogues with the Lutheran World Federation in 1965. Second, the pope considered that "certain concerns of Luther in regard to reform and renewal have found echo with Catholics in various ways, as, for example, when the Second Vatican Council speaks of the necessity for continuous renewal and reform" (Ibid., 101).

Finally, the pope stated, as anticipated by Willebrands in 1968, that "the events surrounding his excommunication left wounds which even today cannot be healed through juridical action. According to the Roman Catholic Church, every excommunication ceases with the death of an individual, since the action itself is to be viewed as a measure taken with respect to an individual during his or her lifetime" (Ibid., 101).[32]

Pope John Paul II's ponderous appreciation of Luther as theologian and reformer leaves more to the future that it takes from the past. Consistent with the directives of the Second Vatican Council and the gestures of Pope Paul VI and his delegate, Cardinal Willebrands, John Paul II has committed the church to a fundamental process of ecumenical consensus-building that of necessity incorporates Lutheran appreciation of the reformer into Catholic theological, magisterial, and pastoral domains. The pope's constant appreciation for the Roman Catholic–Lutheran Joint Commission is significant in this regard. In remarks to that commission in March 1984, he stated that the collaborative research on Luther and his times "are important elements in the reconciliation and growing together of Catholics and Lutherans. They are landmarks on the long and arduous journey that leads us forward" (John Paul II 1984, 12).

John Paul II's third trip to Germany as pope occured from 21 to 23 June 1996 and presented Roman regard for Luther succinctly on the 450th anniversary of his death. Deeply appreciative of broader scholarly and ecclesial discussions on doctrinal condemnations of the sixteenth century and the doctrine of justification, to be discussed in the final section of this chapter, the pope prized highly Luther's attention to scripture and spiritual renewal of the church. Mirroring a central theme in the *Ut Unum Sint*, he noted that "Luther's call for Church reform in its original meaning was an appeal for repentance and renewal, which must begin in the life of every individual." Recognizing political and economic interference in the Catholic activity of the Reformation, the pope claimed that Luther's passion interfered in his work, accelerating a radical criticism of the church. The pope sustained Catholic magisterial interest in greater clarity about the correlation of personal faith, biblical truth, and ecclesial tradition in Luther, stating that "Luther's thought was characterized by a strong emphasis on the individual, which weakened the awareness of the community's requirements" (John Paul II 1996, 157).

The actual state of the current Catholic magisterial image of Luther is incomplete without greater specification of the abiding concerns about Luther's theology. The clear assumption of Catholic coresponsibility for the Reformation and the presupposition of a largely religiously motivation in Luther do not displace the fact that much of the magisterial reserve regarding the reformer results from sharp theological differences that continue to have a significant and direct impact on Catholic ecclesiological doctrine. These concerns are articulated most completely by Cardinal Joseph Ratzinger (b.1927), appointed by Pope John Paul II as prefect of the Congregation for the Doctrine of the Faith in November 1981. Cardinal Ratzinger's overall opinion of Luther is reflected in a comprehensive interview in August 1984 that produced an assessment of Luther's work in terms of the cardinal's official duties: "Yes, I do think that even today we would have to speak to him [Luther] very seriously, and that today too his teaching could not be regarded as 'Catholic theology'" (Ratzinger 1985, 157).

Ratzinger's assessments emerged from a correlation of historical, doctrinal, and ecumenical concerns that coincide with, yet do not undermine, the opinions of Pope John Paul II. The cardinal echoes the postconciliar axiom that Catholics bear some responsibility for the

Reformation and that, in part, Luther's reformational impulse and ideas were spiritually correct.

> While it unmasked the domination of money and power that stood behind the practice of stipends and prebends and the theology oriented toward this, [it] could not encompass the legacy of the early Church. . . . It should be noted that what we encounter in this early work of Luther, the reformer, is an extreme example of an impassioned protest seeking a suitable outlet; much of what he said here was expressed more calmly and brought into harmony with the legacy of the primitive Church. (Ratzinger 1987, 259–260)

Thus Ratzinger isolates the fundamental magisterial concern about Martin Luther today: Luther's theology seems to exclude more of fundamental Catholic tradition than it includes. Ratzinger specifies doctrinal questions regarding ecclesiology, the structure of faith, and Christology to show a side of Luther that overshadows his great strides in liturgical, catechetical, and devotional venues.

Ecclesiological incompatibility is clearly the dominant concern. In studying Luther's "polemical opus of revolutionary radicality" Cardinal Ratzinger first emphasized that Luther's attention on the local community shrank from the full Catholic tradition of *communio* evident in hierarchical and sacramental traditions that are the taproot of Catholicism (Ratzinger 1984, 212). Severing affiliation with the universal church that is joined interiorly by the eucharist and externally in a hierarchical communion, both Christ's gifts, Luther's theology is imperiled in the same way as the Donatists whom Augustine battled in the fourth century (Ratzinger 1986, 243). Thus, he asserted that the benefit of the reformer's emphasis on hearing the Word of God is mitigated by the isolation of the community in which it is audible (Ratzinger 1987, 291).

Likewise, Ratzinger argued that the ecclesiological restriction in Luther's theology is evident in his aberration from the received eucharistic tradition. In understanding the mass as a promise of salvation by God rather than a sacrifice of praise, he asserted that "we cannot fail to see that the Eucharist was reduced to the only aspect that was for Luther the core and content of the Christian faith: the reliable, incommunicable assurance to the individual's troubled conscience that his sins have been forgiven" (1987, 260). Again, Luther is seen to diminish the sacramental priesthood by eliminating its offering of the eucharistic sacrifice in preference of the duty to preach the Word of God. Ratzinger considers this merely functional ministry to be incompatible with the notion of sacramental character inherited from Augustine and refined in the Middle Ages (Ibid., 247–249).

Regarding the structure of faith, Ratzinger believes that the question of personal salvation is so prominent for Luther that the patristic tradition of the communal faith of Christians is radically undermined by Luther's assertion of justification by faith alone (1984, 217). This modification of tradition is seen in Luther's understanding of faith itself, which the cardinal asserts is a fundamental upsetting of the union of the theological virtues of faith, hope, and love. Ratzinger prefaces his assessment by stating that a mere shift in theological ideas did not provide enough momentum to bring about the changes that were begun by Luther's work; only a new religious experience can accomplish such change and Luther indeed provided it—he was more than an academician (1988, 111). Ratzinger states, however, that "I would say that the dialectic of Law and Gospel expresses most poignantly Luther's new experience and that it illustrates most concisely the contradiction with the Catholic concepts of salvation, Scripture and Church." Thus, he analyzes, faith becomes an individual's activity, shorn from the judgment of the Catholic church and dissociated from the demands of love; the certainties of faith and hope collapse into each other (Ratzinger 1984, 219–220).

Finally, Ratzinger detects an inadequate appreciation by Luther of Chalcedonian christology in the Catholic tradition

> which not only knew Christ as the God who descended to earth and in whom God empties himself even unto the abyss of death but also included God's acceptance of man, who, in the God-man, became capable of responding to God precisely as man and, in Christ, could again become sacrifice. For Jesus Christ, in whom are united the law and the gospel, is not just the promise of forgiveness; he is also the gathering together of the dispersed Adam into the *communio* of *agape*. (1987, 261)

While formally presented in a theological rather than magisterial forum, Cardinal Ratzinger's serious objections to Luther's theology show the principles of a real limitation in the official Catholic embrace of Luther as well as the complexities of postconciliar Catholicism. Ecumenical zeal is never to displace doctrinal clarity. Ecumenical initiatives are to transcend but not to ignore the past. This tension is illustrated clearly in Cardinal Ratzinger's own modified position regarding the Catholic recognition of the Augsburg Confession on its 450th anniversary. In 1976 Ratzinger, then professor of dogmatic theology at Regensburg and soon to become Archbishop of Munich, affirmed the opinion of his student, Vinzenz Pfnür, that Catholic recognition would presume that the Lutheran statement of faith can be seen as intending an evangelical Catholicism that could be appreciated as a particular form of Christianity with a legitimate independence of Catholicism. He clearly was leaning toward recognition (Ratzinger 1977, 204–205). In 1982 the new prefect of the Congregation for the Doctrine of the Faith perceived that a clearer Protestant recognition of the Augsburg Confession was prerequisite before the Catholic church could act. Especially significant for the cardinal was (1) a determination of how foundational Luther's writings are for the statement, and (2) to what degree the confession is a separate ecclesiological text apart from Luther's positions, especially as evident in the Smalcald articles (Ratzinger 1987, 220–223). Thus he concluded that

> Since the notion of "recognition" almost of necessity awakens false expectations, it should, in my opinion, be abandoned; since, in addition, the CA [*Confessio Augustana*, Augsburg Confession] cannot be considered in isolation, it would be better to speak of a dialogue about the theological and ecclesial structure of the Protestant-Lutheran confessional writings and their reconcilability with the doctrine of the Catholic Church. (Ibid., 228)

The integration of Christian diversity under Catholic unity is a constant feature of Ratzinger's ecumenical perspective. In an interview in 1983 regarding Luther and the unity of the churches, he stated that "The actual goal of all ecumenical endeavors must naturally be to convert the plurality of the separate denominational churches into the plurality of local churches which, in reality, form one church despite their many and varied characteristics" (Ratzinger 1984, 225). Accordingly, the general magisterial commitment to historical veracity and theological dialogue with Luther must be seen as a singularly fundamental step toward the reconciliation of churches. One cannot underestimate the importance of ecclesiological doctrines for the Roman Catholic magisterium. The mechanisms and intermediate actions of this reconciliation into the church of Christ that subsists in the Catholic church are unclear, but the ultimate status of the various churches is not. As has Pope John Paul II, Ratzinger has argued that the Second Vatican Council has already integrated many of Luther's concerns and other Protestant impulses into the Catholic church (1986, 242). For the Roman magisterium under Pope John Paul II,

Luther rightly taught and anticipated evangelical reform but miscal-
culated the doctrinal and ecclesial context to sustain it.

Trajectories in Magisterial Appreciation of Luther

Actual Roman magisterial statements about Luther reveal that he is
considered to be a reformer and theologian of significant Christian
authority. As clearly, it appears that an abandonment of theological
criticisms about Luther does not occur along with an increased
expectancy of convergence about him in Catholic-Lutheran dialogues. All spokesmen for the magisterium discussed herein have not
disguised the difficulties of ascertaining the theological compatibility
of Luther with Catholic doctrine nor have they underestimated the
fragile and tenuous nature of building Christian unity. Clearly,
additional developments of the magisterial opinion about Luther
depend heavily on the work of interconfessional scholarship with
special consideration for the work of the Roman Catholic–Lutheran
Joint Commission. While this commission works in its own right and
does not obligate the magisterium to specific positions, it exists under
Roman auspices.[33] While not defining magisterial prerogatives about
Luther, theological and historical consensus enunciated by the international joint commission on the Augsburg Confession, Luther, and
the doctrinal condemnations of the sixteenth century provide concrete possibilities for future magisterial statements about Luther.

Theological Consensus

The Roman Catholic–Lutheran Joint Commission produced an
evaluation of the Augsburg Confession, "All Under One Christ," on
23 February 1980. That document was the centerpiece of a flurry of
activity surrounding the 450th anniversary of the Lutheran statement
of faith which, along with Luther's *Small Catechism*, constitute the
grounds for membership in the Lutheran World Federation.[34] "All
Under One Christ" asserted that the *confessio* represented an ecumenical endeavor in 1530 and functions as a basic consensus of Christian
truths for Lutherans and Catholics today, although it leaves both
denominations with unsettled questions. The Joint Commission
stated that "Reflecting on the Augsburg Confession, therefore, Catholics and Lutherans have discovered that they have a common mind on
basic doctrinal truths which points to Jesus Christ, the living center
of our faith" (Roman Catholic–Lutheran Joint Commission 1982,
38–39). While the document does not mention Luther or his role in
the production of the confession, the enthusiastic comment on the

agreement by Pope John Paul II shows that the development of Catholic and Lutheran unity is linked to but not defined by the Catholic image of Luther. Although questions exist regarding the relationship of Luther's teachings with his successors' doctrines, it is clear that the magisterium finds the "evangelical catholicity" of the Augsburg Confession to be a readily acceptable place for development of unity.

"Martin Luther—Witness to Jesus Christ" was released on 6 May 1983 by the Joint Commission during the quincentennial of Luther's birth. Signed by cochairmen Bishop Hans L. Martensen of Denmark and Professor George A. Lindbeck of Yale University, the document reflected the broadest consensus of scholarship in an irenic and easy-to-read manner. The document opened with a statement on the lessening of Christian polemics both for and against Luther in the twentieth century and the development of an image of Luther as a teacher of faith and a reformer. It then stipulated his fundamental evangelical insights, noting a Christocentric focus derived from the Bible and the singularly important principle of justification by faith alone. It stated that "As witness to the gospel Luther proclaimed the biblical message of God's judgment and grace, of the scandal and the power of the cross, of the lostness of human beings and of God's act of salvation" (Roman Catholic–Lutheran Joint Commission 1983, 85).

The third section, entitled "Conflict and Schism in the Church," considered the Reformation to have begun amid Luther's novel interpretation of the gospel with "no understanding for his concerns among the ecclesiastical and theological authorities either in Germany or in Rome." Increased polemics from both sides are noted, a call for continuing study and repentance is issued, and an exhortation for common commitment to the positive aspects of the Reformation is deemed essential. Section four admitted Lutheran overemphasis of Luther's polemics over pastoral and theological insights, some misap-propriations of his theology (e.g., "isolation of the Bible from its churchly context") and posited a Lutheran recognition of Luther's limitations (e.g., overt anti-Semitism and harsh antipapalism). The document concluded with a recognition of the common features of Luther's reform and the modern Catholic renewal due to the Second Vatican Council, positing a common need to recognize God's sover-eignty, our sinfulness, and the need for forgiveness.

For this study, the fact that this statement was followed by the critical commentary of the Reverend Alois M. Kothgasser, SDB, in the Secretariat for Christian Unity's *Information Service*, its official publication, is notable. The calm rehearsal of scholarship on Luther and his modern Roman Catholic reception as well as the obvious lack of overstatement in the Joint Commission's statement was an attempt to reach the tamest consensus. While they are not formal magisterial statements, Kothgasser's critical remarks, solicited by the Secretariat and appended to the Vatican Secretariat's publication of the historic document, reinforce the difficult fact that profound theological differences between Luther and Catholic doctrine figure very prominently into Catholic and Lutheran reconciliation.

Rev. Kothgasser, professor of dogmatics at the Salesian College of Philosophy and Theology at Benediktbeuern, praised the statement as "on the whole [a] well balanced text" (1983, 88).[35] His criticism includes into two basic assertions: (1) that Luther's reduction of Christian tradition has been overlooked in the statement, and(2) that official reception of a theological consensus regarding Luther is quite minimal. Kothgasser asserted that the document's statement that Luther "was led by his intense study of Scriptures to a renewed discovery of God's mercy in the midst of the fears and uncertainties of his time" (§ 8) would read more accurately as "in the midst of his personal fears and the uncertainties of the time," thereby emphasizing the personal nature of Luther's discovery that then hardened into anti-ecclesiastical polemics (Ibid., 89). Likewise he criticized the assertion that Luther's witness always points beyond his own person (§ 12) as a failure to reckon with substantial arguments about the reformer's individual subjectivism (Ibid., 90). This concern about Luther's subjectivity is the fulcrum from which the reformer's weaknesses about objective Catholic doctrine are highlighted. Kothgasser argued that the pivotal discovery of justification by faith alone is a "happy and successful synthesis [of the Christian message of salvation], but at the same time also an abbreviating and narrowing reduction of the whole" (Ibid., 89). Echoing Cardinal Ratzinger's positions, he argues that emphasis on *sola Scriptura* diminishes ecclesial tradition and reduces the sacramental nature of Christianity. Blame for the split in Christianity thus shifts more heavily onto Luther. Contending the Joint Commission's statement that "It was not Luther's understanding of the gospel by itself which brought about conflict and schism in the church (§ 13)," Kothgasser stated that "it was precisely this absolutized and unilaterally and polemically sustained 'sola scriptura' that led to even stronger polarization and, as sole criterion of salvific truth, could not but encounter resistance in view of the Universal Church's marked sense of tradition." Consequently, Kothgasser rejected the commission's assertion that "[Luther] maintained throughout all conflicts his trust in God's promise to keep his church in truth" (§ 14) because "the statements made in this paragraph practically amount to an apology and absolution of Martin Luther and give inadequate expression to the permanently 'apostolic structure' of the Church" (Ibid., 90).

Kothgasser ended his criticism of the document by questioning its commemoration of Luther's deathbed humility and trust in God when the reformer stated "We are beggars. This is true" (§ 27). Rather, Kothgasser stated that "One should also take note of the fact that, according to the testimony of Justas Jonas, Luther's last prayer, the words of which have been handed down, still presented the pope as a persecutor of Jesus Christ: and this inevitably raises the question, often posed in the past, whether Luther could 'forgive,' whether he could 'love his enemies' and practice true humility."[36]

Kothgasser's second general criticism asserted a more minimal ecclesial reception of theological and magisterial statements on Lutheran matters than the Joint Commission allows, highlighting a muted reception of their own "All Under One Christ" and Cardinal Willebrands's statement on Luther at Évian as examples. Further, he queried whether the Protestant principle of "freedom and protest" in itself precludes the binding nature of the Lutheran confessions and Luther's catechisms for Protestants. Thus, the fact of the Second Vatican Council and the lack of a similarly universal and binding modern event for Protestants is construed as an added burden to full ecclesial reception (Ibid., 91). He stated further that the commission's statements regarding Lutheran recognition of Luther's limitations should enlarge to consider limitations in Luther's basic principles, presumably those he enumerated (Ibid., 90).

A third significant source for potential developments in Roman opinion about Luther is found in magisterial participation in scholarly reviews of doctrinal condemnations of the sixteenth century, particularly the Vatican's approval of the Joint Declaration on the Doctrine of Justification in June 1998. Roman interest in reviewing doctrinal condemnations is comprehensively evident in the unpublished 1992 study of the Pontifical Council for Promoting Christian Unity (PCPCU, formerly the Secretariat for Promoting Christian Unity) which evaluated the 1985 German investigation, *The Condemnations of the Reformation Era: Do They Still Divide?* The German study was constituted after the 1980 visit of the pope to Germany with the interest of promoting ecumenical cooperation in Sunday services, eucharistic fellowship, and mixed marriages. The mutual letter of commission by Bishop Eduard Lohse and then-Archbishop Joseph

Ratzinger, Chairmen of the German Joint Ecumenical Commission, to the Ecumenical Study Group of Protestant and Catholic Theologians stated that "According to the general conviction, these so-called condemnations no longer apply to our partner today. But this must not remain merely private persuasion. It must be established by the churches in binding form" (Lehmann and Pannenberg 1990, 169). Thus, as Karl Lehmann, Catholic participant and bishop of Mainz, had stated during the Luther-year "The complete Luther in the unabridged history of the one church's faith can receive a thoroughly prophetic meaning even for Catholics" (1984, 208).

The PCPCU study document reviewed, criticized, and endorsed the German project that stated after an evaluation of condemnations concerning justification, sacraments, and ministry that the strictures are no longer church-dividing. The "Final Report of the Joint Ecumenical Commission on the Examination of the Sixteenth Century Condemnations" (26 October 1985) stated:

> In the acrimony of the dispute, condemnations were uttered which, according to our now commonly acquired recognition, were even at that time the expressions of an incomplete understanding of the facts on both sides. At all events, they no longer apply to today's partner. (Lehmann and Pannenberg, 186)

In asserting the contemporary inapplicability of some sixteenth-century condemnations, *Condemnations* and PCPCU do diminish their historical validity as officially binding statements. *Condemnations* stated that their contemporary nonapplicability is derived from several factors: significant misunderstandings of the opposite party's position, polemical overstatement which current ecumenical commitments belie, theological developments that have moved both parties toward converging rather than diverging positions, and hermeneutical evaluations that now produce like meanings from different thought-patterns despite their dissimilar words. Thus, current ecumenical inquiry explains a genuine although diverse unity that escapes sixteenth-century fears. This is illustrated, for example, in the debates regarding justification:

> In the sixteenth century, Catholic theology was afraid that the result of the Reformers' doctrine of justification could be summed up as: no freedom, no new being, no ethical endeavor, no reward, no church (depreciation of baptism). Protestant theology was afraid that the result of the Catholic doctrine of justification could be summed up as: the triviality of sin, self-praise, a righteousness

of works, purchasable salvation, a church intervening between God
and human beings. (Ibid., 40–41)

For our purposes, the particular consideration given to Luther in
both documents demonstrates the theological seriousness that he
receives from Catholics today and reveals continuing issues for
ecumenical and magisterial evaluation. While Luther is implied but
never named specifically in condemnations pronounced by Tridentine
canons, *Condemnations* especially emphasized that often either the
council understood Luther inadequately, according to a secondhand
or restricted range of texts, or that subsequent Catholic theological
development has complemented Luther. In either case, certain condemnations regarding justification, sacraments, and ministry have
become null or at least mitigated.

Condemnations asserted, for example, that the Decree on Justification canon 6 condemns the position that God is the origin of original
sin in a real sense, based on appeal to exaggerated statements of Luther
and Melanchthon that were later modified and corrected. Further,
these are absent from Lutheran Confessions (Ibid., 43). Similar
exaggeration is made regarding Luther's emphasis on persons passivity before God in the reception of grace (Ibid., 46). The Decree on
Justification canon 4 stated that "If anyone says that a person's free
will when moved and roused by God, gives no cooperation by
responding to God's summons and invitation to dispose and prepare
itself to obtain the grace of justification; and that it cannot, if it so
wishes, dissent, but, like something inanimate, can do nothing at all
and remains merely passive: let him be anathema" (Tanner, 679).

Condemnations also asserted that the Tridentine fathers condemned
positions that did not fully express Luther's thought. While it is often
difficult to ascertain Luther's thought systematically due to the
polemical and spontaneous nature of his writing, *Condemnations*
argued that significant aspects of the reformer's theology remain
unconsidered, thus causing a mismatch of Tridentine canons and
Luther's actual positions. This is often due to the nearly exclusive
reliance on compendia of texts produced before 1530 that were later
collated by Catholic controversialists. Thus, for example, the Decree
on Justification canon 27 anathematized anyone who "says that there
is no mortal sin save that of unbelief; or that grace, once received, is
lost by no other sin, however serious and enormous, than that of
unbelief" based on a fair reading of Luther's *Babylonian Captivity* of
1520 (Tanner 1990, 681). However, this excluded Luther's retraction
of absolute subjective certainty in the Smalcald Articles. Regarding

eucharistic theology, *Condemnations* suggested that Trent's assertion of transubstantiation is not a direct antithesis to what Luther taught, often termed consubstantiation (Lehmann and Pannenberg, 89). Similarly, *Condemnations* asserted that the Council of Trent underestimated the ecclesiological thought of Luther and the Lutheran confessions due to exclusive reference to the earlier writings of the reformer (Ibid., 78).

Beyond a considerable degree of unfamiliarity with Luther, *Condemnations* asserted that contemporary historical and exegetical studies reveal more complementarity between the reformer's and Catholic positions than was evident in the midst of controversy. Catholic concerns about justification *sola fide*, eucharistic theology, and priesthood are especially prominent. While "distinguishing teachings" exist regarding justification (e.g., full vs. partial impairment of human nature, imputed vs. forensic justification, strict vs. relative identity of original sin and concupiscence) it can be shown that a certain compatibility exists regarding the previously divisive issue of moral works. *Condemnations* stated that "Luther rejected talk about justification on the basis of 'faith formed by love' *(fides caritate formata)* but did so because he was afraid of the view that something humanly ethical could play a decisive part in the salvific process, not out of disparagement of God's love. It was a nominalist doctrine that human beings can love God above everything simply of their own natural powers." Modern hermeneutical efforts reveal further that "Protestant talk about justification through faith corresponds to Catholic talk about justification through grace; and on the other hand, Protestant doctrine understands substantially under the word "faith" what Catholic doctrine (following 1 Cor. 13:13) sums up in the triad of faith, hope, love" (Ibid., 52).[37]

Luther's denial of the sacrificial element in the mass, anathematized in Trent's Decree on the Sacrifice of the Mass canons 1–4, need not be church-dividing today in light of contemporary linkage of the singularly effective cross of Christ *(sacrificium)* and the commemorative nature of the sacrifice of the mass *(sacramentum)* (Ibid., 114). Also, *Condemnations* stated that Luther's assertion that the mass was instituted for forgiveness of sins is mismatched by the Decree on the Eucharist canon 5 that perceived a reduction of full Catholic teaching on the richness of the eucharist. Specifically, current New Testament studies support Luther's idea, it argued, when "forgiveness of sins" is fully located in Luther's thought and when suitable scriptural synonyms (dawn of the rule of God, *koinonia*) are employed (Ibid., 111–112).

In consideration of Luther on ministry, *Condemnations* unequivocally stated that the reformer's employment of the term *antichrist*
regarding the papacy was "substantially unjustified even under the
conditions of the sixteenth century, if the way in which the papacy saw
itself is precisely evaluated" (Ibid., 158). Considering the sacramental
character of priesthood, Trent anathematized "anyone [who] says the
holy Spirit is not given through holy ordination, and so bishops say
Receive the holy Spirit in vain; or that no character is imprinted by it;
or that someone who was once a priest can become a layman again"
(Tanner 1990, 744). Before 1522 Luther had restricted the passing of
the Spirit strictly to baptism but after that saw a special gift of the Spirit
in connection with the laying on of hands. Thus *Condemnations*
argued for an increased compatibility of Catholic doctrine and Luther
on priesthood, especially with the Second Vatican Council's stronger
connection of priest to bishop as delegate and authorized proclaimer
of the Gospel (*Presbyterorum ordinis* § 7–8).

Magisterial Collaboration with Theological Consensus

While the German Joint Commission's study considered the
Tridentine and Lutheran confessional condemnations broadly, its
provided interfaith analysis of Luther that the Roman magisterium
had sought since Vatican II. While a focused magisterial investigation
of the reformer is yet to be published, the evaluation of the German
study by the Pontifical Council for Promoting Christian Unity
highlights significant theological and historical issues for Luther's
magisterial audience.

The pontifical study endorsed the findings of the German Ecumenical Study Group as a "research of the highest scientific quality."[38]
The PCPCU study examined the findings of *Condemnations* and
presented its own reading and evaluation of the Council of Trent
consistent with Catholic ecumenical principles: it affirmed that a
legitimate Christian theological pluralism exists in accord with a
hierarchy of truths (Pontifical 1992, 8). For purposes of this investigation, the PCPCU study evaluated the Council of Trent's teachings
regarding Martin Luther often like *Condemnations* but also proposed
concerns about the reformer that need additional investigation before
added claims about the nullification or restriction of sixteenth-
century Catholic condemnations can be made.

As did *Condemnations*, PCPCU's study stated that the polemical
environment of the sixteenth century prevented fully accurate understandings of divergent theological positions and adds that the very

definition of heresy is much restricted today from the very broad medieval definition, which included the attitude of disobedience toward ecclesial authorities as well as the rejection of divine Catholic truths, the corpus of which included everything relating to our salvation. Thus the Tridentine anathemas often appear today as too broad and sweeping (Ibid., 9–10).

The pontifical study commented on significant oversights and reductions of Luther's thought by the Council of Trent, especially regarding justification and sacraments. It stated that the council's essential grasp of Luther on justification was drawn from his writings of 1518–26, thus eliminating his retraction of the permanence of grace received at baptism (Ibid., 14). Also, PCPCU stated that the Decree on Justification canon 19 that anathematizes one who says that "the ten commandments in no way apply to Christians" suffers from an inadequate understanding of Luther's dialectic on law and gospel. It speculated that Catholic understanding of this dialectic in accord with Augustine's distinction between liberty of *(libertas)* and freedom of the will *(liberum arbitrium)* would more fully grasp Luther's intent (Ibid., 25). Thereby, the *fact* of the graced life, emphasized by Luther, is more recognized than the *state* of the will faced with the actual demands of the gospel.

In another Tridentine oversight, the pontifical study found that the Decree on Penance canon 3 defended the absolute efficacy of the sacrament that Luther himself never challenged; rather, he considered penance as a consequence of baptism rather than a separate sacrament (Ibid., 64). PCPCU asserted further that once one concedes that Luther's determination of sacramental authenticity was linked to a narrow interpretation of Augustine's teaching on the sacrament as a visible sign, a sign that the reformer did not find in scripture, his position need not be seen in conflict with Catholic teaching. (Ibid., 101). Similarly the pontifical study said that the council "gravely misunderstood" Luther's replacement of the tripartite sacrament (contrition, confession, satisfaction) with the doctrine of penance in two parts, the terrors of conscience and belief (Ibid., 65–66, 100).

PCPCU also subscribed to the principle that convergences in nonpolemical modern theology and ecclesial doctrinal reformulations demonstrate a clear convergence in some positions of Trent and Luther. Thus, when the Decree on Penance canon 7 stated that "For the forgiveness of sins in the sacrament of penance it is not necessary by divine law to confess each and all mortal sins *which are remembered after due and careful consideration*" (emphasis mine), it met a similar concern of Luther regarding the impossibility of remembering one's sins, restricting Lateran IV's scrupulous requirement of confessing "all sins" (Ibid., 67–68).[39]

Regarding the ordination of priests, Luther's condemnation of ordaining priests through anointing of hands and a presentation of chalice and paten, the instruments of sacrifice, is seen as inappropriate today because the practice was modified in 1947 by Pius XII who considered the imposition of hands to be the essential aspect of ordination (Pontifical 1992, 87).

The evaluation for the PCPCU is not a full, systematic consideration of Martin Luther and was not designed to be. However, its review of the canons of Trent regarding the Lutheran Reformation did confirm significant tensions in thought between Catholicism and Luther that deserve further investigation, primarily ecclesiological. Thus Luther's emphasis on forensic justification through the sole efficacy of Christ provides difficulties for Catholicism that emphasizes the mediatorial role of the church, particularly through the sacraments, especially baptism (Ibid., 21). Correspondingly, Luther's restrictions on human lawmaking bump frequently into the Catholic understanding of ecclesial polity with its restricted but clear appreciation of canon law and laws of the church (Ibid., 98). Finally, the pontifical study realizes that "the Catholic view of Tradition as a way in which Scripture is more thoroughly understood and made operative in the Church, is not shared by Lutherans" (Ibid., 102).

By thorough consideration of Trent and Luther on justification by faith begun in 1985, however, the pontifical study prepared for the remarkable approval by the Vatican and the Lutheran World Federation in June 1998 of the Joint Declaration on the Doctrine of Justification. Of Luther's cardinal doctrine and central concern to the magisterium of the sixteenth century, uniquely vital to the church's health, the declaration stated that "on the basis of their dialogue the subscribing Lutheran churches and the Roman Catholic Church are now able to articulate a common understanding of our justification by God's grace through faith in Christ" (Joint Declaration 1998, 120). Namely, "together we confess: By grace alone, in faith in Christ's saving work and not because of any merit on our part, we are accepted by God and receive the Holy Spirit, who renews our hearts while equipping and calling us to good works" (Ibid., 122).

In their first-ever authorized acceptance of theologians' ecumenical consensus, the Vatican and Lutheran World Federation did not erase their historical alienation but agreed that the conditions to look beyond it are readily present. Veteran ecumenists from both confessions marveled at the breakthrough, with Catholic George Tavard stating that "The anathema project underlines the necessity for all churches to function in another way than in the past" (Tavard 1997, 59). Lutheran Harding Meyer named the new way evident in the joint declaration on justification as one of "reconciled diversity" from which solutions to remaining issues will come (Meyer 1997, 166).[40]

Overall, trajectories in magisterial regard of Luther confirm official Catholic subscription to the Second Vatican Council's model of ecumenical dialogue as the way to Christian unity, even regarding one of the most neuralgic persons in Christian tradition. While preliminary in many ways to a comprehensive historical and ecumenical statement on the German reformer, these statements reveal a most deliberative, engaging, and appreciative view of Luther as reformer and theologian.

CONCLUSION

Roman Catholic magisterial appreciation of Martin Luther is a necessary consequence of the Second Vatican Council's ecclesiology of communion that ushered in Catholic ecumenical principles designed to forge Christian unity rather than to lament its historical demise. This ecclesiology neither abandons the fundamental conviction about Catholic hierarchical communion as the paradigm of Christian unity nor asserts that the previous exercise of hierarchical authority is the determinant model for future reconciliation. Significant in the Catholic anticipation of Christian unity is the principle of collaborative interdenominational reconciliation. This collaboration invests the hope for unity into dialogues that discover authentic yet diverse commonplaces in Christianity as they simultaneously discharge the notion that Catholic ecumenism expects a submissive return to an unchanged Rome.

Development of a transformative mentality regarding ecumenism in the Roman magisterium has reversed the previous assessment of Luther as heresiarch by appreciating first the various historical causes of Luther's biblical theology, polemical attitudes, and church-dividing doctrinal statements. This mentality has also discarded reactionary and triumphant caricatures of Roman Catholicism which often had been displayed after the Catholic Reformation and had precluded any appreciative evaluation of Protestant reformers. Tentative and nuanced magisterial appreciation of Luther as a prophetic reformer is made possible by repenting for the historical lapses of the curia, however unspecified, and by appreciating connections between Luther and the nascent reforms produced by the Second Vatican Council.

Further, the definite yet restricted acknowledgment of Luther as a Christian theologian by Rome proceeds from the awareness that his experiences of faith are profound and that they are advanced in his theological analysis. The collaborative investigation of Luther by Catholics and Lutherans is essential to Roman ecumenical efforts to grasp the reformer's analysis. The fact *that* Luther taught novel theology, so central in the mentality of the Catholic reformation, is displaced increasingly by a deep concern for *what* Luther taught, a concern previously matched only by Cardinal Cajetan at Augsburg.

Luther has been found to be an ardent defender of biblical faith, especially the Pauline doctrine of salvation by absolute trust in God's promise manifest in the cross and resurrection of Jesus Christ. He is recognized as an honest, if not prudent, observer of pastoral conditions in the sixteenth-century church who is not wholly or even primarily responsible for the ecclesiastical fractures which ensued. The German reformer is often commended by the magisterium for his pastoral skills and spiritual persuasiveness concerning the merciful love of God given in the revealed Word of God and corresponding tradition. Luther is understood by the magisterium as a theologian whose contributions to profound examination of the Christian faith have been underestimated, if not misunderstood. In concert with Pope John Paul II's millennial ecumenism, Archbishop Justin Rigali of Saint Louis stated at Concordia Seminary in February 1996, "We realize the sinfulness of some Catholic church leaders in the sixteenth century and today, and recognize that the alienation between our two communities calls us all to repentance. Just as Luther called for reform in the church of his day, so Vatican II called the church to reform in our own day" (Rigali 1996, 63).

A new elasticity in Catholic magisterial regard of Luther does not eliminate the ecclesiological reservation that most deeply character-ized Rome's initial objection in Prierias's first review in 1518. In contrast, however, Rome's qualifications are now more pensive than polemical, geared for persuasive dialogue rather than personal invec-tive. Vatican II's ecclesiology of communion, which authorized Rome's rapprochement with Luther, is also the precise location of continuing magisterial anxiety with the reformer. The Roman con-cern that Luther's theology reduces the full wealth of Christian tradition available in the Catholic church is the hub of continuing concern about Martin Luther's catholicity but it does not belie its recognition of Luther's outstanding faith.

5

PERSPECTIVE

Yet however much human culpability has damaged communion, it
has never destroyed it. In fact, the fullness of the unity of the
Church of Christ has been maintained within the Catholic Church
while other Churches and ecclesial Communities, though not in
full communion with the Catholic Church, retain in reality a
certain communion with it.
—Pontifical Council for Promoting Christian Unity[1]

The Roman Catholic magisterial image of Luther after the Second
Vatican Council is established through typically Catholic sensibilities: an appeal to basic ecclesiological doctrines that substantiate the
Catholic vision of life from generation to generation and the celebration of past persons and events that represent the grandeur of the faith
announced by Jesus Christ. This study has considered magisterial
evolution regarding Luther as a process by which resentment against
him has been cauterized due to the development of an ecclesiology of
communion in *Lumen gentium*, its ecumenical application in *Unitatis
redintegratio*, and subsequent interconfessional dialogues. This recovery of a more profoundly biblical notion of the mystical body of Christ
allows recognition of Christian holiness wherever baptized persons
respond to the Holy Spirit of the Christian trinity. Moreover, deep
magisterial appreciation of Luther proceeds from acknowledgment of
his reforming impulses and his genuine dedication to the common life
in the Spirit enunciated in the Word of God and corresponding
tradition.

Together with the reorientation of Catholic ecclesiology at the
Second Vatican Council, papal and curial statements during recent
Luther-celebrations have produced clear evidence that Luther is seen
by the magisterium as an authentic reformer and perceptive theologian rather than the misguided renegade who was excommunicated.
Acknowledgment of Catholic complicity in crimes against the faith in
the sixteenth century and fresh consideration of Luther's diversified
theology, especially his spiritual and pastoral legacy, have removed a
veneer of Catholic righteousness in ecumenical matters and estab-

lished strong magisterial desire for theological and doctrinal clarity in future Christian reconciliation. It is also clear that this appreciation of Luther is exploratory and somewhat fragile. The statements by Cardinal Willebrands have been often more generous than those of Cardinal Ratzinger whose denial of Luther's Roman Catholicity poses significant challenges, not to say obstacles, to Lutheran-Catholic ecumenical discussions.

While concern for Luther's Roman Catholicity is not to be underestimated, it does not undermine the surety of Roman appreciation of him. Magisterial understanding of Luther in conjunction with the reforms of Vatican II provides significant commonplaces, for example, biblical spirituality, liturgical awareness, and evangelical catechesis. Moreover, the doctrinal issues investigated by sanctioned Catholic-Lutheran dialogues have exposed significant convergences that are indismissible. However, it is equally clear that the measurement of Luther's ecclesiological divergence by the magisterium will test the borders of plurality allowed by Vatican II's ecclesiology of communion.

At the onset, this study raised two specific issues related to the magisterial image of Luther that can now be addressed: correlation of this image to the pace of Catholic ecumenical progress and the role of the Catholic press in ecumenical progress regarding Luther.

Assertions of ecumenical tardiness due to Roman intransigence have occurred since the immediate years after Vatican II. In the summer of 1992 the Congregation for the Doctrine of the Faith's positions in "Some Aspects of the Church Understood as Communion" provoked similar criticisms. In discouraging a merely sociological and antihierarchical understanding of Vatican II's ecclesiology the document also asserted that "Since, however, communion with the universal church, represented by Peter's successor, is not an external complement to the particular church, but one of its internal constituents, the situation of those venerable Christian communities also means their existence as particular churches is wounded" (Congregation 1992, 111).[2] The assertion of the wounded nature of non-Catholic churches prompted many Protestants to accuse Rome of regression to preconciliar standards.[3] Subsequently, Cardinal Edward Cassidy, president of the Pontifical Council for Promoting Christian Unity, explained the relative limits of the letter's ecumenical comments and reiterated Catholic commitment to the ecumenical principles established since Vatican II (1993, 736–744).

Assertions of Roman sluggishness are correct as much as the initial euphoria produced by simple magisterial gestures in the conciliar

1960s have given way naturally to the deliberative process of articulating doctrinal convergences. In fact, the mutual practice of Lutherans and Catholics to go slow but steady, evident in the Lutheran caution regarding Catholic recognition of the Augsburg Confession, for example, is itself a principle of ecumenical dialogues.

But what of Catholic ecumenical prospects? Regarding Luther, this study has shown that the ecclesiological concerns that in various ways promoted the reformer's excommunication in 1521 remain the single most important issue regarding his magisterial rehabilitation. The perception that Luther's ecclesiology is probably not consonant with that of contemporary Catholicism is, however, open for discussion. Questions regarding the reception, implementation, and status of his thought for Lutheran churches are also important. In view of the appreciation developed for other aspects of Luther's life in the church illustrated herein, it seems premature to criticize the speed of magisterial ecumenical progress. Especially important for continued progress will be magisterial activity subsequent to the Joint Declaration on the Doctrine of Justification in 1998. Failure by both Lutherans and Catholics to achieve swifter progress, given the pregnancy offered by the work of the Joint Commission and the studies of the condemnations, would verify allegations of tardiness.

Regarding the role of the Catholic press in ecumenical progress regarding Luther, this study has shown that media who take their lead from magisterial teaching cannot ignore the definitive Catholic appreciation of Martin Luther. The scope, consistency, and urgency of magisterial appreciation of Luther as reformer and theologian are hallmarks of postconciliar ecumenism. To parrot lapsed polemics or to shun the constructive emphasis of ecumenical dialogue with all its difficulties would create, in effect, a second and inauthentic magisterium.

An example of this quasi-magisterial approach in Catholic media is evident in John J. Mulloy's editorial, "The Pope, Luther, and Ecumenism," which appeared in the *Wanderer* shortly after the pope's trip to Scandinavia in 1989. Mulloy stated:

> Another question relates to the Pope's referring to the "need for a new evaluation of Luther and his teaching," and his "praising Luther for his profound faith." Should not the Pope have made clear that what he meant by Luther's profound faith is not the same thing as the faith of the Catholic Church, that there is a most important line of division which separates the two? Otherwise, unwise ecumenists may jump to the conclusion that there is no

significant difference between them, and thus that the way is now
open for reunion of the Catholic and Lutheran churches on the
basis of Luther's teaching. (Mulloy 1989, 4)

Finally, how do I justify labeling the recent Roman magisterial
image of Luther as a prophet rather than merely a reformer or a
teacher? Martin Marty has argued that redefined Catholic-Protestant
relations after the Second Vatican Council should be thought of as a
more positive social contract where persuasion takes precedent over
coercion in matters dominated by the practical and spiritual aspects
rather than doctrinal ones (1991, 21). One can first say that success
in preserving the whole Catholic tradition thus demands an image
that is biblical, comprehensive both historically and doctrinally, and
elastic. In our time when apologists for doctrine are needed increasingly, Martin Luther can be best described to Catholics as an authentic
prophet whose fundamental work was highlighting the gospel that
had become eclipsed by the church authorized to proclaim it. Like
men described in the Old Testament, Luther was eccentric yet
brilliant, banal yet prayerful, unsystematic yet focused.[4] As earlier
prophets had urged the recovery of Mosaic traditions within events
that encapsulated their lives, so Luther's life provided novel expressions of faith that purified Catholic tradition even as it promoted
disruption among Christians.

In terms of the New Testament, James Atkinson considers Martin
Luther to be a "prophet of the Church catholic" because God revealed
the gospel to him with a unique clarity known through God's
"terrifying and stark otherness" (1983, 44). He views Paul as Luther's
only comparable prophetic Christian colleague and asserts that neither Protestant nor Roman Catholic can exclude a rare person of such
charisma in their understanding the gospel of Christ (Ibid., 68). In the
light of the gospel that Paul and Luther preach, their personalities are
negligible for the faithful today.

One can further understand the magisterial assessment of Luther as
a Roman Catholic prophet by exploring beyond Atkinson's understandings of Luther's prophetic persona and vital message. Recent
scholarship on the social location of biblical prophets more accurately
nuances the contemporary Roman regard for Luther by correlating to
a profound Catholic sensibility illustrated throughout this discussion—the gospel of Jesus Christ is nurtured in a visibly unified society
of the faithful.

Robert W. Wilson discusses societal factors that are essential to the
authentic activity of the biblical prophet. At least three factors

promote or inhibit this intermediary's contribution to the ancient Israelite faith. First, as with Atkinson, prophecy is a social experience where supernatural power is presumed to influence human affairs. Prophecy is essentially about divine communication to those who seek to bridge the gap between spiritual and ordinary realms. Second, Wilson emphasizes that the biblical prophet operates in social conditions that require their service, that is, some stress or rapid social change. Thus a charismatic individual is cherished amid tumultuous events, and somehow integrated into society, because they uniquely resolve normally uninterpretable threats to social order. Third, consequently, the prophet's actions are encouraged or at least tolerated (Wilson 1980, 28–30).

Wilson advances our awareness of both the biblical intermediaries and Luther's Roman Catholicity by perceiving a meaningful continuum of their social locations, from peripheral to central. The peripheral intermediary operates on society's fringes because they may be involved with minor spirits, lack social status, or otherwise display behavior that is unappreciated by the official religion. Official religion tolerates increasingly the peripheral prophet when their activity is limited to a minority group, itself vital for the prophet's well-being, and when traditional wisdom is confirmed or proposed innovations promote social stability (Ibid., 68–73). The centrally-located prophet offers official links between mainstream society and the spirit world, often seeking to regulate the pace of social change by affirming traditional wisdom or collaborating in political activity (Ibid., 84).

Thomas W. Overholt considers the social dynamics of the prophetic act, emphasizing that these same dynamics exist in various cultures outside the biblical world. He considers how the supernatural, the prophet, and the audience interact, particularly in terms of feedback from prophet to supernatural and from audience to prophet (23). Thus both the prophet's and audience's reactions influence what is communicated. Consequently, prophecy is perceived to be absent when a society is disinterested, ignoring the prophet or crediting their communication as fanaticism or insanity (160). However, Overholt asserts, prophecy is a continuing potentiality in a society, based on its beliefs and past experience (160).

Luther may be seen as an authentic prophet by the Catholic church today because the Second Vatican Council authorized an expanded and more diverse interpretation of Catholic society, particularly through an ecclesiology of communion that is imaged with the biblical metaphor of the body of Christ.[5] Luther has moved into the Christian prophetic continuum as defined by the Catholic magisterium insofar as his insights have become peripheral rather than nonexistent for the Catholic majority group. This movement is especially confirmed in Catholic statements about Luther in the 1980s and about Luther's cardinal insight, justification by faith alone, in the 1990s. Magisterial concerns about Luther are about the Catholic degree, not the Christian fact, of his prophetic activity in the sixteenth century. The Catholic question about Luther is about how far to the Catholic center of Christianity will he and his evangelical theology be located.

One anticipates an added advance of Luther toward the center of a Catholic prophetic continuum as the magisterium establishes even higher expectations of Christian unity. Pope John Paul II stated to Dr. Gottfried Brakemeier, president of the Lutheran World Federation, in June 1997, anticipating Lutheran and Roman Catholic consensus on justification documented in 1998,

> Because it is the will of Christ that we should seek unity, there can be no turning back on the path of ecumenism. The Lord of history invites all Christians to celebrate with joy the forthcoming Third Millennium of Redemption. We are called to respond to this special *kairos* of God with generosity and an unshakable trust in the surpassing power of grace. Nor can we be satisfied simply with tolerance or mutual understanding. Jesus Christ, he who is and who is to come, asks of us a visible sign of unity, a joint witness to the liberating truth of the Gospel. (1997)

The Roman Catholic magisterium activated a perception of Martin Luther as a Christian prophet by introducing doctrinal emphases that resonate, if not validate, his essential theological insights. This increased elasticity of Catholic perceptions was introduced at Vatican II in terms of Catholic affirmations about the vital importance of the Word of God for every believer (*Constitution on Revelation* § 22), the call for continuous reform in the church (*Decree on Ecumenism* § 6), and emphasis on the mystery of God as the taproot of Catholic ecclesiology (*Constitution on the Church* § 2). Lutheran and Roman Catholic official affirmation in 1998 that "the subscribing Lutheran churches and the Roman Catholic church are now able to articulate a common understanding of our justification by God's grace through faith in Jesus Christ" extends the conciliar initiative and appreciation of Luther's providential activity, creating a remarkable possibility for Christian evangelization in the new millennium (Joint Declaration § 5).

As the Catholic church seeks to discover ways to evangelize the globe and to restore the integrity of Catholic faith internally and interconfessionally, tensions in faith must be properly defined even as those corrosive perspectives are excised. The heuristic potential of diversified Christian insight is obvious in the magisterial rediscovery of Martin Luther. Additionally, Luther's Roman rehabilitation is a prominent test for developing a more profound implementation of conciliar ecclesiology that reestablished charismatic as well as communal aspects of the church.[6] To consider Luther as a Catholic prophet would provide the doctrinal latitude, ecclesiological fidelity, and ecumenical witness for today's Christians who are less able to debate Luther than to image him.

NOTES

Chapter 1: Introduction

1. *Exsurge Domine* (June 1520), in *Readings in Church History,* ed. Coleman J. Barry (Westminster: Newman, 1985), 634–635.
2. "Pope John Paul II's Letter on the Fifth Centenary of Birth of Martin Luther," *Information Service* 52 (1983): 83.
3. See, for example, Archbishop John F. Whealon, "Luther's 500th Birthday," *The Catholic Transcript,* 9 September 1983, 6; idem, "Father Martin Luther," *The Catholic Transcript,* 23 September 1983, 6; and idem, "Luther's Heritage," *The Catholic Transcript,* 30 September 1983, 6.
4. See, for example, Pope John Paul II to International Joint Catholic-Lutheran Commission [2 March 1985], "From Commemorations for Luther Arises a New Impulse for Reconciliation," *L'Osservatore Romano,* 12 March 1984, 5, 12(E); and Pope John Paul II to participants in a study convention on Luther [24 March 1984], "United Christians for a United Europe," *L'Osservatore Romano,* 30 April 1984, 10(E).
5. Important surveys include Gottfried Maron's *Das Katholische Lutherbild der Gegenwart, Bensheimer Hefte* 58 (Göttingen: Vandenhoeck und Ruprecht, 1982) and Richard Stauffer's *Le Catholicisme à la découverte de Luther: L'évolution des recherches catholiques sur Luther de 1904 au 2me Concile du Vatican* (Neuchâtel: Delachaux et Niestlé, 1966); this was edited and translated by the author as *Luther as Seen by Catholics* (Richmond: John Knox, 1967).
6. Similar sentiments are echoed in Letters to the Editor entitled "The Truth About Luther," *Priest* 12/3 (March 1956): 282–284, 286, 288; cf. Robert McAfee Brown, "The Reformer, Seen In a New Perspective," *Christianity and Crisis,* 3 October 1983, 349–350.
7. See, for example, "A New Trial for Martin Luther?," *Tablet,* 16 October 1965, 1168; Robert E. Burns, "Is war over between the opposite sects?," *U.S. Catholic* 49 (February 1984): 2; Gordon Rupp, "Catholics Think Again," *Tablet,* 31 December 1983, 1102; and John Todd, "Man or monster?," *Tablet,* 7 January 1984, 7–8.
8. Four months later, Father Ginder reinforced these sentiments, writing that "None of them [Protestants] will admit that he was a lewd satyr whose glandular demands were the ultimate cause of his break with Christian truth" (1956, 134).
9. Archbishop John F. Whealon to American Archbishops and Bishops, 9 September 1983: "It is significant that this anniversary is being observed not in a unilateral, reformation spirit, but in an ecumenical spirit that does not overlook the Catholicism of Luther and hope that in God's mysterious designs Martin Luther may guide both our churches to unity in Christ."
10. Gerard J. M. van den Aardweg, a Dutch psychologist, argued that Luther's psychological state clouded his spiritual perceptions and impeded any development of theological tenets in "Martin Luther's neurotic complex," *Homiletic and Pastoral Review* 85 (October 1984): 65–68. Matthew V. Reilly, OP, offered Luther as an example of the disaster which ensues upon rejection of the Church's authority in *Homiletic and Pastoral Review* 88 (July 1988): 17–22.
11. "The Facts Behind Reformation Sunday," *Sign* (December 1950): 7–8. The more genteel variety characterized Luther as one seduced by fame, e.g., J. D.

Conway's "What Would You Like to Know About the Church?," *Catholic Digest* 27 (March 1963): 146–151. The more virulent variety depicted Luther as the originator of totalitarianism in political authority through rejection of ecclesial authority; see William Thomas Walsh, "From Luther to Hitler," *Sign* (February 1940): 395–397. The linkage of Luther and Hitler is not uncommon: Richard Ginder, "Right or Wrong," 5; Michael Kent, "Propaganda, Past and Present: Luther and Hitler," *Catholic World* 159 (September 1944): 515–521; "Martin Luther, 1546–1946: his role in the disintegration of Christendom," *Tablet*, 16 February 1946, 82–84; and Peter Weiner, "Martin Luther: Hitler's Spiritual Ancestor," Win the Peace Pamphlet 3, London: Hutchinson, 1945. A notable counter-perspective is offered by Gordon Rupp, *Martin Luther: Hitler's Cause—or Cure?, In reply to Peter F. Wiener* (London: Lutterworth, 1945) and Freidrich Heer, *Gottes erste Liebe, 2000 Jahre Judentum und Christentum: Genesis des österreichischen Katholiken Adolf Hitler* (Vienna, 1967).

12. Interestingly, Mondin quotes the Danish Lutheran philosopher Søren Kierkegaard (1813–55) to introduce sentiments that strongly resemble those of Catholic polemics, including comments about Luther's theological skill, sexual stability, and exaggerated subjectivism.

Chapter 2: Luther and
Roman Catholic Theologians in the Twentieth Century

1. *Luther und Luthertum in der ersten Entwickelung,* vol. 1/2 (Mainz: von Kirchheim, 1906), 797.
2. *The Reformation in Germany,* vol. 1, trans. Ronald Walls (New York: Herder and Herder, 1968), 431.
3. "Luther and the Catholic Tradition," *Lutheran Theological Seminary Bulletin* 64 (1984): 18.
4. See, for example, Cardinal Jan Willebrands, "Ecumenical Dialogue Today: An Overview," *Origins* 17 (1988): 565–573; Pope John Paul II, "Pope John Paul II's Letter on the Fifth Centenary of Birth of Martin Luther," *Information Service* 52 (1983): 83. In this time of often tenuous relations between theologians and magisterial authorities, cooperative initiatives in ecumenism may provide insights into the magisterial-theological relationship as a happy byproduct. See also chapter 1, note 4 above.
5. Other models for exploring this shift are available in Yves M.-J. Congar, *Dialogue Between Christians* (Westminster: Newman, 1964), 358–371; Edward D. McShane, "Martin Luther," *Thought* 41 (Spring 1966): 104–116; Otto Hermann Pesch, "Twenty Years of Catholic Luther Research," *Lutheran World* 13 (1966): 303–316; and Gary K. Waite, "Catholic Reappraisals of Luther," *Ecumenist* 21 (November–December 1982): 9–13. An overview of Protestant historiography on Luther is found in Roland Bainton, "Interpretation of the Reformation," *American Historical Review* 99 (1960): 74–84.
6. See Ruth Kleinman, *Saint François De Sales and the Protestants* (Geneva: E. Droz, 1962).
7. See *Seven-headed Luther,* ed. Peter Newman Brooks (Oxford: Clarendon, 1983) for a contemporary discussion of Luther's greatness based on the seven-headed image.

8. Cochläus produced extensive criticisms of other reformers as well. Concerning his work against Melanchthon, for example, see Ralph Keen, "The Arguments and Audiences of Cochläus's *Philippica VII*," *Catholic Historical Review* LXXVIII (1992): 371–394.

9. The elder Pistorius (d. 1583) was a prominent Protestant theologian and minister who served alongside Melanchthon and Bucer in the Diet of Regensburg in spring 1541.

10. Both men would be taken to task by the Protestant Veit Ludwig von Seckendorff (1626–92) in his *History of Lutheranism* (1692); see Ernst Walter Zeeden, *The Legacy of Luther*, trans. Ruth Mary Bethell (Westminster: Newman, 1954), 55–64.

11. Bossuet is criticized for this rather benign view of Luther by Marie-Joseph Lagrange, who relies heavily on the interpretation of Heinrich Denifle, in *Luther on the Eve of His Revolt* (New York: Cathedral Library Association, 1918), 1–2.

12. A brief survey is found in W. J. Sparrow Simpson, *A Study of Bossuet* (London: S. P. C. K., 1937), 38–47. Bossuet's focus on the issues separating Catholics and Protestants is also seen in his *Exposition of the Faith* (1671) and in his correspondence on reunion with the philosopher of Hanover, Gottfried Wilhelm von Leibniz (1646–1716) which ran from 1683 to 1700. See Simpson, 165–185; Bonaventura Malatesta, "Leibniz and the Problem of Christian Unity," Unitas 17/1 (1965): 17–27(E); and, Zeeden, *The Legacy of Luther*, 65–80.

13. Further, he links Lutheranism to gnosticism, juxtaposing their mutual principles of radical corruption, predestination, and a distinction between faith and morality. See Herve Savon, Johann Adam Möhler: *The Father of Modern Theology* (Glen Rock, NJ: Paulist, 1966), 83–93.

14. Döllinger, *Die Reformation, ihre innere Entwicklung und ihre Wirkungen im Umfang des lutherischen Bekenntnisses*, vol. III (Frankfurt: Minerva, 1962).

15. Döllinger's *Der Papst und das Concil* (1869; ET, 1870–73), published with the pseudonym Janus, was placed on the Index of Forbidden Books on November 26, 1869 just prior to the council.

16. Peter Iver Kaufman stated that "Döllinger insinuated that not only had Luther misrepresented the Catholic position and distorted the biblical balance between faith and works but also that Luther's aversion to his own parodies of Catholic moral theology impelled him to neglect 'the common life of the world' and to rely exclusively on faith's consolations"; see "'Unnatural' Sympathies? Acton and Döllinger on the Reformation," *Catholic Historical Review* 70 (1984): 549.

17. Julius Köstlin (1826–1902), professor of church history at the University of Halle/Wittenberg, was the prime Protestant respondent to Janssen with his *Luther und Johannes Janssen: Der deutsche Reformator und ein ultramoner Historiker* (Halle, 1883).

18. Denifle's credentials are listed in Aubrey Gwynn, "Martin Luther: A Reappraisal," *Studies* 51 (Fall 1962): 349. In fact, Protestants anticipated the publication of the book as they hoped it would have contributed to a more positive Catholic view of Luther insofar as it was to be based on primary sources. Ironically, Denifle is best known for this massive study of Luther when his most enduring scholarship was accomplished in medieval studies. An interesting sketch of his scholarly stature and his influence at the Vatican Archives can be found in Owen Chadwick's *Catholicism and History: The Opening of the Vatican Archives* (New York: Cambridge University Press, 1978).

19. Further, Iserloh quotes Hubert Jedin: "this book was a moral and scientific execution of the renegade Augustinian by a true-blue Dominican." A more popular Catholic castigation of the reformer is found in William Loughnan's "The Luther Celebration" and "Martin Luther" in *Month* 49 (1883): 153–165, 305–321.

20. *Quellenbelege: Die abendländischen Schriftausleger bis Luther über Justitia Dei (Rom. 1.17) und Justificatio: Beitrag zur Geschichte der Exegese, der Literatur und des Dogmas im Mittelalter*, Mainz.

21. A list of Protestant responses to Denifle's charges of Luther's monastic failure is in J. M. Reu, *Thirty-five Years of Luther Research* (New York: AMS, rep. 1970), 125 n. 36.

22. In 1908 Wilhelm Braun criticized Denifle's narrow understanding of the concept in Luther with his *Die Bedeutung der Concupiszenz in Luthers Leben und Lehre* (Berlin). See Gordon Rupp, *The Righteousness of God: Luther Studies* (London: Hodder and Stoughton), 24–25.

23. See Karl Holl (1866–1926), "Was verstand Luther unter Religion?," *Gesammelte Aufsätze zur Kirchengeschichte I: Luther* (Tübingen, 1921); Otto Scheel, *Dokumente zur Luthers Entwicklung* (Tübingen, 1911) and Martin Luther: Von Katholizismus zur Reformation (Tübingen, 1916); and, J. M. Reu, *Thirty-five Years of Luther Research*, 1–7.

24. David Steinmetz stated that the shorter *Martin Luther: His Life and His Work* (1955) was distributed by the Knights of Columbus to thousands of public libraries throughout America in *Concordia Journal* 11/2 (1985): 46. The Knights of Columbus could not confirm this action in a letter from Susan H. Brosnan, Archivist for the Knights of Columbus, New Haven to author, 10 July 1989.

25. Extended overviews of the French image of Luther are Ernst Benz, "Das Lutherbild des Franzoesischen Katholizismus," *Zeitschrift für Religions und Geistesgeschichte* 4 (1952): 1–19; Albert Greiner, "Luther vu par les Francias du XIXe du XXe siècles," *Francia* 5 (1977): 708–713; Paul M. Minus, "The Contemporary Catholic Reconsideration of Protestantism in French-speaking Europe" (Ph.D. diss., Yale, 1962); and Stauffer, *Le catholicisme à la découverte de Luther*, 19–38, 91–106.

26. In his *Brève Histoire des Hérésies*, he would describe Luther as "a man of passionate feeling and possessed an ardent and impetuous heart, together with a fertile mind lacking the faculty of clear thought and served by an astounding assurance; his was a popular and captivating eloquence, though often trivial; by temperament he was violent, incapable of restraint, poise of loyalty towards an adversary, and yet a lover of material order, of civil and religious discipline. Added to this, he had a vivid imagination haunted by strange visions and irresistible obsessions; he has sometimes been called the *doctor hyperbolicus*—'the excessive doctor'"; see *Heresies and Heretics*, vol. 136 of *Twentieth Century Encyclopedia of Catholicism*, trans. Roderick Bright (New York: Hawthorne, 1959), 80.

27. See also *Luther et le Lutheranisme*, 4 vols., trans. and ed. Jacques Paquier (Paris: Picard, 1910–13).

28. *Revue Biblique* (1915): 456–484 and (1916): 90–120; see *Luther on the Eve of His Revolt*, trans. W. S. Reilly (New York: Cathedral Library Association, 1918).

29. After serving as the French ambassador to the Vatican from 1945 to 1948, Maritain taught at Princeton University from 1948 to 1956.

30. See chapter 1 of *Integral Humanism: Temporal and Spiritual Problems*, trans. Joseph W. Evans (University of Notre Dame Press, 1969). Yves M.-J. Congar

stated of Maritain's work on Luther that it "is a good example of an a priori method. I doubt that Maritain has read more than thirty pages of Luther. He has not really tried to understand the *positive religious meaning* of his desire for reform" (Patrick Granfield, *Theologians at Work* [New York: Macmillan, 1967], 244).

31. See also his "The Witness of History," *Truth* 35 (February 1931): 20–21 where Clayton makes no attempt to assign coresponsibility for the Reformation to Catholicism. Cf., Joseph Clayton, *The Protestant Reformation in Great Britain* (Milwaukee: Bruce, 1934), 1–33.

32. A most succinct study of the Catholic scholarly attitudes towards Luther can be gained by comparing this article in the *Catholic Encyclopedia* of 1913 with that by John P. Dolan in *New Catholic Encyclopedia* of 1967 (New York: McGraw-Hill). F. M. Quealy stated three years before the emergence of *The New Catholic Encyclopedia* that "Much of the English-speaking church is still being fed on the misconceptions and misrepresentations of the Denifle-Grisar tradition" (*Ecumenist* 3/2 [1964]: 39).

33. The classic history for this period is *A History of the Ecumenical Movement, 1517–1948,* ed. Ruth Rouse and Stephen Charles Neill (Philadelphia: Westminster, 1954); see also William Rausch, *Ecumenism: A Movement Towards Church Unity* (Philadelphia: Fortress, 1985) and Thomas Sartory, *The Oecumenical Movement and the Unity of the Church,* trans. Hilda C. Graef (Westminster: Newman, 1963).

34. Leonard Swidler stated that "the book was to be a supplement to the fourth volume of the periodical *Una Sancta* . . .; because of difficulties with Rome it did not appear as part of *Una Sancta*. Von Martin said, 'What is presented here is no longer an "Una Sancta" periodical: it forgoes for the time the attempt to find a united *objective* ground on which the Christians of separated faiths can meet each other'" ("Catholic Reformation Scholarship," 193).

35. "Was der betende Luther der ganzen Christenheit zu sagen hat" [What Luther has to Say to the Whole of Christendom as a Man of Prayer], *Luther in ökumenischer Sicht,* ed. Alfred von Martin (Stuttgart), 187–188.

36. "Gutes an Luther und Übles an seinen Tadlern [Good Points in Luther and Bad Points in His Critics]," *Luther in ökumenischer Sicht,* ed. Alfred von Martin (Stuttgart), 9–19. Merkle was a pioneer in more scholarly and less polemical Catholic studies of the Enlightenment as well; see Georg Schwaiger, "Catholicism and the Enlightenment," *Progress and Decline in the History of Church Renewal,* vol. 27 of *Concilium: Theology in the Age of Renewal* (New York: Paulist, 1967), 91–92.

37. See Klaus Ganzer, "Der Beitrag Sebastian Merkles zur Entwicklung des katholischen Lutherbildes," *Historisches Jahrbuch* 105/1 (1985): 171–188.

38. His *Die Erforschung der kirchlichen Reformationsgeschichte seit 1876: Leistungen und Aufgaben der deutschen Katholiken* (Münster) reviewed the works of German Catholic scholars from Janssen through 1910. Most recognized for his outstanding history of the Council of Trent, Jedin would therein confirm Merkle's claims for Luther's context in the sixteenth century. He agreed with Kiefl that Luther was an instrument of Providence and also pointed out that Luther is not condemned by name in the Tridentine decrees.

39. *Die Reformation in Deutschland,* 2 vols. (Freiburg-im-Bresgau); subsequent editions came in 1942, 1948, 1962, 1965, and 1982. English translation by

Ronald Walls, *The Reformation in Germany*, 2 vols. (New York: Herder and Herder, 1968). An imprimatur was granted by the bishop of Freiburg in 1948.

40. Lortz's interpretation of the influence of Ockhamism on Luther has been a constant source of scholarly debate. Counterpoints to Lortz and Janz are found in Leif Grane, *Modus Loquendi Theologicus, Luthers Kampf um die Erneuerung der Theologie* (1515–1518) (Leiden: Brill, 1975) and Bernhard Lohse, *Martin Luther: An Introduction to His Life and Work*, trans. Robert Schultz (Philadelphia: Fortress, 1986). John L. Farthing's *Thomas Aquinas and Gabriel Biel* (Durham: Duke University Press, 1988) supports Lortz and Janz by arguing that Gabriel Biel's Pelagian anthropology is quite different than Aquinas's thoroughly Augustinian view (173).

41. *The Reformation: A Problem for Today*, trans. John C. Dwyer (Westminster: Newman, 1964); *How the Reformation Came*, trans. Otto M. Knab (New York: Herder and Herder, 1964). The most succinct statement of his views is found in *Die Reformation: Thesen als Handreichung bei ökumenischen Gesprachen* (Meitangen b. Aug.; 2nd ed., 1946) with English version in *Eastern Churches Quarterly* 7 (1947): 76–91. Some have stated that Lortz encountered problems in republishing *Die Reformation in Deutschland* caused by the church authorities (Iserloh 1966, 12; Wicks 1969a, 276). Jedin speculated that Lortz might have been refused publication for works which would have been immediately translated (1967a, 91).

42. Protestant criticisms of Lortz have often focused on his tendency to excuse Luther for his shortcomings due to the condition of the church as well as Luther's alleged subjectivism and immature grasp of Catholic tradition. Thus, they resent that Luther is ultimately seen to have little theological promise. See Kenneth Hagen, review of *The Reformation in Germany*, *Theological Studies* 30 (1969): 717–719; Leif Grane, *Contra Gabrielem* (Copenhagen, 1962): 28–30; Wilhelm Pauck, "The Catholic Luther," *Luther, Erasmus, and the Reformation* (New York: Fordham University Press, 1969), 52; and idem, "Luther's Catholic Critics," *Union Seminary Quarterly Review* 10 (1955): 1–10.

43. Three vols. (Münster). The work bore an imprimatur. There is no English translation and nearly all copies originally published were burned in an air raid on Munich (Loewenich 1959, 280).

44. Reformation, *Katholische Reform und Gegenreformation*, vol. 4 of *Handbuch der Kirchengeschichte* (Freiburg: Herder, 1967); "The Protestant Reformation," in vol. 5 of *History of the Church*, trans. Anselm Biggs and Peter W. Becker (New York: Seabury, 1980), 3–295, 327–339.

45. *Luther zwischen Reform und Reformation: der Thesenanschlag fand nich statt* Münster: Aschendorff, (1966; 3rd. ed., 1968), trans. Jared Wicks (Boston: Beacon, 1968). Iserloh first presented this claim in a lecture in Mainz on 8 November 1961 (Wicks 1970, 35). Thurman L. Smith affirms Iserloh's thesis with an analysis of the seventeen coins depicting Luther posting the theses (of 750 Reformation-coins struck from the sixteenth century until the present day), arguing that little numismatic attention is paid to the notion of a posting until the two hundredth anniversary of the Reformation in 1717. Smith speculates that Melanchthon's preface to the second volume of Luther's collected works is probably the source of the legend in "Luther and the Iserloh Thesis from a Numismatic Perspective," *Sixteenth Century Journal* 20 (1989): 183–201. Among Iserloh's contributions to the study of Catholic respondents to Luther are *Die Eucharistie in der Darstellung des Johannes Eck* (1950), *Johannes Eck (1486–*

1543): Scholastiker, Humanist, Kontroverstheologe (1981), and the edition of various primary texts in the *Corpus Catholicorum* on Eck (1982) and Johann Dietenberger, OP, (1985) as well as a compendium of secondary studies in *Katholische Theologen der Reformationszeit* (1985).

46. An extended discussion of Protestant reception of this claim is found in Gordon Rupp, review of *Luther zwischen Reform und Reformation*, *Journal of Theological Studies* (1968): 360–369; see also John Jay Hughes in *Journal of Ecumenical Studies* 6 (1969): 443–445 and Steven E. Ozment in *Church History* 38 (1969): 532–533.

47. Rolf Decot is a leading student of Manns; see Decot, "Martin Luther in katholischen Theologie," *Theologie der Gegenwart* 26/2 (1983): 73–83 and Rolf Decot and R. Vinke, *Zum Gedenken an Joseph Lortz (1887–1975)* (Stuttgart: Steiner, 1989).

48. *Du protestantisme à l'Église*, vol. 27 of *Unam Sanctam* (Paris: Éditions du Cerf); the third English edition appeared in 1959, trans. A. V. Littledale (Westminster Newman, 1956).

49. *Le procès Luther 1517–1521* (Paris: Fayard), trans. by John Tonkin (St. Louis: Concordia, 1978). Olivier has also argued that Luther anticipated Theodor W. Adorno's concept of negative dialectic and, correspondingly with an emphasis on Luther's understanding of grace, the solution to modernity's tendency toward nihilism; see "Luther's Challenge to Roman Catholicism," in *Luther and Learning: The Wittenberg University Luther Symposium*, ed. Marilyn J. Harran (London: Associated University Presses, 1984), 115–132.

50. *La Foi de Luther: la cause de l'évangile dans l'Église* (Paris: Beauchesne), trans. John Tonkin (St. Louis: Concordia, 1982).

51. *A la Rencontre du Protestantisme*; cf., Edward F. Hanohoe, *Catholic Ecumenism* (Washington D.C.: Catholic University Press, 1953).

52. Tavard's claim for Luther's short-sighted theology is found extensively in *Holy Writ or Holy Church: The Crisis of the Protestant Reformation* (New York: Harper and Brothers, 1959) where he considers Luther's principle of *sola Scriptura* to break with Christian tradition's that correlated scriptural and ecclesial sources for biblical interpretation (80–89).

53. Kenneth Hagen, review of *Man Yearning for Grace: Luther's Early Spiritual Teaching* in *Theological Studies* 31 (1970): 190–192 and the review by Steven Ozment in *Journal of Ecumenical Studies* 7 (1970): 365–367. Hagen criticizes Wicks for his poorly substantiated contention that Luther lies in a Catholic Augustinian-Bernardine context. Ozment faults Wicks for a short-sighted grasp of Luther's insight, arguing that a more properly constructed formula of Luther's position (to replace *fides caritate formata*) would reveal the authentic foundation of Luther's faith as *fides certitudine promissionis Dei formata*.

54. See Carl E. Braaten, "A Lutheran View of the Catholic Dialogue with Luther," *Dialog* 11 (1972): 299–303.

55. See Donald K. McKim, review of *Luther and His Spiritual Legacy* (Wilmington, DE: Michael Glazier) in *Theological Studies* 45 (1984): 570–571.

56. An overview of the work's central positions is found in Wicks's "Roman Reactions to Luther: The First Year (1518)," *Catholic Historical Review* 69 (1983): 521–562.

57. *Justification, La doctrine de Karl Barth et une réflexion Catholique* (Einsiedeln, 4th ed., 1964), trans. Thomas Collins, Edmund E. Tolk, and David Granskou (New

York: Thomas Nelson, 1964). See John Kiwiet's *Hans Küng, Makers of the Modern Theological Mind* (Waco, TX: Word, 1985), 15–50.

58. "I here gladly, gratefully and publicly testify not only that you have adequately covered all significant aspects of justification treated in the ten volumes of my *Church Dogmatics* published so far [1932–1955], and that you have fully and accurately reproduced my views as I myself understand them; but also that you have brought all this beautifully into focus through your brief yet precise presentation of details and your frequent references to the larger historical context. Furthermore, your readers may rest assured—until such time as they themselves might get into my books—that you have me say what I actually do say and that I mean it in the way you have me say it" (Küng, *Justification*, xix). See the positive reception by Catholics in B. R. Brinkmann, S.J., "Karl Barth and Justification," *Irish Theological Quarterly* 25 (1958): 274–284 and F. T. Gignac, review of *Justification: The Doctrine of Karl Barth and a Catholic Reflection, Review for Religious* 24 (1965): 661–662. Bibliography of additional reactions is available in Pesch 1966, 310.

59. Vol. 1 of *Beiträge zur ökumenischen Theologie*, ed. H. Fries (Munich: Hüber,1967); trans. McSorley, *Luther: Right or Wrong?* (Westminster: Newman; Minneapolis: Augsburg, 1967). This book was the first volume in a new series on ecumenism sponsored by the Ecumenical Institute of the University of Munich. Cf., McSorley, "Luther's Central Concern," *One in Christ* 3 (1967): 429–435.

60. Vol. 2 of *Beiträge zur ökumenischen Theologie*, ed. H. Fries (Munich: Hüber, 1968).

61. His earliest efforts are "Ein katholisches Anliegen an evangelische Darstellungen der Theologie Luthers," *Catholica* 16 (1962): 304–316 and "Freiheitsbegriff und Freiheitslehre bei Thomas von Aquin und Luther," *Catholica* 17 (1963): 197–244.

62. (Mainz: Matthias Grünewald, 1967). The heart of his argument is found in "Existential and Sapiential Theology—the Theological Confrontation between Luther and Thomas Aquinas," *Catholic Scholars Dialogue with Luther* (1970, 61–81). A partial English translation of the dissertation by Gottfried Krodel is *The God Question in Thomas Aquinas and Martin Luther* (Philadelphia: Fortress, 1972).

63. An overview of the consultation is given by Mark Ellingsen, "Ecumenical Consultation on Luther," *Journal of Ecumenical Studies* 19 (1982): 865–867.

64. See "'Ketzerfurst' und 'Vater im Glauben': Die seltsamen Wege katholischer 'Luther-rezeption'," in *Weder Ketzer nach Heileger*, ed. H. F. Geisser (Regensberg: Pustet, 1982).

65. Congar's evaluation of German Catholic Luther-scholarship is available in "Church Reform and Luther's Reform, 1517–1967," *Lutheran World* 14 (1967): 351–359; chapter 17 of *Chrétiens en dialogue*; "L'Église catholique et Luther," *Unité des Chrétiens* 38 (1980): 17–19; and "Encore Luther et l'oecuménisme," *Revue sciences philosophique et théologique* 68 (1984): 115–124.

66. Congar's dynamic ecclesiology, and his indebtedness to Möhler and Newman, is also expressed in a more meditative fashion in "True and False Reform in the Church," *Oratre Fratres* 23 (1948–49): 252–259. Cf., Paul D. L. Avis, *The Church in the Theology of the Reformers* (Atlanta: John Knox, 1981) 21–24.

67. See chapter four of Congar's *Tradition and Traditions: An Historical and Theological Essay*, trans. Michael Naseby and Thomas Rainborough (New York: Macmillan, 1966).

68. See Paul Hacker (1913–79), *Das Ich im Glauben bei Martin Luther* (Graz: Styria, 1966) with English selection by author, *The Ego in Faith: Martin Luther and the Origin of Anthropocentric Religion* (Chicago: Franciscan Herald, 1970); Theobald Beer, *Der fröhliche Wechsel und Streit: Grundzüge der Theologie Martin Luthers* (Einsiedeln: Johannes Verlag, 1980); and Remigius Bäumer, "Das Zeitalter der Glaubensspaltung," in *Kleine deutsche Kirchengeschichte*, ed. Bernhard Kötting (Freiburg: Herder, 1980), 53–79. Discussion of the relative merits of these works is found in Gottfried Maron, "An Evangelical Expression Regarding Catholic Luther Research," in *Luther's Ecumenical Significance*, 59–60 and in Maron, *Das Katholische Lutherbild der Gegenwart*, 30–38. A critical review of Hacker by Jared Wicks is found in *Theological Studies* 28 (1967): 374–376. Critical reviews of Bäumer and Beer by Iserloh are in *Catholica* 36 (1982) 101–114 and by Wicks in *Theological Digest* 31 (1984): 315–324. Beer has stated, for example, that "If the Council of Trent had known about these texts [by Luther concerning Christ's dual natures] there would certainly have been formal condemnations" ("Luther?: Manichean Delirium," *30 Days* 1992/2, 57).

69. Antonio Socci argued that the successors of Lortz exercise collective censorship on opponents of their revised historiography. He cites the adverse treatment of Remigius Bäumer who wrote a critical essay on Luther in a book of church history published on the eve of Pope John Paul's visit to Germany in 1980 as well as the marginalization of Theobald Beer who asserts that Luther rejected the church's doctrines on Trinity, the Incarnation, and the personal unity of Jesus Christ after 1509 ("Luther is 'One of Us'," *30 Days* 1992/2, 60–61).

70. Pesch chronicles various magisterial statements made during the Luther-year of 1983 and considers their sentiments rather inconclusive in "Erträge des Luther-Jahres für die katholische systematische Theologie," in *Zur Bilanz des Lutherjahres*, ed. Peter Manns (Stuttgart: Steiner, 1986).

Chapter 3: Luther and the
Roman Catholic Magisterium in the Sixteenth Century

1. *Readings in Church History*, ed. Coleman J. Barry (Westminster: Newman, 1985), 705.

2. "Cardinal Pole's Eirenikon," trans. Vincent McNabb, *Dublin Review* 198 (January 1936): 152. Reginald Pole (1500–58), last Catholic Archbishop of Canterbury, was one of three presiding papal legates at the council.

3. Indulgences were not preached in Wittenberg to avoid competing with Elector Frederick whose relic collection there was a source of personal pride and the community's spiritual activity. Robert E. McNally also notes that the rivalry between Elector Frederick and the House of Hohenzollern precluded their toleration of any aid to Albrecht, the latter's rising star ("The Ninety-five Theses of Martin Luther, 1517–1967," *Theological Studies* 28 [1967]: 448). Extensive accounts of events before October 1517 are given in Martin Brecht, *Martin Luther: His Road to the Reformation, 1483–1521*, trans. James Schaff (Philadelphia: Fortress, 1985); Robert Herndon Fife, *The Revolt of Martin Luther* (New York: Columbia University Press, 1957); Scott H. Hendrix, *Luther and the Papacy: Stages in a Reformation Conflict* (Philadelphia: Fortress, 1981); and Erwin

Iserloh in *Reformation and Counter Reformation*, trans. Anselm Biggs and Peter W. Becker (New York: Crossroad, 1980).

4. See Nikolaus Paulus, *Geschichte des Ablasses in Mittelalter*, 3 vols. (1922–23) and *Indulgences as a Social Factor in the Middle Ages*, trans. J. Elliot Ross (1922).

5. The tenuous theological and canonical claim for papal jurisdiction over the faithful in purgatory is discussed in Robert W. Shaffern, "Learned Discussions of Indulgences for the Dead in the Middle Ages," *Church History* 61 (1992): 367–381. Shaffern posits an alliance of Albert and Thomas Aquinas with successive proponents of papal jurisdiction against Bonaventure and successive opponents of papal jurisdiction. Shaffern later discusses popular appreciation and practice of indulgences as a saintly imitation of Christ in "Indulgences and Saintly Devotionalisms in the Middle Ages," *Catholic Historical Review* 84 (1998): 643–661.

6. "Sobald das Geld in Kasten klingt; Die Seele aus dem Fegfeuer springt." See thesis 27.

7. The fact that ecclesiastical-monarchical relations stymied the enforcement of the magisterial policies regarding Luther and his followers is discussed in William J. Wright, "Mainz versus Rome: Two Responses to Luther in the 1520s," *Archiv für Reformationsgeschichte* 82 (1991): 83–104. Wright contends that insufficient curial understanding of Albrecht's qualifications coupled with its overestimation of Charles V's *imperium*, which was expected to be a remedy on the order of the relatively successful Spanish Inquisition, aided the Lutheran challenge.

8. The original summons is lost but a probable facsimile is found in Robert E. McNally, "The Roman Process of Martin Luther: A Failure in Subsidiarity" in *The Once and Future Church: A Communion of Freedom*, ed. James A. Coriden (New York: Alba, 1971), 120–123.

9. Leo's *Postquam ad aures* of 23 August had ordered Cajetan to detain Luther pending further orders while his *Cum nuper* of 11 September introduced the procedure of a hearing, not to say debate (Iserloh 1980, 55–56). It is commonly argued that Rome's need for Frederick's support in imperial decisions concerning a tax to fund a war with the Turks and the impending election of a new emperor prompted the concession.

10. See Luther's account of Augsburg in *Luther's Works* 41: 253–92.

11. See a crisp account of the Leipzig Disputation in James Atkinson, *The Trial of Luther* (New York: Stein and Day, 1971), 60–78.

12. See H. Roos, "Die Quellen der Bulle 'Exsurge Domine'," *Theologie in Geschichte und Gegenwart*, ed. J. Auer and H. Volk (Munich: Zink, 1957), 909–926.

13. Jesuamirtham Narchison argues that this invocation demonstrates the success of papal restoration after the conciliarist controversies, from the Council of Florence (1438–45) to Lateran V (1512–17) in "Papal Authority in *Exsurge Domine*" (PhD diss., Lutheran School of Theology at Chicago, 1974), 44–45. He argues further that the extended reference to the affiliation of Germany and the papacy is a Roman assertion of ultimate authority in the Holy Roman Empire which is traceable to the *translation imperii* of Pope Innocent III in 1202 when the pope intervened to settle the German civil war thus establishing the primacy of church over state (105–106).

14. The illegitimacy of appeals to a general council over papal authority was established by Pope Pius II (1405–64, pope from 19 August 1458) in the bull *Execrabilis* (18 January 1460).

15. Prierias's statements regarding the papacy are often extreme, as one reads in his *Summa summarium*, "And if at any time a temporal emperor has given [something] to the pope as Constantine did to Sylvester, it is not a donation but a restitution. Conversely, however, if the pope has given [something] to the emperor it was not in recognition of his supremacy but only for the conservation of the peace. Imperial power is conceded by God. It is from God mediately through the pope" (Scionti 1967, 95).

16. See *Vollständige Reformations Acta und Documenta* II, ed. Valentin Ernst Locher (Leipzig, 1723), 14–15.

17. The demise of conciliarism and the evolution of strongly papal thought is associated with Nicholas of Cusa (1401–64) and the classical restorationist, Juan de Torquemada (1563–1624) with his *Summa de ecclesia* (1453). See Steven Ozment, *The Age of Reform, 1250–1550* (New Haven: Yale University Press, 1980), 172–179.

18. This conviction was already at work in the *Misuse* and in the *Divine Institution of the Pontifical Office*, where he took up "the subject of the rightful primacy of Peter and his successors, the Roman pontiffs, a primacy held in possession for untold ages in the resplendent light of the Gospel but now assailed by arguments upsetting those less grounded in Scripture" (Wicks 1978, 105). Cajetan's *Five Articles of Luther—Justification for Their Condemnation* of 1521, a defense of five condemnations from *Exsurge Domine* which had merited criticism by Catholics, also demonstrated a more deliberate and consistent reference to scripture. Four of the five articles concern themes and positions which surfaced at Augsburg and are already discussed herein (Ibid., 145–152).

19. See Peter Fabisch, "Johannes Eck and die Publikationen der Bullen 'Exsurge Domine' und 'Decet Romanum Pontificem'," *Johannes Eck (1486–1543) im Streit der Jahrhunderte*, ed. Erwin Iserloh (Münster: Aschendorff, 1988), 74–107.

20. Against Luther's and Karlstadt's conclusion that Eck had contradicted himself by vacillating on the legitimate activity of the will apart from grace, Walter Moore argues that Eck's nuanced distinctions were unappreciated by the reformers ("Protean Man: Did John Eck Contradict Himself at Leipzig?," *Harvard Theological Review* 72 [1979]: 245–266). A helpful synopsis of Luther's stance on the papacy just before and at Leipzig is found in Zdenko Zlatar's "On the origins of Luther's break with Rome: a badly-put question," *Parergon* 14 (1996): 57–84.

21. Brecht understates the situation wonderfully when he states that "It is difficult for one to call this viewpoint [of Luther] an essentially revolutionary one, although it did stand in extreme tension with the dominant theory of the church at that time" (322).

22. Publication details can be found in Nelson H. Minnich's "On the Origins of Eck's 'Enchiridion'," in *Johannes Eck (1486—1543) im Streit der Jahrhunderte*, ed. Erwin Iserloh (Münster: Aschendorff, 1988), 37–73.

23. His most vehement work is found in *Against the Roman Papacy, An Institution of the Devil* of 1545 (*Luther's Works* 41: 257–376). See chapter four of Mark U. Edwards, *Luther's Last Battles: Politics and Polemics, 1531–46* (Ithaca: Cornell University Press, 1983).

24. The emergence of imperial visitations to assure that parishes in electoral Saxony and Hesse conformed to evangelical theology in preaching, morality, and church administration also demonstrated a decisive break from Catholic authority. Instructions for visitation by Elector John of Saxony in spring 1526 and 1527

were complemented by Philip Melanchthon's "Instruction to the Visitors of Pastors" in March 1528 (Johann M. Reu, *The Augsburg Confession* [Chicago: Wartburg, 1930], 4–23).

25. A brief history and useful collection of pertinent documents is found in Reu's *The Augsburg Confession*. The *Confutatio* would reject the twenty-eight articles of the *Confessio*, echoing the now standard arguments for the meritorious value of good works, the hierarchical-historical nature of the church, and eucharistic sacrifice and transubstantiation, among other doctrines. See *Die Confutatio der Confessio Augustana, Corpus Catholicorum 33*, ed. Herbert Immenkötter (Münster: Aschendorff, 1979) and Edward D. O'Connor, "The Catholic Response to the Augsburg Confession," *Communio (US)* 7 (1980): 178–186.

26. John Eck believed that most doctrinal disagreements between Lutherans and Catholics were more verbal than real and asserted that there were ways which Lutheran positions could be interpreted acceptably. For the most part, this first colloquy between the German Lutherans and Catholics dissolved because of the clash of biblical and ecclesial principles of authority, especially concerning whether the church had been delegated by Christ to allow or forbid communion in the chalice (Catholics) or whether the biblical institutions of the eucharist mandated the chalice for all (Lutheran). See Jared Wicks, "The Lutheran *forma ecclesiae* in the Colloquy at Augsburg, August 1530," in *Christian Authority*, ed. G. R. Evans (Oxford: Clarendon, 1988), 160–203.

27. Dermot Fenlon, *Heresy and Obedience in Tridentine Italy: Cardinal Pole and the Counter-Reformation* (Cambridge: Cambridge University Press, 1972), 46–47. Fenlon states that these evangelical Catholics were committed to (1) refuting a false dichotomy in the Lutherans' opposition of scriptural and ecclesial authorities, (2) refuting antipapal applications of scriptural primacy, and (3) integrating scripture more fully in the life of the church. Jedin testifies to the general preoccupation with justification by faith in the 1530s (366–367).

28. Matheson states that "Surprising, at first sight at least, is the relatively high estimate which Contarini had of Eck, although he had, of course, the advantage of not knowing him very well" (94). His judgment of the Catholic controversialists is particularly harsh as he states that "Their message was a dourly traditionalist one, their style painfully pedestrian, their reactions of Pavlovian predictability" (4).

29. Luther's rejection of the article on justification ought to have been expected in light of his general opposition to ambiguous statements of evangelical doctrine that might transgress the *Confessio Augustana* (1530); this is particularly evident in his *Smalcaldic Articles* (1536) which express evangelical identity in Luther's own thought. Kenneth Hagen argues that this statement ought to be seen as a personal testament of Luther's as well as a confessional document of Lutherans insofar as it professes publicly, in the manner of patristic *ennaratio*, the essential Christian doctrine. See "The Historical Context of the Smalcald Articles," *Concordia Theological Quarterly* 51 (October 1987): 245–253.

30. See Luther's *Against the Roman Papacy, An Institution of the Devil* of March 1545 in *Luther's Works* 41: 257–376. Luther's bitter estimation of the council's integrity is appreciated in light of the council's tardy appearance after he was first apprised of its coming in a personal visit from the papal representative Peter Vergerio on 13 November 1535; this announcement was followed in December 1536 by the *Articles of Smalcalden*. The League of Smalcalden rejected participation in February 1537 (Jedin, *History I*, 298). Historical surveys are found in

Erwin Iserloh, "Luther and the Council of Trent," *Catholic Historical Review* LXIX (1983): 563–576; Robert McNally, "The Council of Trent and the German Protestants," *Theological Studies* 25 (1964): 1–22; and, Wilhelm Pauck, "Protestant Reactions to the Council of Trent" in *The Heritage of the Reformation* (New York: Oxford University Press, 1968), 145–161.

31. See George Tavard, *Holy Writ or Holy Church: The Crisis of the Protestant Reformation* (New York: Harper, 1959), 195–209.

32. In scholastic thought, a cause is "anything responsible for change, motion or action" (*Dictionary of Philosophy*, 1960 ed., s.v. "Cause"). Aquinas, based on Aristotle, asserted that there are four essential causes which are conditions of all being: the formal, material, final, and efficient causes. The formal and material causes are *intrinsic*, that is, they are constitutive of a thing. The formal cause is the pattern by which a thing is made; for Trent, it is the justice of God. The material cause is the actual material out of which a thing is made; Trent refers to the "meritorious cause" of Christ crucified. The final and efficient causes are *extrinsic* causes as they are external to the thing itself. The final (and most important cause) defines the purpose or goal of a thing; in this case, the glory of God and of Christ and life everlasting. The efficient cause brings the thing into existence; in this case, God *per se*. The principle of efficient causality states further that everything that exists does so through the agency of an already existing thing. An efficient cause actively brings something new into being. Aquinas conceived efficient causality to be twofold. The *principal efficient cause* makes the effect according to the formal cause. Thus God justifies persons according to his justice. The *instrumental efficient cause* is subordinate to the principal efficient cause and brings about the effect insofar as it carries the motion of the agent (*Summa theologiae* III. 62. 1). Herein lies the significance of the sacraments of baptism and penance for Catholics. In stating that sacraments are the causes of justifying grace, Trent, like Aquinas, asserted that sacraments are the efficient causes of grace. God is the principal efficient cause and the sacrament, as a sign in itself, is the instrumental efficient cause.

33. Canons 4–9 place a special edge on the council's rejection of Luther while preserving the policy of not denoting particular reformers by name. Rejection of the theory of double justice posited by Seripando at the council is chronicled in Hubert Jedin, *Papal Legate at the Council of Trent: Cardinal Seripando*, trans. Frederic C. Eckhoff (St. Louis: Herder, 1947), 326–392. The unique significance of this most thoughtful conciliar document is attested to in Giuseppe Alberigo, "The Council of Trent: New Views on the Occasion of the Fourth Centenary," in *Concilium: Theology in the Age of Renewal* 7 (Glen Rock, NJ: Paulist, 1965), 6.

34. The brief debate regarding indulgences is discussed in Peter J. Beer, "What Price Indulgences?," *Theological Studies* 39 (1978): 526–535.

35. A brief history of catechetics is found in Joseph A. Jungmann, *Handing on the Faith: A Manual of Catechetics*, trans. A. N. Fuerst (New York: Herder and Herder, 1959).

36. The investigation of Tridentine spiritual classics offers another avenue for assessing the impact of the conciliar teachings. Saint Francis de Sales (1567–1622), for example, begins Book III of his treatise *On the Love of God* by stating that "The sacred Council of Trent assures us that the friends of God, proceeding from virtue to virtue, are day by day renewed, that is, they increase by good works in the justice which they have received by God's grace and are more and more

justified, according to those heavenly admonitions; He that is just let him be justified still: and he that is holy, let him be sanctified still (Apocalypse 12:11)" (*The Book of Christian Classics*, ed. Michael Williams [New York: Liveright, 1933], 225).

37. A discussion of effective Catholic catechesis in contrast to a less effective Protestant counterpart is presented in Geoffrey Parker, "Success and Failure During the First Century of the Reformation," *Past and Present* 136 (1992): 41–82.

38. While the catechisms were generally unpolemical, Canisius's *Falsifications of the Word of God* (1571) heartily countered Flacius Illyricus's *The Magdeburg Centuries* (1559–74) which argued that the Lutheran church is the church of the apostles (Brodrick 1935, 664–711). In July 1577, Luther himself merited an uncharacteristic barb from the Dutch Jesuit who referred to the reformer as "a hog in heat" (Brodrick 1935, 744).

39. See Gustavo Galeota, "Genesi, Sviluppo e Fortuna delle *Controversiae* di Roberto Bellarmino," in *Bellarmino e la Controriforma*, ed. Romeo di Maio et al (Sora: Centro di Studi Sorani, 1990), 6–48.

40. Comparison to Athanasius is made by Alban Goodier, "Bellarmine: Defender of the Faith," *Month* 157 (1931): 482. Bellarmine's strongly papal ecclesiology is evident in his *De potestate Summi Pontificis in rebus temporalibus* (1610) and *De officio principis christiani* (1598).

Chapter 4: Luther and the
Roman Catholic Magisterium in the Twentieth Century

1. *L'Osservatore Romano*, 1 June 1987, 4(E).
2. *Acta Sanctae Sedis* 4: 132–136. Earlier Pius IX's Holy Office had forbidden English Catholic participation in London's *Association for the Promotion of the Unity of Christendom*, founded in 1857, because the non-Catholics had presumed a catholicity of faith which the Holy See determined to exist only in the Roman communion. The Anglican sponsors were thereby considered heretics. See *Apostolicae sedi* (16 September 1864) in *Acta Sanctae Sedis* 2: 657–622 with English translation by Edward Hanahoe, S.A. in *Unity Studies* 14 (1954): 7–10. The Holy Office later reiterated "by an absolute necessity, that the faith and communion of the Roman Church be accepted." This assertion to 198 Anglican clerics who had responded to the earlier declaration is found in *Quod vos* of 8 November 1865 (Hanahoe 1954, 11–16). On 4 September 1869 Pius IX reinforced his earlier remarks; he told Archbishop Henry Edward Manning of Westminster, who had been queried as to the possibilities of Protestant justification of their beliefs at the council by a Scottish minister, that "by the inspiration of divine grace, they [non-Catholic dissenting Christians] shall perceive their own danger, and shall seek God with their whole heart, they will easily cast away all preconceived and adverse opinions; and, laying aside all desire of disputation, they will return to the Father from whom they have long unhappily gone astray" ("Per Ephemerides," *Unitas* 11/2 [1959]: 135).
3. Leo seemed to encourage non-Catholic reunion by conversions in the United States as he stated, regarding Protestant dissenters, that "Surely we ought not to desert them nor leave them to their fancies; but with mildness and charity draw

them to us, using every means of persuasion to induce them to examine closely every part of Catholic doctrine, and to free themselves from preconceived notions"; *Acta Sanctae Sedis* 27: 387–399; English translation in Carlen 2: 369.

4. Leo likened the difficulties of the modern age to the spirit of revolution and the consequent loss of faith and decline in morals in his *Militantis ecclesiae* of 1 August 1897 which celebrated the third centenary of the death of St. Peter Canisius; *Acta Sanctae Sedis* 30: 3–9 with English translation in Carlen 2: 419–423.

5. *Provida matris* (5 May 1895) dedicated a novena for Christian unity on the nine days between the feasts of Ascension and Pentecost (*Acta Sanctae Sedis* 27: 645–647). *Divinum illud munus* mandated this practice annually for the universal church (Leo XIII 1981, 2: 416).

6. Randolph Harrison McKim, Episcopal Rector at the Church of the Epiphany at Washington D.C., argued against the historical validity of papal infallibility and considered Pope Leo XIII to be "helplessly in the grip of the absolutism which he represents"; see *Leo XIII at the Bar of History* (Washington, DC: Gibson, 1897), 12.

7. An interpretation of Pius X's profound rejection of Luther is found in Liam Brophy's "St Pius X—The Embodied Counter-reformation," *Social Justice Review* 47 (June 1954): 75–78.

8. Pius IX's *Apostolicae sedi* and *Quod vos* are cited as precedents in *Acta Apostolicae Sedis* 11 (1919): 309–316.

9. The octave received extension and indulgences with *Romanorum pontificem* of 25 February 1916; see *Acta Apostolicae Sedis* 9 (1917): 61–62. The motu proprio *Orientalis catholici* of 15 October 1917 erected the Oriental Institute; *Acta Apostolicae Sedis* 9 (1917): 531–533.

10. The militant tone of Pius XI's encyclical was echoed in many parish pulpits shortly thereafter. See, for example, the sermon by Francis X. Talbot, SJ, at Saint Ignatius Church, Manhattan in *Catholic Mind* 26 (1928): 73–79. Various styles of Protestant disappointment are introduced in Oliver Stratford Tomkins, "The Roman Catholic Church and the Ecumenical Movement, 1910–1948," in *A History of the Ecumenical Movement, 1517–1948* (Philadelphia Westminster, 1967), 682–684.

11. Rev. Henry St. John, OP, maintains that Pius XII was able to accelerate Catholic ecumenical involvement because the long-standing ecclesiological concerns of Catholics had finally been matched seriously by Protestant ecclesiological awareness at the world ecumenical conferences at Oxford and Edinburgh in 1937; see "The Catholic Church and Ecumenism," *Blackfriars* 33 (1952): 411–420.

12. Like his predecessors, Pius XII found it easier to recognize the legitimacy of Eastern non-Catholics who had maintained apostolic succession. See, for example, *Orientalis ecclesiae* (9 April 1944) in *Acta Apostolicae Sedis* 36 (1944): 129–144; English translation in *The Papal Encyclicals*, 5 vols, ed. Claudia Carlen (Wilmington, NC: McGrath), 4: 81–88; and *Sempiternus rex Christus* (8 September 1951) in *Acta Apostolicae Sedis* 43 (1951) 625–644; English translation in ibid., 4: 203–211.

13. Illustration of previous directives for practical Catholic ecumenism is found in T. Lincoln Bouscaren, SJ, "Co-operation with Non-Catholics Legislation," *Theological Studies* 3 (1942): 475–512. Developments in Catholic cooperation with non-Catholics are explored further in John Courtney Murray, SJ, "Intercredal Co-operation: Some Further Views," *Theological Studies* 4 (1943): 100–111 and

"Intercredal Co-operation: Its Theory and Organization," *Theological Studies* 4 (1943): 257–286.

14. Earlier reiteration of ecclesiastical authorization of Catholic participation in non-Catholic ecumenical affairs is found in the Holy Office's *Cum compertum* of 5 June 1948 in *Acta Apostolicae Sedis* 40 (1948): 257 with English translation in *Homiletic and Pastoral Review* 49 (1948): 71.

15. George Tavard highlights the importance of the term "separated brethren" when he highlights the fact that the councils use of *fratres sejuncti* rather than *fratres separati* presents a relationship of estrangement rather than strict separation, thus demonstrating the active presupposition of partial communion throughout the council's deliberations; see "Reassessing the Reformation," *One in Christ* 19 (1983): 360.

16. Avery Dulles notes that the former Cardinal Montini's Lenten letter to the archdiocese of Milan in 1962 mirrored John XXIII's goals for the council; see "Pope Paul's Ecumenical Perspective," *Catholic World*, October 1964: 15–16.

17. The idea of a council had twice been presented to Pope Pius XII and it seems that John XXIII had counsel on 2 November 1958 with Cardinal Ernesto Ruffini who had, with Cardinal Alfredo Ottaviani, lobbied Pius XII. See Peter Hebblethwaite, *Pope John XXIII: Shepherd of the Modern World* (Garden City, NY: Doubleday, 1985), 306–324.

18. The official modification from "brothers of separated Churches" to "the faithful of separated communities" is discussed in Hebblethwaite 1985, 320–324.

19. Pope John XXIII's conceptualization of a return to Catholic communion is clearly evident in *Ad Petri Cathedram* (29 June 1959) as well as *Aeterna Dei sapientia* (11 November 1961). Identical affirmations are found in his first public address of 29 October 1958 and coronation homily of 4 November 1958; see *Hac trepida hora* in *Acta Apostolicae Sedis* 50 (1958): 839–841; English translation in *The Pope Speaks* 5 (1958–59): 135–138; and, *Venerabiles Fratres* in *Acta Apostolicae Sedis* 50 (1958): 884–888; English translation in *The Pope Speaks* 5 (1958–59): 139–142. See also his exhortation to Rev. Angelus Delahunt, Superior General of the Franciscan Friars of the Atonement, during the Chair of Unity Octave 1959 in *The Pope Speaks* 6 (1960): 85–86.

20. Cf., *Aeterna Dei sapientia* (11 November 1961) § 40: "But mark this well: unless the faithful remain bound together by the same ties of virtue, worship, and sacrament, and all hold fast to the same belief, they cannot be perfectly united with the Divine Redeemer, the universal Head, so as to form with Him one visible and living Body," in *The Papal Encyclicals*, 5 vols., ed. Claudia Carlen (Wilmington, NC: McGrath, 1981), 5: 95.

21. Rejection of past polemics and expectant hope for future dialogues are evident in the popes remarks to observers in Session III; see *Cette nouvelle recontre* (29 September 1964) in *The Pope Speaks* 10 (1965): 127–129. See remarks near the close of the council, *Voici que* (4 December 1965) in *The Pope Speaks* 11 (1966): 36–40.

22. See Alois Grillmeier, "Chapter II: The People of God," in *Commentary on the Documents of Vatican II*, 5 vols., ed. Herbert Vorgrimler (New York: Herder and Herder, 1967), 1: 171–175; and, Joseph Ratzinger, *Theological Highlights of Vatican II*, trans. Henry Traub et al (New York: Paulist, 1966), 44–49.

23. Protestant recognition of the opportunity for Christian unity provided by the council is evident in Carl E. Braaten, "Rome, Reformation, and Reunion," *Una Sancta* 23/2 (1966): 3–8; *Vatican Council II: The New Direction*, ed. Oscar

Cullmann (New York: Harper and Row, 1968); Robert E. Cushman [observer for the World Methodist Council], "Prospects of Ecumenism," *Duke Divinity School Review* 30 (Winter 1965): 59–74; Charles J. Keating, "The Implications of the New Climate," *Princeton Seminary Bulletin* (February 1967): 15–18; *Dialogue on the Way*, ed. George Lindbeck [observer for the Lutheran World Federation] (Minneapolis: Augsburg, 1965); and, *Challenge … and Response: A Protestant Perspective of the Vatican Council*, ed. Warren Quanbeck (Minneapolis: Augsburg, 1966).

24. An example of the pope's own reconsideration of divisive Christian history is found in his *Sacrorum indulgentiarum doctrinae* (1 January 1967) which established norms for the postconciliar practice of indulgences and included a frank admission that they had occasionally been granted too readily in the past for "sordid purposes of gain"; see *The Pope Speaks* (1967): 54–63.

25. A catalogue of the pope's highly symbolic meetings is found in Brian Hearne's "Pope Paul VI and Christian Unity," *Doctrine and Life* 28 (1978): 585–596. Especially interesting for Catholic relations with Protestant Christians is the pope's visit to the World Council of Churches at Geneva in June 1969; see Cardinal Willebrands's "Importance of an Ecumenical Visit," *L'Osservatore Romano*, 26 June 1969, 5(E). A review of Catholic participation in ecumenical dialogues is found in Cardinal Willebrands' "Ecumenism: The Mixed Commissions and Their First Results," *L'Osservatore Romano*, 10 January 1974, 4(E); and, "Ecumenical Dialogue Today: An Overview," *Origins*, 28 January 1988, 565–573.

26. The English translations of the German "Er mag uns darin gemeinsamer Lehrer sein" are insufficient as they reduce substantially the new assessment of the reformer. For example, the translation in *American Benedictine Review* read "In this we could all learn from him that God must always remain the Lord. . . ." (209).

27. Hans Küng urged that excommunications be lifted from all reformers in May 1977 in *Toward Vatican III: The Work That Needs to Be Done*, ed. David Tracy et al (New York: Seabury, 1978), 78.

28. Michaelis had first proposed lifting the excommunication in a letter to Cardinal Bea during the interim between the first and second sessions of Vatican II. Later, he proposed formal revocation of excommunication to occur on 3 January, 1971, 450 years after the formal excommunication by *Decet Romanum pontificem*; see *Materialdienst des Konfessionskundlichen Instituts* 21 (1970): 34–36 and "Die Kontroversen um die Bannaufhebung," *Concilium* 12 (1976): 525–533. The VELKD's directing body declined, stating that it is "not the function of the VELKD's directing body to pressure the Vatican in such difficult theological and juridical matters" (*Lutheran World Federation Report* 22/79: 13). In an interview on Vatican Radio in the fall of 1965, German Lutheran pastor Max Lackmann suggested a retrial of Martin Luther regarding excommunication, which he termed "premature and harsh" (*Tablet*, 16 October 1965, 1168). A summary of Catholic and Lutheran reactions to the idea of revoking the excommunication is found in Erwin Iserloh's "Aufhebung des Lutherbannes?," *Lutherprozess und Lutherbann*, ed. Remigius Bäumer (Münster: Aschendorff, 1972), 69–80.

29. While the thoughts of Pope John Paul I, Pope Paul VI's immediate and short-lived successor, cannot be known, the reaffirmation of an ecumenical outreach based on an ecclesiology of communion is evident in the traditional "Urbi et

Orbi" speechof 27 August 1978 (*Origins*, 7 September 1978, 180) and the installation homily of 3 September 1978 (*Origins*, 14 September 1978, 196).

30. High interest in Luther is also espressed on 31 May, 1980 to Christian leaders in Paris (*L'Osservatore Romano*, 9 June 1980, 3E) and on 29 April 1985 to leaders of the American Lutheran Church (*L'Osservatore Romano*, 13 May 1985, 8–9E).

31. The issue of formal Catholic recognition of the *Confessio Augustana* was a very significant ecumenical debate from the time of its first proposal to the Roman Catholic-Lutheran Joint Commission in January 1974 by Vinzenz Pfnür and the subsequent affirmation by the Ecumenical Episcopal Commission of Münster in June 1974 and the Lutheran World Federation in June 1977 at Dar-es-Salaam. Despite a significant force of consensus regarding Catholic, including Archbishop Joseph Ratzinger of Munich, recognition of the common Lutheran confession as a common statement of faith did not occur formally, in large measure because of the prematurity for ecclesiastical links on other levels which such an extraordinary measure would demand. See Walter Kasper, "The Augsburg Confession in Roman Catholic Perspective," *LWF Report* 6/7 (December 1979): 163–187; Harding Meyer et al, "Roman Catholic 'Recognition' of the Confessio Augustana," *LWF Report* 9 (June 1980): 117–122; and, Vinzenz Pfnür, "Anerkennung der Confessio Augustana durch die katholische Kirche?," *Internationale katholische Zeitschrift* 4/4 (1975): 298–307.

32. This assessment on Luther's excommunication is consistent with that of Cardinal Joseph Ratzinger, prefect of the Congregation for the Doctrine of the Faith in "Luther and the Unity of the Churches," *Communio* 11 (1984): 213. The concern for Luther's excommunication from Lutherans was still active after Pope Paul VI's response to the Memorandum of Worms in 1971. In July 1979 Dr. Reinhard Leuze, lecturer in systematic theology at Munich, sought revocation of Luther's excommunication for the five hundredth anniversary of his birth in "Den Bann über Luther aufheben," *Lutherische Monatshefte*, July 1979: 404–407. In a remarkable gesture on 1 March 1986, Rev. Boerre Knudsen of Balsfjord, Norway, a participant in an international pro-life conference at Rome, knelt before the pope at the Vatican and requested Luther's release from excommunication; see *Lutheran World Information* 10/86 (1986): 4. Professor Won Young Ji of Luther Seminary at Seoul protested any such Lutheran request in *Lutheran World Information* 13/86 (1986): 6 and *Concordia Journal*, November 1986, 203–204.

33. The assertion of the independent and nonobligatory character of dialogue commissions vis-à-vis the magisterium is found, for example, in Cardinal Willebrands, "Panorama of the Ecumenical Scene to 1971," *L'Osservatore Romano*, 16 November 1972, 7(E); "Ecumenism: The Mixed Commissions and Their First Results," *L'Osservatore Romano*, 10 January 1974, 4(E); and "Address to the Convention of the Lutheran Church in America (3 July 1984)," ed. William G. Rusch (New York: Lutheran Church of America, n.d.), 10–11.

34. An overview of the issues and documents produced is found in "Lutheran/ Roman Catholic Discussion of the Augsburg Confession," *Lutheran World Report* 10 (August 1982).

35. The Secretariat requested Rev. Kothgasser's opinion as is evident in a letter from Alois M. Kothgasser, SDB, to author, 9 September 1993.

36. Michael B. Lukens argues that the report of Johann Landau, the Catholic apothecary who treated Luther on his deathbed, confirms the accuracy of Jonas's

report in "Luther's Death and the Secret Catholic Report," *Journal of Theological Studies* 41 (1990): 545–563.

37. Supporting documents for positions of the German Ecumenical Study Group were published in 1989–90 and are available in English as *Justification by Faith: Do the Sixteenth-Century Condemnations Still Apply?*, ed. Karl Lehmann and trans. Michael Root and William G. Rusch (New York: Continuum, 1997).

38. "Evaluation for the Pontifical Council for Promoting Christian Unity of the Study Lehrverurteilungen — kirchentrennend?," (Vatican City: Pontifical Council for Promoting Christian Unity, 1992, photocopy), 92.

39. *Constitutions of Lateran IV* § 21 in Tanner 1990, 245. Kilian McDonnell, OSB, argues that Lateran IV (1215) and Luther share the same concern for a pastorally sensitive recollection of sins and that abuses were spawned from imprudent applications of Lateran IV's doctrine and the standards of subsequent confessional manuals. Thus, McDonnell argues, Luther and Angelus de Clavisio's *Summa de casibus conscientiae*, which he burned with *Exsurge Domine* and canon law in December 1520, both reject in principle merely juridical approaches to penance; see "The *Summae Confessorum* on the Integrity of Confession as Prolegomena for Luther and Trent," *Theological Studies* 54 (1993): 405–26.

40. The Vatican's Congregation for the Doctrine of the Faith offered an analysis of remaining issues on justification itself, naming three issues. First, how can Luther's anthropology that specifies persons as simultaneously acceptable to God and sinful be reconciled with Catholic anthropology that posits a true transformation of the Christian? Second, how can the doctrine of justification function with singular importance in Lutheran ecclesiology and be integrated into the more complex Catholic ecclesiology with its Trinitarian, Christological, and sacramental differences? Finally, what might the churches discover upon extending biblical investigations of justification beyond the Pauline corpus? See "Official Catholic Response to Joint Declaration," *Origins* 28: 130–32.

Chapter 5: Perspective

1. Directory for the Application of Principles and Norms on Ecumenism (25 March 1993) § 18 (Washington, DC: United States Catholic Conference, 1993).

2. See a summary of the document's salient points in Cardinal Joseph Ratzinger's "Ultimately there is one basic ecclesiology," *L'Osservatore Romano*, 17 June 1992, 1, 10(E).

3. In addition to the acrimony acknowledged by Cardinal Cassidy, see Peter Hebblethwaite, "Rome reduces ecumenism to 'return to Rome'," *National Catholic Reporter*, 2 October 1992, 14.

4. The upshot of this prophetic image is reformational rather than hagiographical as was the case in Melanchthon's eulogy at Luther's funeral on 22 February 1546. See *Corpus Reformatorum* 11 (Braunschweig, 1834), 726–34 with English translation in *A Melanchthon Reader*, trans. Ralph Keen (New York: Peter Lang, 1988), 89–96.

5. Specific extension of Christ's prophetic office beyond the hierarchy to the laity is found in *Lumen gentium* (1964) § 35 and *Apostolicam actuositatem* (1964) § 9. Pope John Paul II teaches likewise regarding theologians in *Redemptor hominis* (1979) § 19.

6. See Yves M.-J. Congar, *The Word and the Spirit*, trans. David Smith (San Francisco: Harper and Row, 1986).

References

Accattoli, Luigi. 1998. *When a Pope Asks Forgiveness*. Translated by Jordan Aumann. New York: Alba House.

Adrian VI. 1969. Instruction to the nuncio Chieregati. In *The Catholic Reformation: Savonarola to Ignatius Loyola*, edited by John C. Olin. Westminster: Christian Classics.

Ahern, Eugene. 1966. The Ecumenical Spirit of the First Vatican Council. *Irish Ecclesiastical Record* 5/106:265–285.

Alberigo, Giuseppe. 1988. The Council of Trent. In *Catholicism in Early Modern History*, edited by John O'Malley. St. Louis: Center for Reformation Research.

Atkinson, James. 1970. Review of *Luther: Right or Wrong?* by Harry J. McSorley. *Scottish Journal of Theology* 23:99–101.

———. 1971. *Trial of Luther*. New York: Stein and Day.

———. 1983. *Martin Luther: Prophet to the Church Catholic*. Grand Rapids: Eerdmans.

Aubert, Roger. 1981. Ultramontane Progress and Final Gallican Resistance. In *The Church in the Age of Liberalism*. Vol. 8 of *History of the Church*, edited by Hubert Jedin. New York: Crossroad.

Bagchi, David V. N. 1991. *Luther's Earliest Opponents, Catholic Controversialists, 1518–1525*. Minneapolis: Fortress.

Barry, Coleman J., ed. 1985. *Readings in Church History*. Westminster: Newman.

Bea, Augustin. 1964. *Unity in Freedom: Reflections on the Human Family*. New York: Harper and Row.

———. 1969. *Ecumenism in Focus*. London: G. Chapman.

Bell, G. K. A. 1955. *Documents on Christian Unity, A Selection from the First and Second Series, 1920–30*. London: Oxford University Press.

Belloc, Hilaire. 1920. *Europe and the Faith*. New York: Paulist.

Böhmer, Heinrich. 1946. *The Road to the Reformation*. Translated by John W. Doberstein and Theodore G. Tappert. Philadelphia: Muhlenberg.

Bornkamm, Heinrich. 1983. *Luther in Mid-Career, 1521–1530*. Translated by E. Theodore Bachmann. Philadelphia: Fortress.

Bouyer, Louis. 1956. *The Spirit and Forms of Protestantism*. Translated by A. V. Littledale. Westminster: Newman.

Bradley, Robert I. 1990. *The Roman Catechism in the Catechetical Tradition of the Church*. Lanham: University Press of America.

Brecht, Martin. 1985. *Martin Luther: His Road to the Reformation, 1483–1521*. Translated by James L. Schaff. Philadelphia: Fortress.

———. 1991. *Martin Luther: Shaping and Defining the Reformation, 1521–1532*. Translated by James L. Schaaf. Minneapolis: Fortress.

Brodrick, James. 1935. *Saint Peter Canisius, S.J., 1521–1597*. New York: Sheed and Ward.

———. 1961. *Robert Bellarmine: Saint and Scholar*. Westminster: Newman.

———, ed. 1971. *Documents of Vatican Council I, 1869–1870*. Collegeville: Liturgical Press,.

Brown, Robert McAfee. 1983. Review of *Luther: A Life* by John M. Todd. *Theology Today* 40 (April): 58–62 .

Cassidy, Edward. 1993. The Measure of Catholic Ecumenical Commitment. *Origins* 22:736–744.

Castelli, Jim, and Joseph Gremillion. 1987. *The Emerging Parish: The Notre Dame Study of Catholic Life Since Vatican II*. San Francisco: Harper and Row.

Christopherson, Kenneth E. 1985. Review of *Cajetan und die Anfänge der Reformation* by Jared Wicks. *Sixteenth Century Journal* 16:387.

Clinton, Farley. 1983. Kueng Postures as a New Luther. *The Wanderer*, 17 November.

Congar, Yves M.-J. 1939. *Divided Christendom*. Translated by M. A. Bousfield. London: Geoffrey Bles.

———. 1963. Ecumenical Experience and Conversion: A Personal Testimony. In *The Sufficiency of God: Essays on the Ecumenical Hope in Honor of W.A. Visser't Hooft*, edited by Robert C. Mackie and Charles C. West. Philadelphia: Westminster.

———. 1964. *Dialogue Between Christians*. Translated by Philip Loretz. Westminster: Newman.

———. 1982. *Diversity and Communion*. Translated by John Bowden. Mystic, CT: Twenty-Third.

———. 1983. *Martin Luther, sa foi, sa réforme: Etudes de théologie historique*. Paris: Cerf.

———. 1988. *Fifty Years of Catholic Theology: Conversations with Yves Congar*. Edited and introduced by Bernard Lauret. Philadelphia: Fortress.

Congregation for the Doctrine of the Faith. 1992. Some Aspects of the Church Understood as Communion. *Origins* 22:108–112.

Coriden, James A., ed. 1985. *Code of Canon Law: A Text and Commentary*. New York: Paulist, 1985.

Cristiani, Léon. 1936. The Protestant Revolution. In Vol. 4 of *European Civilization: Its Origin and Development*, edited by Edward Eyre. London: Oxford University Press.

———. 1962. *The Revolt Against the Church*. Vol. 78 of *Twentieth Century Encyclopedia of Catholicism*. Translated by R. F. Trevett. New York: Hawthorne.

Dallman, W. 1943. Kiefl on Luther. *Concordia Theological Monthly* 16:481–487.

Denifle, Heinrich. 1917. *Luther and Lutherdom from Original Sources*. Translated by Raymond Volz. Somerset, OH: Torch.

Dickens, A. G., John M. Tonkin, and Kenneth Powell. 1985. *The Reformation in Historical Thought*. Oxford: Basil Blackwell.

Döllinger, Johann Joseph Ignaz. 1872. *Lectures on the Reunion of Churches*. Translated by H. N. Oxenham. New York: Pott, Young, and Co.

Dulles, Avery. 1965. Luther's Unfinished Reformation. *Catholic Mind* 63:32–35.

Eck, John. 1979. *Enchiridion of Commonplaces Against Luther and Other Enemies of the Church*. Translated by Ford Lewis Battles. Grand Rapids: Baker.

Edwards, Mark U. 1994. *Printing, Propaganda, and Martin Luther*. Berkeley: University of California Press.

Evenett, Henry. 1957. *The Reformation*. Vol. 27 of *Tracts on Comparative Religion*. London: Catholic Truth Society.

Faulkner, John. 1905. Luther and His Latest Critic. *American Journal of Theology* 9:359–373.

Feiner, Johannes. 1968. The Decree on Ecumenism: Commentary on the Decree. In *Commentary on the Documents of Vatican II*. Vol. 2. Edited by Herbert Vorgrimler and translated by William Glen-Doepel et al. New York: Herder.

Fenlon, Dermot. 1972. *Heresy and Obedience in Tridentine Italy: Cardinal Pole and the Counter-Reformation.* Cambridge: Cambridge University Press.

Fife, Robert Herndon. 1957. *The Revolt of Martin Luther.* New York: Columbia University Press.

Finley, Mitch. 1983. Luther seen as obedient rebel. *National Catholic Reporter,* 11 November.

Fraenkel, Pierre. 1967. John Eck's Enchiridion of 1525 and Luther's Earliest Arguments Against Papal Primacy. *Studia Theologica* 21:110–163.

Fries, Heinrich. 1986. Unity in View?: 20 Years after the Council. *Theology Digest* 33:107–111.

Gallup, George, Jr., and Jim Castelli. 1987. *The American Catholic People: Their Beliefs, Practices, and Values.* Garden City: Doubleday.

Ganss, Henry George. 1913. Luther. *Catholic Encyclopedia.* New York: Encyclopedia Press.

Ginder, Richard. 1955. Right or Wrong: Christ and Luther—Two Founders. *Our Sunday Visitor,* 30 October, 4–5.

———. 1956. Should We Speak or Hold Our Tongue? *Priest* 12 (February): 133–136.

Gleason, Elizabeth. 1969. Sixteenth-Century Italian Interpretations of Luther. *Archiv für Reformationsgeschichte* 60:160–173.

Gregory XVI. 1981. Inter praecipuas. English translation in *The Papal Encyclicals.* 5 vols. Edited by Claudia Carlen. Wilmington, NC: McGrath.

Grisar, Hartmann. 1916–17. *Luther.* Translated by E. M. Lamond. St. Louis: B. Herder.

———. 1955. *Martin Luther: His Life and Work.* Translated by Frank J. Eble. Westminster: Newman.

Gritsch, Eric W. 1966. Review of *Martin Luther: A Biographical Study* by John M. Todd. *Archiv für Reformationsgeschichte* 57:257–258.

———. 1988. Joseph Lortz's Luther in Luther Research. Paper read at American Catholic Historical Association, 18 December.

Hagen, Kenneth. 1987. The Historical Context of the Smalcald Articles. *Concordia Theological Quarterly* 51 (October): 245–253.

Häring, Bernard. 1967. Theologian Asks Pardon for Luther. *St. Anthony Messenger* 75 (November):10.

Hebblethwaite, Peter. 1983. At Luther fest: a good word was said by all. *National Catholic Reporter,* 25 November.

———. 1985. *Pope John XXIII: Shepherd of the Modern World.* Garden City: Doubleday.

———. 1993. *Paul VI: The First Modern Pope.* New York: Paulist.

Hempsall, David S. 1973. Martin Luther and the Sorbonne, 1519–21. *Bulletin of the Institute of Historical Research* 46:28–40.

Hendrix, Scott. 1981. *Luther and the Papacy: Stages in a Reformation Conflict.* Philadelphia: Fortress.

Hillerbrand, Hans J. 1969. Martin Luther and the Bull Exsurge Domine. *Theological Studies* 30:108–112.

———, ed. 1978. *The Reformation: A Narrative History Related by Contemporary Observers and Participants.* Grand Rapids: Baker.

Holy Office. 1950. *Ecclesia Catholica:* Instruction to Bishops on the Ecumenical Movement (20 December 1949). *Jurist* 10:206–213.

————. 1952. Suprema haec sacra. *American Ecclesiastical Review* 127 (1952): 307–315.

Horgan, Thaddeus. 1983. Martin Luther: His Legacy and Lessons for Christian Unity. *St. Anthony Messenger* 91 (November): 12–16.

Hughes, Philip. 1947. *The Revolt Against the Church: Aquinas to Luther.* Vol. 3 of *A History of the Church.* New York: Sheed and Ward.

————. 1957. *A Popular History of the Reformation.* Garden City: Image.

Iserloh, Erwin. 1966. Luther in Contemporary Catholic Thought. In *Do We Know the Others?* Translated by Eileen O'Gorman. Vol. 14 of *Concilium: Theology in the Age of Renewal,* edited by Hans Küng. New York: Paulist.

————. 1968. *The Theses Were Not Posted.* Translated by Jared Wicks. Boston: Beacon.

————. 1980. The Protestant Reformation. In *Reformation and Counter-Reformation.* Vol. 5 of *History of the Church,* edited by Hubert Jedin. New York: Crossroad.

————. 1983. Luther and the Council of Trent. *Catholic Historical Review* 69:563–576.

Jabusch, Willard. 1961. A Second Look at Luther. *St. Jude Magazine* 27 (August): 33–36.

Janz, Dennis R. 1983. *Luther and Late Medieval Thomism: A Study in Theological Anthropology.* Waterloo: Wilfrid Laurier University Press.

————. 1998. Syllogism or Paradox: Aquinas and Luther on Theological Method. *Theological Studies* 59:3–21.

Jedin, Hubert. 1957–61. *A History of the Council of Trent.* 2 vols. Translated by Dom Ernest Graf. New York: Thomas Nelson.

————. 1962. Council of Trent and Reunion: Some Historical Notes. *Heythrop* 3 (January): 3–14.

————. 1966. Luther: A New View. *Chicago Studies* 5:53–63.

————. 1967a. Changes Undergone by the Image of Luther in Catholic Works on Ecclesiastical History. In *Martinus Luther: 450th Anniversary of the Reformation.* Bad Godesberg: Inter Nationes.

————. 1967b. *Crisis and Closure of the Council of Trent: A Retrospective View from the Second Vatican Council.* Translated by N. D. Smith. London: Sheed and Ward.

John XXIII. 1960. In sollemnis. *The Pope Speaks* 6:379.

————. 1961. Humanae salutis. *The Pope Speaks* 7:353–361.

————. 1962–63. Notre recontre. *The Pope Speaks* 8:226.

————. 1981. Ad Petri Cathedram. English translation in *The Papal Encyclicals.* 5 vols. Edited by Claudia Carlen. Wilmington, NC: McGrath.

John Paul II. 1980a. *Addresses and Homilies Given in West Germany.* Translated by National Catholic News Service. Washington, DC: United States Catholic Conference.

————. 1980b. General Audience on Augsburg Confession. *L'Osservatore Romano,* 7 July, English edition.

————. 1983a. Address of Pope John Paul II at the Lutheran Church in Rome. *Information Service* 52:94–95.

————. 1983b. Pope John Paul II's Letter on the Fifth Centenary of Birth of Martin Luther. *Information Service* 52:83.

————. 1984. To Members of Catholic-Lutheran Commission. *L'Osservatore Romano,* 12 March, English edition.

————. 1987. Homily of Mass at Augsburg. *L'Osservatore Romano*, 1 June, English edition.

————. 1989. Pope John Paul II and Ecumenism: The Pastoral Journey to the Nordic Countries. *Information Service* 71:83–110.

————. 1994. As the Third Millennium Draws Near. *Origins* 24:401+.

————. 1995. Ut Unum Sint. *Origins* 25:49+.

————. 1996. Pope John Paul II's Third Pastoral Visit to Germany. *Information Service* 93:154–158.

Joint Declaration on the Doctrine of Justification. 1998. *Origins* 28:120–127.

Kamm, Henry. 1983. Pope Praises Luther in an Appeal for Unity on Protestant Anniversary. *New York Times*, 6 November, national edition.

Kaufman, Peter Iver. 1984. 'Unnatural' Sympathies? Acton and Döllinger on the Reformation. *Catholic Historical Review* 70:547–559.

Kelly, John J. 1984. Fallacy about our brother, Martin Luther. *Homiletic and Pastoral Review* 84 (April): 61–64.

Kloppenburg, Bonaventure. 1974. *Ecclesiology of Vatican II.* Translated by Matthew O'Connell. Chicago: Franciscan Herald.

Kothgasser, Alois. 1983. 'Martin Luther—Witness to Jesus Christ': Comments and Questions. *Information Service* 52:88–92.

Küng, Hans. 1964. *Justification: The Doctrine of Karl Barth and a Catholic Reflection.* Translated by Thomas Collins, Edmund E. Tolk, and David Granskou. New York: Thomas Nelson.

————. 1983. Twenty Years of Ecumenical Theology—For What? In *Twenty Years of Concilium: Retrospect and Prospect*, edited by Paul Brand, Edward Schillebeeckx, and Anton Weiler. Vol. 170 of *Concilium: Religion in the Eighties*. New York: Seabury.

Lagrange, Marie-Joseph. 1918. *Luther on the Eve of His Revolt: A Criticism of Luther's Lectures on the Epistle to the Romans Given at Wittenberg in 1515–1516.* Translated by W. S. Reilly. New York: Cathedral Library Association.

Lehmann, Karl. 1984. The focus of discussion today: Luther and the unity of the churches. *Communio* 11:208.

Lehmann, Karl and Wolfhart Pannenberg, eds. 1990. *The Condemnations of the Reformation Era: Do They Still Divide?* Translated by Margaret Kohl. Minneapolis: Fortress.

Leo X. 1970. *Decet Romanum Pontificem.* In *Martin Luther*, edited by E. G. Rupp and Benjamin Drewery. New York: St. Martin's.

————. 1985. *Exsurge Domine.* In *Readings in Church History*, edited by Coleman Barry. Westminster: Newman.

Leo XIII. 1903. *The Great Encyclical Letters of Pope Leo XIII.* Edited by John J. Wynne. New York: Benziger.

————. 1981. Aeterni Patris. English translation in *The Papal Encyclicals.* 5 vols. Edited by Claudia Carlen. Wilmington, NC: McGrath.

Lindberg, Carter. 1972. Prierias and His Significance for Luther's Development. *Sixteenth Century Journal* 3 (October): 45–64.

Loewenich, Walther. 1959. *Modern Catholicism.* Translated by Reginald Fuller. London: Macmillan.

Lortz, Joseph. 1947. Reformation: theses put forward as a friendly approach for oecumenical conversations. *Eastern Churches Quarterly* 7:76–91.

————. 1948–49. The Catholic Attitude Towards the Reformation. *Oratre Fratres* 23:455–461.

————. 1968. *Reformation in Germany*. 2 vols. Translated by Ronald Walls. New York: Herder.

————. 1970. The Basic Elements of Luther's Intellectual Style. In *Catholic Scholars Dialogue with Luther*, edited by Jared Wicks, SJ. Chicago: Loyola University Press.

Lukens, Michael B. 1988. Lortz's View of the Reformation and the Crisis of the True Church. Paper read at the American Catholic Historical Society, 28 December.

Luther, Martin. 1957a. Explanations of the Ninety-five Theses, 1518. In *Luther's Works* 31, edited by Harold J. Grimm and translated by Carl W. Folkemer. Philadelphia: Fortress.

————. 1957b. Proceedings at Augsburg, 1518. In *Luther's Works* 31, edited and translated by Harold J. Grimm. Philadelphia: Fortress.

————. 1963. *Letters I*. Vol. 48 of *Luther's Works*, edited and translated by Gottfried Krodel. Philadelphia: Fortress.

————. 1966a. Against Hanswurst, 1541. In *Luther's Works* 41, edited and translated by Eric W. Gritsch. Philadelphia: Fortress.

————. 1966b. Against the Roman Papacy, An Institution of the Devil, 1545. In *Luther's Works* 41, edited and translated by Eric W. Gritsch. Philadelphia: Fortress.

————. 1972. Lectures on Romans, 1515. In *Luther's Works* 25, edited by Hilton C. Oswald and translated by Walter G. Tillmanns and Jacob A. O. Preus. St. Louis: Concordia.

"Luther's Justification." 1983. *America*, 26 November, 322.

Maddox, Randy L. 1984. Review of *Justification: An Ecumenical Study* by George Tavard. *Theological Studies* 45:736–737.

Manns, Peter. 1970. Absolute and Incarnate Faith—Luther on Justification in the Galatians Commentary of 1531–1535. In *Catholic Scholars Dialogue with Luther*, edited by Jared Wicks, SJ. Chicago: Loyola University Press.

————. 1983. *Martin Luther: An Illustrated Biography*. Translated by Michael Shaw. New York: Crossroad.

————. 1984. The Validity and Theological-Ecumenical Usefulness of the Lortzian Position on the 'Catholic Luther'. In *Luther's Ecumenical Significance*, edited by Harding Meyer and Carter Lindberg. Philadelphia: Fortress.

Maritain, Jacques. 1929. *Three Reformers: Luther, Descartes, Rousseau*. New York: Charles Scribner's Sons.

Marty, Martin E. 1991. Never the Same Again: Post-Vatican II Catholic-Protestant Interactions. *Sociological Analysis* 52,1:13–26.

Marty, Myron A. 1968. *Lutherans and Roman Catholicism*. Notre Dame: University of Notre Dame Press.

Matheson, Peter. 1972. *Cardinal Contarini at Regensburg*. Oxford: Clarendon.

Maxcey, Carl E. 1979. Double Justice, Diego Laynez, and the Council of Trent. *Church History* 48:269–278.

McBride, Alfred. 1983. Martin Luther: The Man Who Began the Reformation. *St. Anthony Messenger* 91 (November): 17–19.

McCue, James F. 1984. Review of *Martin Luther, sa foi, sa réforme* by Yves M.-J. Congar. *Theological Studies* 45:180.

McDonnell, Kilian. 1983. Lutherans and Catholics on Justification. *America*, 3 December, 345–348.

McGinness, Frederick J. 1995. *Right Thinking and Sacred Oratory in Counter-Reformation Rome*. Princeton: Princeton University Press.

McHugh, John, and Charles J. Callan, eds. and trans. 1934. *Catechism of the Council of Trent for Parish Priests*. New York: Joseph F. Wagner.

McNally, Robert E. 1967. The Ninety-Five Theses of Martin Luther. *Theological Studies* 28:439–480.

McNeill, John Thomas. 1967. Early Roman Catholic Reactions to Protestantism. In *A History of the Ecumenical Movement, 1517–1948*, edited by Ruth Rouse and Stephen Charles Neill. Philadelphia: Westminster.

McSorley, Harry J. 1967. *Luther: Right or Wrong?* Westminster: Newman and Minneapolis: Augsburg.

Meyer, Harding. 1997. Consensus in the Doctrine of Justification. *Ecumenical Trends* 26:165–168.

Minus, Paul M. 1976. *The Catholic Rediscovery of Protestantism: A History of Roman Catholic Ecumenical Pioneering*. New York: Paulist.

Misner, Paul. 1980. Augsburg, Then and Now. *Journal of Ecumenical Studies* 17:483–491.

Mondin, Battista. 1972. Luther and the Catholic Church. *L'Osservatore Romano*, 3 February, English edition.

Mulloy, John J. 1989. The Pope, Luther, And Ecumenism. *The Wanderer*, 20 July.

Niebuhr, Reinhold. 1949. The Rising Catholic-Protestant Tension. *Christianity and Crisis* 9,14:107.

No Canonization for Luther. 1968. *St. Anthony Messenger* 76:11.

Oberman, Heiko. 1963. Interview by John B. Sheerin. *Catholic World* 197:100–106.

O'Hare, Patrick. 1916. *The Facts About Luther*. New York and Cincinnati: Frederick Pustet.

O'Malley, John W. 1979. Lutheranism in Rome, 1542–43—The Treatise by Alfonso Zorrilla. *Thought* 54:262–273.

Outler, Albert. 1986. Protestant Observer at Vatican II Surveys Ecumenism Today. *Origins* 16:253–257.

Overholt, Thomas W. *Channels of Prophecy: The Social Dynamics of Prophetic Activity*. Minneapolis: Fortress, 1989.

Palmer, Paul F., ed. 1959. *Sacraments and Forgiveness: History and Doctrinal Development of Penance, Eucharist and Indulgences*. Westminster: Newman.

Parker, T. H. L. 1964. Review of *The Law and the Gospel in Luther: A Study of Martin Luther's Confessional Writings* by Thomas McDonough. *Journal of Theological Studies* 15:439–441.

Pauck, Wilhelm. 1961. *The Heritage of the Reformation*. New York: Oxford University Press.

Paul VI. 1963a. Ea quae. *The Pope Speaks* 9:9.

———. 1963b. Salvete fratres. *The Pope Speaks* 9:125–141.

———. 1964a. Nous sommes profondément. *The Pope Speaks* 9:230–233.

———. 1964b. To pilgrims at Trent. *Doctrine and Life* 14:493–494.

———. 1966a. General audience of 19 January. *Unitas* 18:42.

———. 1966b. Voici que le. *The Pope Speaks* 11:36–40.

———. 1967. Nous vous saluons. *The Pope Speaks* 12:97–102.

———. 1968. General audience of January 24. *American Ecclesiastical Review* 159:59.

———. 1973. Homily at an ecumenical prayer service at Santa Maria in Vallicella at Rome. *The Pope Speaks* 17:329.

————. 1978a. General audience on January 18. *L'Osservatore Romano*, 26 January, English edition.

————. 1978b. Last Will of Pope Paul VI. *Origins* 8:175–176.

————. 1981. Ecclesiam Suam. English translation in *The Papal Encyclicals*. 5 vols. Edited by Claudia Carlen. Wilmington, NC: McGrath.

Persson, Erik. 1963. The Reformation in Recent Roman Catholic Theology. *Dialog* 2 (1): 24–31.

Pesch, Otto Hermann. 1966. Twenty Years of Catholic Luther Research. *Lutheran World* 13:303–316.

————. 1970. Existential and Sapiential Theology—the Theological Confrontation between Luther and Thomas Aquinas. In *Catholic Scholars Dialogue with Luther*, edited by Jared Wicks, SJ. Chicago: Loyola University Press.

————. 1984a. Luther and the Catholic Tradition. *Lutheran Theological Seminary Bulletin* 64 (1): 3–21.

————. 1984b. The Lutheran Luther—A Catholic Possibility? In *Luther's Ecumenical Usefulness*, edited by Harding Meyer and Carter Lindberg. Philadelphia: Fortress.

————. 1985. Free by Faith: Luther's Contribution to a Theological Anthropology. In *Martin Luther and the Modern Mind*, edited by Manfred Hoffman. New York: Edwin Mellen.

Peter, Carl J. 1986. The Church's Treasures (*Thesauri Ecclesiae*) Then and Now. *Theological Studies* 47:251–272.

Pfürtner, Stephen. 1964. *Luther and Aquinas on Salvation*. Translated by Edward Quinn. New York: Sheed and Ward.

Pius X. 1981. Pascendi dominici gregis. English translation in *The Papal Encyclicals*. 5 vols. Edited by Claudia Carlen. Wilmington, NC: McGrath.

Pius XI. 1981a. Caritate Christi compulsi. English translation in *The Papal Encyclicals*. 5 vols. Edited by Claudia Carlen. Wilmington, NC: McGrath.

————. 1981b. Mortalium animos. English translation in *The Papal Encyclicals*. 5 vols. Edited by Claudia Carlen. Wilmington, NC: McGrath.

————. 1981c. Ubi arcano Dei consilio. English translation in *The Papal Encyclicals*. 5 vols. Edited by Claudia Carlen. Wilmington, NC: McGrath.

Pius XII. 1945. Four Hundred Years After Trent. *Tablet*, 22 December.

————. 1948. Wie hätten Wir. *L'Osservatore Romano* 8 September, Italian edition.

————. 1957. Almost fifty years. *Unitas* 9: 259–261.

————. 1981a. Humani generis. English translation in *The Papal Encyclicals*. 5 vols. Edited by Claudia Carlen. Wilmington NC: McGrath.

————. 1981b. Mediator dei. English translation in *The Papal Encyclicals*. 5 vols. Edited by Claudia Carlen. Wilmington, NC: McGrath.

————. 1981c. Mystici corporis Christi. English translation in *The Papal Encyclicals*. 5 vols. Edited by Claudia Carlen. Wilmington, NC: McGrath.

————. 1981d. Summi pontificatus. English translation in *The Papal Encyclicals*. 5 vols. Edited by Claudia Carlen. Wilmington, NC: McGrath.

Pontifical Council for Promoting Christian Unity. 1992. *Evaluation for the Pontifical Council for Promoting Christian Unity of the Study Lehrverurteilungen — kirchentrennend?* Vatican City. Photocopy.

————. 1993. Directory for the Application of Principles and Norms on Ecumenism (25 March). Washington, DC: United States Catholic Conference.

Pope Preaches From Lutheran Pulpit in Rome. 1983. *The Wanderer*, 22 December.

Ratzinger, Joseph. 1977. The Future of Ecumenism. *Theology Digest* 25:200–205.

————. 1984. Luther and the unity of the churches. *Communio* 11:210–226.

————. 1985. *The Ratzinger Report: An Exclusive Interview on the State of the Church.* Translated by Salvator Attanasio and Graham Harrison. San Francisco: Ignatius.

————. 1986. The Ecclesiology of the Second Vatican Council. *Communio* 13:239–252.

————. 1987. *Principles of Catholic Theology: Building Stones for a Fundamental Theology.* Translated by Sister Mary Frances McCarthy. San Francisco: Ignatius.

————. 1988. *Church, Ecumenism and Politics: New Essays in Ecclesiology.* Translated by Robert Nowell. New York: Crossroad.

Reu, Johann M. 1930. *The Augsburg Confession.* Chicago: Wartburg.

Richgels, Robert W. 1980. The Pattern of Controversy in a Reformation Classic. *Sixteenth Century Journal* 2 (2): 3–15.

Rigali, Justin. 1996. Presentation of Archbishop Justin Rigali on February 7, 1996 at Concordia Seminary. *Ecumenical Trends* 25:61–64.

Robinson, Carol Jackson. 1983. Happy Birthday, Martin Luther. *The Wanderer*, 10 November.

————. 1984a. Pleasing Martin Luther. *The Wanderer*, 19 January.

————. 1984b. Who Is the Common Doctor of the Church: Thomas Aquinas or Martin Luther? *The Wanderer*, 8 November.

————. 1985. Rahner in Context III. *The Wanderer*, 31 October.

Roman Catholic–Lutheran Joint Commission. 1982. 'All Under One Christ': Statement on the Augsburg Confession. *LWF Report* 10 (August): 34–43.

————. 1983. Martin Luther—Witness to Jesus Christ. *Information Service* 52:84–88.

Rupp, Gordon. 1953. *The Righteousness of God: Luther Studies.* London: Hodder and Stoughton.

Russell, William R. 1994. Martin Luther's Understanding of the Pope as the Antichrist. *Archiv für Reformationsgeschichte* 85:32–44.

Schlink, Edmund. 1965. The Decree on Ecumenism. In *Dialogue on the Way*, edited by George Lindbeck. Minneapolis: Augsburg.

Scionti, Joseph N. 1967. Sylvester Prierias and His Opposition to Martin Luther. Ph.D. diss., Brown University.

Scrutator. 1985. The men who run the Vatican (4): Dedicated ecumenist. *Tablet*, 21 September.

Sixtus IV. 1970. *Salvator noster.* In *Martin Luther*, edited by E. G. Rupp and Benjamin Drewery New York: St. Martin's.

Sly, Julie. 1983. Lutheran, Catholic talks picking up momentum. *National Catholic Register*, 20 October.

Sly, Julie and Charlotte Hays. 1983. Martin Luther, 500 years later. *National Catholic Register*, 13 November.

Spitz, Lewis W. 1971. Review of *Luther in der katholischen Dogmatik* by August Hasler. *Archiv für Reformationsgeschichte* 62:139–141.

Stacpoole, Alberic. 1988. Early Ecumenism, Early Yves Congar, 1904–1940. *Month* 21:502–510, 623–631.

Stauffer, Richard. 1966. *Le catholicisme à la découverte de Luther: L'évolution des recherches catholiques sur Luther de 1904 au 2me Concile du Vatican.* Neuchâtel: Delachaux et Niestlé.

————. 1967. *Luther As Seen by Catholics.* Vol. 7 of Ecumenical Study Series. Richmond: John Knox.

Stransky, Thomas F. 1986. Surprises and Fears of Ecumenism: Twenty Years after Vatican II. *America*, 25 January, 44–48.

Swidler, Leonard. 1965. Catholic Reformation Scholarship in Germany. *Journal of Ecumenical Studies* 2:189–204.

Synod of Bishops. 1985. The Final Report. *Origins* 15:444–450.

Tanner, Norman P., ed. 1990. *Decrees of the Ecumenical Councils*. Washington: Georgetown University Press.

Tappert, Theodore G., ed. and trans. 1959. *The Book of Concord*. Philadelphia: Fortress.

Tatlow, Tissington. 1967. The World Conference on Faith and Order. In *A History of the Ecumenical Movement, 1517–1948*, edited by Ruth Rouse and Stephen Charles Neill. Philadelphia: Westminster.

Tavard, George. 1955. *The Catholic Approach to Protestantism*. New York: Harper.

———. 1959. *Holy Writ or Holy Church: The Crisis of the Protestant Reformation*. New York: Harper.

———. 1983. Reassessing the Reformation. *One in Christ* 19:355–367.

———. 1997. Ecumenical Implications of the Reassessment of Past Condemnations. *Ecumenical Trends* 26:57–60.

Tavuzzi, Michael. 1997. *Prierias: The Life and Works of Silvestro Mazzolini da Prierio, 1456–1527*. Durham: Duke University Press.

Tinsley, Barbara Sher. 1983. Review of *Luther's Faith: The Cause of the Gospel in the Church* by Daniel Olivier. *Sixteenth Century Journal* 14:539.

Tomaro, John B. 1988. San Carlo Borromeo and the Implementation of the Council of Trent. In *San Carlo Borromeo: Catholic Reform and Ecclesiastical Politics in the Second Half of the Sixteenth Century*, edited by John M. Headley and John B. Tomaro. Washington, DC: Folger.

Van den Aardweg, Gerard J. M. 1984. Martin Luther's Neurotic Complex. *Homiletic and Pastoral Review* 85 (November): 65–68.

Whealon, John F. 1983a. Father Martin Luther. *Catholic Transcript*, 23 September.

———. 1983b. Luther's 500th Birthday. *Catholic Transcript*, 9 September.

———. 1983c. Luther's Heritage. *Catholic Transcript*, 30 September.

Wicks, Jared. 1969a. Luther Through Catholic Eyes. *Chicago Studies* 8:275–285.

———. 1969b. *Man Yearning for Grace: Luther's Early Spiritual Teaching*. Washington, DC: Corpus.

———. 1969c. Review of *Luther in der katholischen Dogmatik* by August Hasler. *Theological Studies* 30:140–142.

———. 1970. *Catholic Scholars Dialogue with Luther*. Chicago: Loyola University Press.

———. 1978. *Cajetan Responds: A Reader in Reformation Controversy*. Washington, DC: Catholic University Press.

———. 1980a. Abuses Under Indictment at the Diet of Augsburg 1530. *Theological Studies* 41:253–321.

———. 1980b. Review of *La Foi de Luther: la cause de l'evangelie dans l'eglise* by Daniel Olivier. *Theological Studies* 41:214–216.

———. 1983a. *Luther and His Spiritual Legacy*. Vol. 7 of Theology and Life. Wilmington, DE: Michael Glazier.

———. 1983b. Roman Reactions to Luther: The First Year (1518). *Catholic Historical Review* 69:521–562.

Willebrands, Jan. 1970a. Cardinal Willebrands Addresses Lutherans. *American Ecclesiastical Review* 163, 3 (1970): 208–209.

———. 1970b. Diversity without Separation. *Tablet*, 24 January.

———. 1972. Panorama of the Ecumenical Scene to 1971. *L'Osservatore Romano*, 16 November, English edition.

———. 1983. Address at quincentenary celebrations at Leipzig. *Information Service* 52:92–94.

———. 1988. Ecumenical Dialogue Today: An Overview. *Origins* 17:565–573.

Williams, George Hunston. 1982. The Ecumenical Intentions of Pope John Paul II. *Harvard Theological Review* 75:141–176.

Wilson, Robert R. 1980. *Prophecy and Society in Ancient Israel*. Philadelphia: Fortress.

Wojtyla, Karol. 1980. *Sources of Renewal: The Implementation of Vatican II*. Translated by P. S. Falla. San Francisco: Harper and Row.

Wrenn, Michael J. 1991. *Catechisms and Controversies: Religious Education in the Postconciliar Years*. San Francisco: Ignatius.

Wright, William J. 1991. Mainz versus Rome: Two Responses to Luther in the 1520s. *Archiv für Reformationsgeschichte* 82:83–104.

Wuthnow, Robert. 1988. *The Restructuring of American Religion: Society and Faith Since World War II*. Princeton: Princeton University Press.

INDEX OF NAMES